On the Origins of Cognitive Science

On the Origins of Cognitive Science

THE MECHANIZATION OF THE MIND

Jean-Pierre Dupuy
translated by M. B. DeBevoise

A BRADFORD BOOK

THE MIT PRESS, CAMBRIDGE, MASSACHUSETTS, LONDON, ENGLAND

This book was set in Adobe Bauer Bodoni by SNP Best-set Typesetter Ltd., Hong Kong.

Library of Congress Cataloging-in-Publication Data

Dupuy, Jean-Pierre, 1941–
[Aux origines des sciences cognitives. English]
On the origins of cognitive science : the mechanization of the mind / Jean-Pierre Dupuy; translated by M. B. DeBevoise.
    p.   cm. — (A Bradford book)
Originally published: Princeton : Princeton University Press, 2000.
Includes bibliographical references and index.
ISBN 978-0-262-51239-8 (pbk. : alk. paper)
1. Cognitive science—History.   I. Title.
BF311.D84513 2009
153—dc22

2008037716

In Memory of Jean Ullmo and Heinz von Foerster

Contents

Preface

TO THE MIT PRESS EDITION

I have set before you life and death,

blessing and curse; therefore choose life,

that you and your descendants may live.

—DEUTERONOMY 30:19

WHEN THIS book first appeared in English in 2000, some reviewers considered its conclusions too pessimistic and its outlook too bleak. For I saw the history of cybernetics—the first great attempt to construct a physicalist science of the mind—as the story of a failure. And indeed cybernetics was soon forgotten, apparently consigned to a dark corner of modern intellectual history—only to reemerge several decades later. In the meantime it had undergone a metamorphosis and now bore the features of the various disciplines that make up what today is known as cognitive science, most of which pretend not to recognize their kinship with cybernetics. And yet it was cybernetics that gave birth to all of them.

The history of cybernetics is undeniably fascinating. Its ambition was unprecedented, the minds who animated it were among the most exceptional of their time, and its heritage was rich and varied. But cybernetics got certain things wrong. It was riddled with contradictions that it did not know how to resolve, if it recognized them at all. Overly confident of its powers, it held itself aloof from other disciplines of the mind that might have pointed it in more promising directions. Today, cognitive science is poised to repeat these errors, I believe, only in a far more dangerous way than before—as though it has learned nothing from the failures of cybernetics. But perhaps this should not come as a surprise, since it does not acknowledge cybernetics as its true source.

More than one reader has been surprised by the seemingly paradoxical character of this book. How, it is asked, can I take an interest in something that I judge to have been a failure? But why should it be any

different with an ecology of ideas than with our personal lives? Do we
not learn chiefly from our own failures? I make no secret of my hostility,
as a philosopher, toward the underlying assumptions of a physicalist
science of the mind. But here again, why should it be any different with
intellectual combat than with other sorts of combat? To create the strongest possible position for oneself, mustn't one know one's adversaries
from the inside, and no less well than they know themselves? Nor do I
hide my fascination with an intellectual movement whose aims I do not
share. I am committed to arguing on behalf of a certain point of view,
but my commitment has nothing to do with that of a scientist dedicated
to advancing the cause of the discipline in which he or she has freely
chosen to work. For I am making an argument *against*. This may be why
my book has puzzled some readers.

It is therefore a book that seeks to disabuse readers of a number of
ideas that I consider mistaken. Cybernetics calls to mind a series of familiar images that turn out on closer inspection to be highly doubtful. As
the etymology of the word suggests, cybernetics is meant to signify control,
mastery, governance—in short, the philosophical project associated with
Descartes, who assigned mankind the mission of exercising dominion over
the world, and over mankind itself. Within the cybernetics movement,
this view was championed by Norbert Wiener—unsurprisingly, perhaps,
since it was Wiener who gave it its name. But this gives only a very partial,
if not superficial idea of what cybernetics was about, notwithstanding that
even a philosopher of such penetrating insight as Heidegger was taken in
by it.

In the pages that follow, I rely on Karl Popper's notion of a metaphysical research program, which is to say a set of presuppositions about the
structure of the world that are neither testable nor empirically falsifiable,
but without which no science would be possible. For there is no science
that does not rest on a metaphysics, though typically it remains concealed.
It is the responsibility of the philosopher to uncover this metaphysics, and
then to subject it to criticism. What I have tried to show here is that
cybernetics, far from being the apotheosis of Cartesian humanism, as
Heidegger supposed, actually represented a crucial moment in its demystification, and indeed in its deconstruction. To borrow a term that has
been applied to the structuralist movement in the human sciences, cybernetics constituted a decisive step in the rise of *antihumanism*. Consider,
for example, the way in which cybernetics conceived the relationship
between man and machine. The philosophers of consciousness were not
alone in being caught up in the trap set by a question such as "Will it be
possible one day to design a machine that thinks?" The cybernetician's
answer, rather in the spirit of Molière, was: "Madame, you pride yourself
so on thinking. And yet, you are only a machine!" The aim of cognitive

science always was—and still is today—the mechanization of the mind, not the humanization of the machine.

A great many things have happened in the eight years separating the second edition of this book from the first that, I fear, only confirm the pessimism of my conclusions and justify the gloominess of my outlook.

I have in mind not so much the intellectual evolution of cognitive science itself as its embodiment by new technologies, or, as one should rather say, its instantiation by ideas for new technologies. For the moment, at least, these technologies exist only as projects, indeed in some cases only as dreams. But no matter that many such dreams will acquire physical reality sooner or later, the simple fact that they already exist in people's minds affects how we see the world and how we see ourselves.

Since this book was first published, I have thought a great deal about the philosophical foundations of what is called NBIC convergence—the convergence of nanotechnology, biotechnology, information technology, and cognitive science—and about the ethical implications of this development. Here I have found many of the same tensions, contradictions, paradoxes, and confusions that I discerned first within cybernetics, and then within cognitive science.[1] But now the potential consequences are far more serious, because we are not dealing with a theoretical matter, a certain view of the world, but with an entire program for acting upon nature and humankind.

In searching for the underlying metaphysics of this program, I did not have far to look. One of the first reports of the National Science Foundation devoted to the subject, entitled "Converging Technologies for Improving Human Performance," summarizes the credo of the movement in a sort of haiku:

> If the Cognitive Scientists can think it,
> The Nano people can build it,
> The Bio people can implement it, and
> The IT people can monitor and control it.[2]

Note that cognitive science plays the leading role in this division of labor, that of thinker—not an insignificant detail, for it shows that the metaphysics of NBIC convergence is embedded in the work of cognitive scientists. It comes as no surprise, then, that the contradictions inherent in cognitive science should be found at the heart of the metaphysics itself.

One of the main themes of the present book is the confrontation between Norbert Wiener and John von Neumann, Wiener embodying the ideas of control, mastery, and design, von Neumann the ideas of complexity and self-organization. Cybernetics never succeeded in resolving the tension, indeed the contradiction, between these two perspectives; more specifically, it never managed to give a satisfactory answer to the problems involved in realizing its ambition of *designing* an autonomous, self-organizing machine. Nanotechnology—whose wildest dream is to reconstruct the natural world that has been given to us, atom by atom—is caught up in the same contradiction.

The most obvious element of the nanotechnological dream is to substitute for what François Jacob called *bricolage*, or the tinkering of biological evolution, a paradigm of design. Damien Broderick, the Australian cultural theorist and popular science writer, barely manages to conceal his contempt for the world that human beings have inherited when he talks about the likelihood that "nanosystems, designed by human minds, will bypass all this Darwinian wandering, and leap straight to *design success.*"³ One can hardly fail to note the irony that science, which in America has had to engage in an epic struggle to root out every trace of creationism (including its most recent avatar, "intelligent design") from public education, should now revert to a logic of design in the form of the nanotechnology program—the only difference being that now it is humankind that assumes the role of the demiurge.

Philosophers—faced with the ambition of emerging technologies to supersede nature and life as the engineers of evolution, the designers of biological and natural processes—may suppose that they are dealing with an old idea: Descartes' vision of science as the means by which man may become the master and possessor of nature. Again, however, this is only part of a larger and more complicated picture. As another influential visionary, the American applied physicist Kevin Kelly, revealingly remarked, "It took us a long time to realize that the power of a technology is proportional to its inherent out-of-controlness, its inherent ability to surprise and be generative. In fact, unless we can worry about a technology, it is not revolutionary enough."⁴ With NanoBio convergence, a novel conception of engineering has indeed been introduced. The engineer, far from seeking mastery over nature, is now meant to feel that his enterprise will be crowned by success only to the extent that the system component he has created is capable of surprising him. For whoever wishes ultimately to create a self-organizing system—another word for life—is bound to attempt to reproduce its essential property; namely, the ability to make something that is radically new.

In her masterful study of the perils facing mankind, *The Human Condition* (1958), Hannah Arendt brought out the fundamental paradox of our age: whereas the power of mankind to alter its environment goes on increasing under the stimulus of technological progress, less and less do we find ourselves in a position to control the consequences of our actions. I take the liberty of giving a long quotation here whose pertinence to the subject at hand cannot be exaggerated—keeping in mind, too, that these lines were written fifty years ago:

> To what extent we have begun to *act into nature*, in the literal sense of the word, is perhaps best illustrated by a recent casual remark of a scientist [Wernher von Braun, December 1957] who quite seriously suggested that *"basic research is when I am doing what I don't know what I am doing."*
>
> This started harmlessly enough with the experiment in which men were no longer content to observe, to register, and contemplate whatever nature was willing to yield in her own appearance, but began to prescribe conditions and to provoke natural processes. What then developed into an ever-increasing skill in *unchaining elemental processes*, which, without the interference of men, would have lain dormant and perhaps never have come to pass, has finally ended in a veritable art of *"making"* nature, that is, of creating *"natural"* processes which without men would never exist and which earthly nature by herself seems incapable of accomplishing. . . .
>
> [N]atural sciences have become exclusively sciences of process and, in their last stage, *sciences of potentially irreversible, irremediable "processes of no return".*[5]

The sorcerer's apprentice myth must therefore be updated: it is neither by error nor terror that mankind will be dispossessed of its own creations, but by *design*—which henceforth is understood to signify not mastery, but nonmastery and out-of-controlness.

Arendt began the same, decidedly prescient book with the following words:

> The human artifice of the world separates human existence from all mere animal environment, but life itself is outside this artificial world, and through life man remains related to all other living organisms. For some time now, a great many scientific endeavors have been directed toward making life also "artificial," toward cutting the last tie through which even man belongs among the children of nature. . . .
>
> This future man, whom the scientists tell us they will produce in no more than a hundred years, seems to be possessed by *a rebellion against human existence as it has been given*, a free gift from nowhere (secularly speaking), which he wishes to exchange, as it were, for something he has made himself.[6]

The nanotechnological dream that began to take shape only a few decades after the utterance of Arendt's prophesy amounts to exactly this revolt against the finiteness, the mortality of the human condition. Human life has an end, for it is promised to death. But not only do the champions of NBIC convergence oppose themselves to fate, by promising immortality; they quarrel with the very fact that we are born. Their revolt against the given is therefore something subtler and less visible, something still more fundamental, than the revolt against human mortality, for it rejects the notion that we should be brought into the world for no reason.

"Human beings are ashamed to have been born instead of made." Thus the German philosopher Günther Anders (Arendt's first husband and himself a student of Heidegger) characterized the essence of the revolt against the given in his great book, first published in 1956, *Die Antiquiertheit des Menschen* (The Antiquatedness [or Obsolescence] of the Human Being).[7] One cannot help recalling here another philosophical emotion: the nausea described by Jean-Paul Sartre, that sense of forlornness that takes hold of human beings when they realize that they are not the foundation of their own being. The human condition is ultimately one of freedom; but freedom, being absolute, runs up against the obstacle of its own contingency, for we are free to choose anything except the condition of being *un*free. Discovering that we have been *thrown* into the world without any reason, we feel abandoned. Sartre acknowledged his debt to Günther Anders in expressing this idea by means of a phrase that was to become famous: man is "to freedom condemned."

Freedom, Sartre held, never ceases trying to "nihilate" that which resists it. Mankind will therefore do everything it can to become its own maker; to owe its freedom to no one but itself. But only things are what they are; only things coincide with themselves. Freedom, on the other hand, is a mode of being that never coincides with itself since it ceaselessly projects itself into the future, desiring to be what it is not. Self-coincidence is what freedom aspires to and cannot attain, just as a moth is irresistably attracted to the flame that will consume it. A *metaphysical self-made man*, were such a being possible, would paradoxically have lost his freedom, and indeed would no longer be a man at all, since freedom necessarily entails the impossibility of transforming itself into a thing. Thus Anders's notion of "Promethean shame" leads inexorably to the obsolescence of man.

Had they lived to see the dawn of the twenty-first century, Sartre and Anders would have found this argument resoundingly confirmed in the shape of NBIC convergence—a Promethean project if ever there was one. For the aim of this distinctively metaphysical program is to place humankind in the position of being the divine maker of the world, the demiurge, while at the same time condemning human beings to see themselves as out of date.

At the heart of the nanotechnological dream we therefore encounter a paradox that, as the present work shows, has been with us since the cybernetic chapter in the philosophical history of cognitive science—an extraordinary paradox arising from the convergence of opposites, whereby the overweening ambition and pride of a certain scientific humanism leads directly to the obsolescence of humankind. It is in the light, or perhaps I should say the shadow, of this paradox that all "ethical" questions touching on the engineering of humankind by humankind must be considered.

In 1964, Norbert Wiener published an odd book with the curious title *God and Golem, Inc.: A Comment on Certain Points where Cybernetics Impinges on Religion.* In it one finds this:

> God is supposed to have made man in His own image, and the propagation of the race may also be interpreted as a function in which one living being makes another in its own image. In our desire to glorify God with respect to man and Man with respect to matter, it is thus natural to assume that machines cannot make other machines in their own image; that this is something associated with a sharp dichotomy of systems into living and non-living; and that it is moreover associated with the other dichotomy between creator and creature. Is this, however, so?[8]

The rest of the book is devoted to mobilizing the resources of cybernetics to show that these are false dichotomies and that, in truth, "machines are very well able to make other machines in their own image."[9]

In recent years, the enterprise of "making life from scratch" has been organized as a formal scientific discipline under the seemingly innocuous name of synthetic biology. In June 2007, the occasion of the first Kavli Futures Symposium at the University of Greenland in Ilulissat, leading researchers from around the world gathered to announce the convergence of work in synthetic biology and nanotechnology and to take stock of the most recent advances in the manufacture of artificial cells. Their call for a global effort to promote "the construction or redesign of biological systems components that do not naturally exist" evoked memories of the statement that was issued in Asilomar, California, more than thirty years earlier, in 1975, by the pioneers of biotechnology. Like their predecessors, the founders of synthetic biology insisted not only on the splendid things they were poised to achieve, but also on the dangers that might flow from them. Accordingly, they invited society to prepare itself for the consequences, while laying down rules of ethical conduct for themselves.[10] We know what became of the charter drawn up at Asilomar. A few years later, this attempt by scientists to regulate their own research lay shattered in pieces. The dynamics of technological advance and the greed of the marketplace refused to suffer any limitation.

Only a week before the symposium in Ilulissat, a spokesman for the Action Group on Erosion, Technology and Concentration (ETC), an environmental lobby based in Ottawa that has expanded its campaign against genetically modified foods to include emerging nanotechnologies, greeted the announcement of a feat of genetic engineering by the J. Craig Venter Institute in Rockville, Maryland, with the memorable words, "For the first time, God has competition." In the event, ETC had misinterpreted the nature of the achievement.[11] But if the Ilulissat Statement is to be believed, the actual synthesis of an organism equipped with an artificial genome ("a free-living organism that can grow and replicate") will become a reality in the next few years. Whatever the actual timetable may turn out to be, the process of fabricating DNA is now better understood with every passing day, and the moment when it will be possible to create an artificial cell using artificial DNA is surely not far off.

The question arises, however, whether such an achievement will really amount to *creating life*. In order to assert this much, one must suppose that between life and nonlife there is an absolute distinction, a critical threshold, so that whoever crosses it will have shattered a taboo, like the prophet Jeremiah and like Rabbi Löw of Prague in the Jewish tradition, who dared to create an artificial man, a *golem*. In the view of its promoters and some of its admirers, notably the English physicist and science writer Philip Ball,[12] synthetic biology has succeeded in demonstrating that no threshold of this type exists: between the dust of the earth and the creature that God formed from it, there is no break in continuity that permits us to say (quoting *Genesis* 2:7) that He breathed into man's nostrils the breath of life. And even in the event that synthetic biology should turn out to be incapable of fabricating an artificial cell, these researchers contend, it would still have had the virtue of depriving the prescientific notion of life of all consistency.

It is here, in the very particular logic that is characteristic of dreams, that nanotechnology plays an important symbolic role. It is typically defined by the scale of the phenomena over which it promises to exert control—a scale that is described in very vague terms, since it extends from a tenth of a nanometer[13] to a tenth of a micron. Nevertheless, over this entire gamut, the essential distinction between life and nonlife loses all meaning. It is meaningless to say, for example, that a DNA molecule is a living thing. At the symbolic level, a lack of precision in defining nanotechnology does not matter; what matters is the deliberate and surreptitious attempt to blur a fundamental distinction that until now has enabled human beings to steer a course through the world that was given to them. In the darkness of dreams, there is no difference between a living cat and a dead cat.

Once again, we find that science oscillates between two opposed attitudes: on the one hand, vainglory, an excessive and often indecent pride; and on the other, when it becomes necessary to silence critics, a false humility that consists in denying that one has done anything out of the ordinary, anything that departs from the usual business of normal science. As a philosopher, I am more troubled by the false humility, for in truth it is this, and not the vainglory, that constitutes the height of pride. I am less disturbed by a science that claims to be the equal of God than by a science that drains of all meaning one of the most essential distinctions known to humanity since the moment it first came into existence: the distinction between that which lives and that which does not; or, to speak more bluntly, between life and death.

Let me propose an analogy that is more profound, I believe, than one may at first be inclined to suspect. With the rise of terrorism in recent years, specifically in the form of suicide attacks, violence on a global scale has taken a radically new turn. The first edition of this book belongs to a bygone era, which ended on September 11, 2001. In that world, even the most brutal persecutor expressed his attachment to life, because he killed in order to affirm and assert the primacy of his own way of living. But when the persecutor assumes the role of victim, killing himself in order to maximize the number of people killed around him, all distinctions are blurred, all possibility of reasoned dissuasion is lost, all control of violence is doomed to impotence. If science is allowed, in its turn, to continue along this same path in denying the crucial difference that life introduces in the world, it will, I predict, prove itself to be capable of a violence that is no less horrifying.

Among the most extreme promises of nanotechnology, as we have seen, is immortality (or "indefinite life extension," as it is called). But if there is thought to be no essential difference between the living and the nonliving, then there is nothing at all extraordinary about this promise. Yet again, Hannah Arendt very profoundly intuited what such a pact with the devil would involve:

> The greatest and most appalling danger for human thought is that what we once believed could be wiped out by the discovery of some fact that had hitherto remained unknown; for example, it could be that one day we succeed in making men immortal, and everything we had ever thought concerning death and its profundity would then become simply laughable. Some may think that this is too high a price to pay for the suppression of death.[4]

The ETC Group's premonitory observation—"For the first time, God has competition"—can only strengthen the advocates of NBIC convergence in their belief that those who criticize them do so for religious reasons. The same phrases are always used to sum up what is imagined to be the heart of this objection: human beings do not have the right to usurp powers reserved to God alone; *playing God* is forbidden.[5] Often it is added that this taboo is specifically Judeo-Christian.

Let us put to one side the fact that this allegation wholly misconstrues the teaching of the Talmud as well as that of Christian theology. In conflating them with the ancient Greek conception of the sacred—the gods, jealous of men who have committed the sin of pride, *hubris*, send after them the goddess of vengeance, Nemesis—it forgets that the Bible depicts man as cocreator of the world with God. As the French biophysicist and Talmudic scholar Henri Atlan notes with regard to the literature about the golem:

> One does not find [in it], at least to begin with, the kind of negative judgment one finds in the Faust legend concerning the knowledge and creative activity of men "in God's image." Quite to the contrary, it is in creative activity that man attains his full humanity, in a perspective of *imitatio Dei* that allows him to be associated with God, in a process of ongoing and perfectible creation.[16]

Within the Christian tradition, authors such as G. K. Chesterton, René Girard, and Ivan Illich see Christianity as the womb of Western modernity, while arguing that modernity has betrayed and corrupted its message. This analysis links up with Max Weber's idea of the desacralization of the world—its famous "disenchantment"—in regarding Christianity, or at least what modernity made of it, as the main factor in the progressive elimination of all taboos, sacred prohibitions, and other forms of religious limitation.

It fell to science itself to extend and deepen this desacralization, inaugurated by the religions of the Bible, by stripping nature of any prescriptive or normative value. It is utterly futile, then, to accuse science of being at odds with the Judeo-Christian tradition on this point. Kantianism, for its part, conferred philosophical legitimacy on the devaluation of nature by regarding it as devoid of intentions and reasons, inhabited only by causes, and by severing the world of nature from the world of freedom, where the reasons for human action fall under the jurisdiction of moral law.

Where, then, is the ethical problem located, if in fact there is one here? It clearly does not lie in the transgression of this or that taboo sanctioned by nature or the sacred, since the joint evolution of religion and science has done away with any such foundation for the very concept of a moral limitation, and hence of a transgression. But that is precisely the problem. For there is no free and autonomous human society that does not rest on some principle of self-limitation. We will not find the limits we desperately need in the religions of the Book, as though such limits are imposed on us by some transcendental authority, for these religions do nothing more than confront us with our own freedom and responsibility.

The ethical problem weighs more heavily than any specific question dealing, for instance, with the enhancement of a particular cognitive ability by one or another novel technology. But what makes it all the more intractable is that, whereas our capacity to act into the world is increasing without limit, with the consequence that we now find ouselves faced with new and unprecedented responsibilities, the ethical resources at our disposal are diminishing at the same pace. Why should this be? Because the same technological ambition that gives humankind such power to act on the world also reduces humankind to the status of an object that can be fashioned and shaped at will; the conception of the mind as a machine—the very conception that allows us to imagine the possibility of (re)fabricating ourselves—prevents us from fulfilling these new responsibilities. Hence my profound pessimism.

Since this book first appeared, I have been saddened by the loss of three dear friends who figured in its conception and publication: the psychiatrist and communication theorist Paul Watzlawick, who was one of the chief disciples of Gregory Bateson; the Chilean neurophilosopher Francisco Varela, cofounder of the theory of autopoietic systems; and finally Heinz von Foerster, a Viennese Jewish immigrant to the United States who, after serving as secretary to the Macy Conferences, the cradle of cybernetics in its first phase, went on to found what was to be called second-order cybernetics. Francisco and Heinz play important roles in the story that I tell in this book. I miss them both terribly.

The first edition of this book was dedicated to my teacher Jean Ullmo, who had passed away long before, as well as to Heinz von Foerster, then still very much alive. I had the good fortune of being able to present Heinz with my book and to see his appreciative reaction to it. To pay him a final homage, I would like to conclude by recounting a very lovely and moving story he told me, one that has a direct bearing on the arguments developed here.

The story takes place in Vienna toward the end of 1945, and it concerns another Viennese Jew, the psychiatrist Viktor Frankl, whose celebrated book *Man's Search for Meaning* was to be published the following year. Frankl had just returned to Vienna, having miraculously survived the Auschwitz-Birkenau camp; in the meantime he had learned that his wife, his parents, his brother, and other members of his family had all been exterminated. He decided to resume his practice. Here, then, is the story as my friend Heinz told it:

> Concentration camps were the setting for many horrific stories. Imagine then
> the incredulous delight of a couple who returned to Vienna from two differ-

ent camps to find each other alive. They were together for about six months, and then the wife died of an illness she had contracted in the camp. At this her husband lost heart completely, and fell into the deepest despair, from which none of his friends could rouse him, not even with the appeal "Imagine if she had died earlier and you had not been reunited!" Finally he was convinced to seek the help of Viktor Frankl, known for his ability to help the victims of the catastrophe.

They met several times, conversed for many hours, and eventually one day Frankl said: "Let us assume God granted me the power to create a woman just like your wife: she would remember all your conversations, she would remember the jokes, she would remember every detail: you could not distinguish this woman from the wife you lost. Would you like me to do it?" The man kept silent for a while, then stood up and said, "No thank you, doctor!" They shook hands; the man left and started a new life.

When I asked him about this astonishing and simple change, Frankl explained, "You see, Heinz, we see ourselves through the eyes of the other. When she died, he became blind. But when he *saw* that he was blind, he could see!"[17]

This, at least, is the lesson that von Foerster drew from this story—in typical cybernetic fashion. But I think that another lesson can be drawn from it, one that extends the first. What was it that this man suddenly saw, which he did not see before? The thought experiment that Frankl invited his patient to perform echoes one of the most famous Greek myths, that of Amphitryon. In order to seduce Amphitryon's wife, Alcmena, and to pass a night of love with her, Zeus assumes the form of Amphytryon.

All through the night, Alcmena loves a man whose qualities are in every particular identical to those of her husband. The self-same description would apply equally to both. All the reasons that Alcmena has for loving Amphitryon are equally reasons for loving Zeus, who has the appearance of Amphitryon, for Zeus and Amphitryon can only be distinguished numerically: they are two rather than one. Yet it is Amphitryon whom Alcmena loves and not the god who has taken on his form. If one wishes to account for the emotion of love by appeal to arguments meant to justify it or to the qualities that lovers attribute to the objects of their love, what rational explanation can be given for that "something" which Amphitryon possesses, but that Zeus does not, and which explains why Alcmena loves only Amphitryon, and not Zeus?[18]

When we love somebody, we do not love a list of characteristics, even one that is sufficiently exhaustive to distinguish the person in question from anyone else. The most perfect simulation still fails to capture something, and it is this something that is the essence of love—this poor word that says everything and explains nothing. I very much fear that the spontaneous ontology of those who wish to set themselves up as the makers or re-creators of the world know nothing of the beings who inhabit it, only lists of characteristics. If the nanotechnological dream were ever to come true, what still today we call love would become incomprehensible.[19]

Jean-Pierre Dupuy
Paris, July 2008

NOTES

1. See Jean-Pierre Dupuy, "Some Pitfalls in the Philosophical Foundations of Nanoethics," *Journal of Medicine and Philosophy* 32, no. 3 (2007): 237–261; Jean-Pierre Dupuy, "Complexity and Uncertainty: A Prudential Approach to Nanotechnology," in *Nanoethics: Examining the Social Impact of Nanotechnology*, ed. John Weckert, et al., 119–131 (Hoboken, N.J.: John Wiley and Sons, 2007); Jean-Pierre Dupuy, "The double language of science, and why it is so difficult to have a proper public debate about the nanotechnology program," foreword to *Nanoethics: Emerging Debates*, eds. Fritz Allhoff and Patrick Lin (Dordrecht: Springer, 2008); and Jean-Pierre Dupuy and Alexei Grinbaum, "Living with Uncertainty: Toward a Normative Assessment of Nanotechnology," *Techné* (joint issue with *Hyle*) 8, no. 2 (2004): 4–25.

2. Mihail C. Roco and William Sims Bainbridge, *Converging Technologies for Improving Human Performance: Nanotechnology, Biotechnology, Information Technology, and Cognitive Science* (Washington, D.C.: National Science Foundation, 2002), 13.

3. Damien Broderick, *The Spike: How Our Lives Are Being Transformed by Rapidly Advancing Technologies* (New York: Forge, 2001), 118.

4. See Kevin Kelly, "Will Spiritual Robots Replace Humanity by 2100?" The Technium, http://www.kk.org/thetechnium/.

5. Hannah Arendt, *The Human Condition* (Chicago: University of Chicago Press, 1958), 231.

6. Ibid., 2–3.

7. See Günther Anders, *Die Antiquiertheit des Menschen*, 2 vols. (Munich: Beck, 1980), 1:21–97.

8. Norbert Wiener, *God and Golem, Inc.: A Comment on Certain Points where Cybernetics Impinges on Religion* (Cambridge, Mass.: MIT Press, 1964), 12.

9. Ibid., 13.

10. The Ilulissat Statement, Kavli Futures Symposium, "The Merging of Bio and Nano: Towards Cyborg Cells," June 11–15, 2007, Ilulissat, Greenland.

11. Carole Lartigue's JCVI team had succeeded in "simply" transferring the genome of one bacterium, *Mycoplasma mycoides*, to another, *Mycoplasma capricolum*, and showing that the cells of the recipient organism could function with the new genome. In effect, one species had been converted into another.

12. See Philip Ball, "Meanings of 'life': Synthetic biology provides a welcome antidote to chronic vitalism," *Nature* 447 (June 28, 2007): 1031–1032.

13. A nanometer is one-billionth of a meter.

14. Hannah Arendt, *Journal de pensée (1950–1973)*, 2 vols., trans. Sylvie Courtine-Denamy (Paris: Seuil, 2005), 2:786.

15. See the section "Concerns about 'Playing God'" in the November 1982 report of the U.S. President's Commission for the Study of Ethical Problems in Medicine and Biomedical and Behavioral Research, "The Social and Ethical Issues of Genetic Engineering with Human Beings," 53–73.

16. Henri Atlan, *Les étincelles de hasard*, 2 vols. (Paris: Seuil, 1999–2003), 1:45.

17. Translated from the German ("Wir sehen uns mit den Augen des anderen. . . . Als er aber erkannte, daßer blind war, da konnte er sehen!"); see Heinz von Foerster, "Mit den Augen des anderen," in *Wissen und Gewissen: Versuch einer Brücke*, ed. Siegfried J. Schmidt, 350–363 (Frankfurt: Suhrkamp, 1993).

18. Monique Canto-Sperber, "Amour," in *Dictionnaire d'éthique et de philosophie morale*, 4th edition, ed. Monique Canto-Sperber, 41 (Paris: Presses Universitaires de France, 2004).

19. Some readers regretted that I did not develop a more provocative argument than the one I merely hinted at here, namely that a marriage of cognitive science and Husserlian phenomenology would have been much more fruitful than the one that was actually consummated between cognitive science and the analytic philosophy of mind and language. But it was not my intention to include my own work or that of my colleagues in the philosophical history that I recount in the pages that follow. The desired argument is laid out in extensive detail in Jean Petitot, Francisco Varela, Bernard Pachoud, and Jean-Michel Roy, eds., *Naturalizing Phenomenology: Issues in Contemporary Phenomenology and Cognitive Science* (Stanford: Stanford University Press, 2000).

Preface

M

Y INTEREST in cybernetics dates from 1976, the year I was fortunate enough to meet the founder of its second phase of activity, Heinz von Foerster, who, as the secretary of the last five Macy Conferences, was responsible for preparing the transcripts of these meetings. Elsewhere I have recounted the circumstances of our encounter, which was decisive in orienting my future research.[1]

At the time, von Foerster was nearing the end of a career almost wholly devoted to what he called "second-order cybernetics," whose home was the Biological Computer Laboratory he had founded two decades earlier at the University of Illinois. Thanks to von Foerster I came into contact with two scientists whose work on self-organization in living organisms had drawn its initial impetus from his own thinking: the French biophysicist Henri Atlan and the Chilean neurophysiologist Francisco Varela.[2] The wave of orthodox cognitive science had not yet reached the shores of France, and so it was the theory of self-organizing systems that first brought together French researchers interested in problems of cognition, not only from the point of view of the life sciences but also from that of the social sciences. Two conferences that I organized during the summer and fall of 1981, one at Cerisy-la-Salle in Normandy, the other at Stanford University, demonstrated the fruitfulness of this approach.[3]

In the meantime the École Polytechnique in Paris had decided, at the urging of the eminent physicist and philosopher of science Jean Ullmo, to set up a center for philosophical research having a strong epistemological component. I was called upon to organize and direct this center, which was to be known as the Centre de Recherche en Épistemologie Appliquée (CRÉA), with a staff chosen from among those who had contributed to the success of the two conferences just mentioned, in particular Atlan and Varela. It is entirely natural, then, that I should dedicate this book to the memory of my teacher, Jean Ullmo, and no less natural that I dedicate it also to Heinz von Foerster, whose contagious enthusiasm had a great influence upon the theoretical orientation that I was led to give CRÉA at the time of its founding.

Theories of self-organization were therefore part of the center's research program from the beginning. At the same time it was clear that, despite their very great interest, they represented only one branch of cognitive science, and a quite marginal one at that. The authorities responsible for supervising scientific research in France had become aware, albeit somewhat belatedly, of the importance of a program of research that cut across long-established disciplinary boundaries, stimulating dialogue and debate among neurophysiologists, linguists, philosophers, economists, anthropologists, and psychologists. CRÉA quickly became one of the leading research centers for cognitive science in France, placing great emphasis on philosophical issues. Its originality by comparison with similar centers elsewhere in the world, particularly in the United States, derives from the fact that it provides a forum for quite varied approaches and paradigms. Both analytic philosophy of mind and language and naturalized phenomenology play an important role in the work of the center; neither one shrinks from looking to mathematical models for inspiration—in this respect following the example of the first cybernetics. As a result of circumstance and institutional politics, research in cognitive science in France came to be focused primarily on neurobiology and artificial intelligence, with the human and social sciences taking a back seat. Here again CRÉA occupies a special place by virtue of the importance it attaches to social cognition, and therefore to social and political philosophy, as well as to the social sciences proper, chiefly economics and anthropology. At the Macy Conferences, as we shall have occasion to see, these last two disciplines conceived their future development in terms of the mechanistic view of the world championed by cybernetics.

It was in this context that I felt the need to reflect upon the origins of cognitive science, all the more since my own work—but also to some extent the force of circumstance—had made me one of its architects. Although the history of science and ideas is not my field, I could not imagine adopting Alfred North Whitehead's opinion that every science, in order to avoid stagnation, must forget its founders. To the contrary, it seems to me that the ignorance displayed by most scientists with regard to the history of their discipline, far from being a source of dynamism, acts as a brake on their creativity. To assign the history of science a role separate from that of research itself therefore seems to me mistaken. Science, like philosophy, needs to look back over its past from time to time, to inquire into its origins and to take a fresh look at models, ideas, and paths of investigation that had previously been explored but then for one reason or another were abandoned, great though their promise was. Many examples could be cited that confirm the usefulness of consulting history and, conversely, the wasted opportunities to which a neglect of history often leads. Thus we have witnessed in recent years, in the form of the theory of deterministic chaos, the rediscovery of Poincaré's dazzling intuitions and early results concerning nonlinear dynamics; the return to macroscopic physics, and the study of fluid dynamics and disordered systems, when previously only the infinitely small and the infinitely large had seemed worthy of the attention of physicists; the revival of interest in embryology, ethology, and ecology, casting off the leaden cloak that molecular biology had placed over the study of living things; the renewed appreciation of Keynes's profound insights into the role of individual and collective expectations in market regulation, buried for almost fifty years by the tide of vulgar Keynesianism; and, last but not least, since it is one of the main themes of this book, the rediscovery by cognitive science of the cybernetic model devised by McCulloch and Pitts, known now by the name of "neoconnectionism" or "neural networks," after several decades of domination by the cognitivist model.

The reasons for my own interest in the history of cognitive science are essentially philosophical. The fact that for a number of years I have directed a major center of research in cognitive science does not in any way imply that I am a convinced materialist. Although I am a rationalist, I nonetheless believe in the autonomy of the soul. I wholly subscribe to Thomas Nagel's view that "a solution to the mind-body problem is nowhere in sight."[4] Nonetheless, as I try to show in the first chapter of this book, the apparent inevitability of a materialist and mechanist solution was not due to any unanswerable philosophical argument but rather to the fact that it was rooted in a conception of the world and of knowledge that had a long history, going back to Hobbes and Vico. Accordingly, a purely philosophical critique of the mechanist materialism of cognitive science does not suffice to undermine its foundations. To do this, it is necessary to know where it came from—hence the present inquiry.

In 1983, the Centre National de la Recherche Scientifique (CNRS) asked me to head up a study group, under the auspices of its Science-Technology-Society program, to investigate the history of theories of self-organization. I put together at once a team whose members included Isabelle Stengers, a chemist as well as a philosopher and historian of science, and the author of a recent book with Ilya Prigogine, whose work on far-from-equilibrium systems had won him the Nobel Prize in chemistry six years earlier.[5] Together we were able to exploit the very rich work done at the Biological Computer Laboratory in Illinois, the mecca of the second cybernetics, Stengers retracing the history of the notion of self-organization in the physical and chemical sciences while I reserved for myself the task of analyzing the transactions of the Macy Conferences, to which I was able to obtain access owing to the generosity of Heinz von Foerster.

On learning that I had embarked on this project, von Foerster gave me the liveliest encouragement, for he was dismayed that the Macy Conferences had so far failed to arouse curiosity among scholars. This situation was rapidly changing, however. An American historian of science, Steve Joshua Heims, had recently decided to reexamine the history of this period as well. I therefore got in touch with him, and we met for the first time the following year, 1984, in Boston. Heims and I remained in close contact during the entire time I worked on the original edition of this book. In 1985 I invited him to give a series of talks at CRÉA in Paris, and in our final CNRS report, transmitted in November that year in the form of two special issues of *Cahiers du CRÉA*, I included an essay by Heims that summarized the argument of his forthcoming book.[6] Without his careful historical research, I could not have successfully completed my own work.

The years went by. In France they were marked above all by the vigorous development of cognitive science and the emergence of CRÉA as an important center. In 1991 Heims published his long-awaited work on the Macy Conferences, *The Cybernetics Group*.[7] Three years later the results of my own research appeared under the title *Aux origines des sciences cognitives*.[8]

The situation of French thought in America, no less than that of American thought in France, is very much a part of the story told in this book. Since 1981 I have divided my time between research at the École Polytechnique and teaching at Stanford University. So that the American reader may better appreciate the perspective I bring to the history of cognitive science, let me quote from a talk that I delivered a few years ago at Stanford on the possibility—and the desirability—of going beyond the schism between the "two cultures."[9] Entitled "Beyond the Dualism between the Cultured Ignorami and the Hidebound Savants," it began by inquiring into what I call, with only mild exaggeration, the "schizophrenia" of American academic life:

> I have been asked to describe what it is like to be divided between two worlds. The division in my case is geographical, since I commute between California and France; but it is also cultural, since even at Stanford I find myself straddling the humanities, dominated by French poststructuralism, and philosophy and social science, dominated by American neopositivism. More fundamentally, I find myself divided—indeed torn—between a number of conflicting allegiances: between my background in logic, mathematics, and physics and my identity as a philosopher committed to the human sciences; between my need to think in terms of formal models and my deeply held conviction that literature is a superior form of knowledge to science; between the two ways of doing philosophy today: "Continental" philosophy—profound, rich, meaningful, but too often willfully obscure, elitist, and, at times, dishonest—and "analytic" philosophy—rigorous, egalitarian, democratic, but too often shallow and tedious—the one pointing toward literature, the other toward science; and, finally, between the narrow professionalism of

American academics, who devote themselves to knowing everything about "fields" so restricted that they often border on nothingness (the hidebound savants of my title), and the distinguished dilettantism of many French intellectuals, who tend to know almost nothing about everything (the cultured ignorami, or "foggy froggies").

Though I am torn, I refuse to be forced to choose between the Scylla of French intellectualism and the Charybdis of American academicism. From the unusual and rather uncomfortable vantage point I occupy on an American university campus, I observe the following oddity: on the one hand, students of literature are initiated into the mysteries of French-style "deconstruction," taught to celebrate the death of the human subject and to repeat ad nauseam that man is not his own master and that such awareness as he may have of his own affairs is severely limited by a sort of tyranny of the unconscious; while at the same time their fellow students in the economic, political, and cognitive sciences learn to systematically reduce social institutions to voluntary agreements between fully conscious and free individuals. It is fortunate for the stability of the system that these students practically never talk to each other—no more often, in fact, than do their professors.

Opposing the rationalist individualism of the American humanities and social sciences, including cognitive science, to the deconstruction of metaphysical humanism that animates the human sciences in France runs the risk of combining the worst aspects of French and American thought. Even if it is institutionally embedded in the heart of the American academy, such a distinction is not tenable philosophically. One of my aims in the present book is to establish just this, by showing that cognitive science represents both the highest expression of Western humanism and the source of its ultimate condemnation.

In addition to Steve Heims, I wish to express my gratitude to my colleagues at CRÉA, whose thinking about cognitive science, in both their published research and the many informal conversations I have been fortunate to have with them over the years, has greatly contributed to my work: Daniel Andler, Paul Dumouchel, Pascal Engel, Françoise Fogelman, Pierre Jacob, Maurice Milgram, Jean Petitot, Joëlle Proust, François Recanati, Dan Sperber, and Gérard Weisbuch; to those who have shown confidence in me by supporting my work and showing great patience when it has gone more slowly than I would have liked: Jean-Michel Besnier, François Gèze, and Dominique Wolton; to my research partners during the first phase of this project, from whom I borrowed a number of insights and discoveries: Isabelle Stengers, Pierre Lévy, and Pierre Livet; and, finally, to Henri Atlan, Francisco Varela, and Heinz von Foerster, who first introduced me to the ideas of cybernetics.

The ethical questions that are posed—and will continue to be posed—by new technologies of the mind, to which I briefly refer in the introduction, have been the object of much debate within a study group that Monique Canto-Sperber and I have recently formed at the École Polytechnique to examine issues in moral philosophy, the Groupe de Recherche et d'Intervention sur la Science et l'Éthique (GRISÉ). I wish to thank Monique from the bottom of my heart for all the encouragement and advice she has given me throughout the course of my work.

The English-language edition of this book is an extensively revised version of the original French edition. It was made possible by the interest shown in my work by three people: the psychotherapist and communication theorist Paul Watzlawick, a disciple of Gregory Bateson and, by virtue of this, an heir to the cybernetic tradition;[10] Michael Arbib, of the University of Southern California, an eminent brain researcher and one of the very few cognitive scientists who, as a faithful disciple of Warren McCulloch, has had the courage to declare—and to brilliantly illustrate in his own work—that the cybernetic paradigm remains a promising alternative, which artificial intelligence and cognitivism have not succeeded in rendering obsolete;[11] and Thomas Pavel, of the University of Chicago, whose efforts to give a fuller and more accurate picture of current French thought than the small portion of it that is known to the literature departments of American universities presently permits are remarkable. To each of them I wish to express my thanks.

Last, but not least, I would like to express my profound gratitude to my translator, Malcolm DeBevoise. "Translator" is not really the right word. Faced with a difficult and dense French text, he repeatedly insisted on clarifications while criticizing my arguments point by point. The result is a book that is very different from the original, clearer, more complete, more candid. In France it is customary for authors not to reveal their motives any more than is strictly necessary, for fear of multiplying openings for critics; in America, I have learned, candor is a mark of the respect an author owes his readers. In this, and in other things, Malcolm has been a demanding tutor.

Jean-Pierre Dupuy
Paris, October 1999

On the Origins of Cognitive Science

The Self-Mechanized Mind

ROM 1946 TO 1953 ten conferences—the first nine held at the Beekman Hotel at 575 Park Avenue in New York, the last at the Nassau Inn in Princeton, New Jersey—brought together at regular intervals some of the greatest minds of the twentieth century. Sponsored by the Josiah Macy, Jr. Foundation, these meetings have since come to be known as the Macy Conferences. The mathematicians, logicians, engineers, physiologists, neurophysiologists, psychologists, anthropologists, and economists who took part set themselves the task of constructing a general science of how the human mind works. What brought them together, what they discussed, and what came of a collaboration unique in the history of ideas— these things form the subject of the present volume.

Every group of this kind adopts a code name as a way of affirming its identity. In the case of the Macy Conferences it was "cybernetics." Today this name has fallen out of fashion, to say the least. Since 1954 the project undertaken by the Cybernetics Group[1] has been carried on under a series of different names, ultimately coming to be known as "cognitive science." Why cognitive science today is ashamed of its cybernetic heritage is one of the chief questions I wish to address.

The Cybernetic Credo

The Cybernetics Group drew exceptional energy and passion from two convictions that were shared by most of its members and that were so novel at the time that the simple fact of defending them made one part of an elitist avant-garde, worshipped by some and demonized by others. These two convictions were based on logical and scientific discoveries that had been made in the immediately preceding decades, the consequences of which the members of the Cybernetics Group intended to exploit to the fullest. In very general terms, which will need subsequently to be made more precise, they held that:

1. Thinking is a form of computation. The computation involved is not the mental operation of a human being who manipulates symbols in applying

rules, such as those of addition or multiplication; instead it is what a particular class of machines do—machines technically referred to as "algorithms." By virtue of this, thinking comes within the domain of the mechanical.

2. Physical laws can explain why and how nature—in certain of its manifestations, not restricted exclusively to the human world—appears to us to contain meaning, finality, directionality, and intentionality.

Inspired by these two articles of faith with a fervor and an enthusiasm rarely matched in the history of science, the founders of the cybernetic movement believed they were in a position to achieve very great things. They thought it possible to construct a scientific, physicalist theory of the mind, and thereby resolve the ancient philosophical problem of mind and matter. They thought themselves capable of reconciling the world of meaning with the world of physical laws. Thanks to them, the mind would at last find its rightful place in nature.

They were neither the first nor the last to conceive of such an ambition. In the past it had generally been philosophers who debated such questions, fraught with metaphysical assumptions and implications. Materialists feared that the slightest hint of dualism would let back in religion, which they abhorred; dualists, for their part, saw in materialism a threat to man's free will. But now scientists and engineers ventured to address what formerly had been philosophical problems. For them, to devise a theory meant to build a model, which was to be constructed not only on paper but in physical form as well. They were persuaded that one truly understands only that which one has made, or is capable of making. Their research program would be realized, they thought, only when—like God, who was supposed to have created the universe—they had succeeded in making a brain that exhibited all the properties associated with the mind. Indeed, one of the most influential works of the cybernetics movement bore the title *Design for a Brain*.[2]

In this book I retrace the exceedingly complex intellectual history of this movement and defend the thesis that contemporary cognitive science is fully rooted in cybernetics. This is not to say that the ideas underlying cybernetics do not differ from those of the rival paradigms that contend within cognitive science today. Ideas have changed to such an extent during the past half-century, in fact, that I feel the need to warn the reader at the outset against a number of serious misunderstandings on the part of cognitive scientists that are the result of interpreting cybernetics in the light of present-day conceptions. It will be well, then, to go back to the two basic convictions mentioned earlier and to examine how they differ from current beliefs.

The cyberneticians' first thesis—that to think is to compute as a certain class of machines do—amounted to analyzing and describing what it is to think, not, as it is commonly supposed, to deciding whether it is possible to conceive of machines that think. The question "Can a machine think?" did not come to the forefront until later, at the beginning of the 1950s, as the research program known as artificial intelligence began gradually to establish itself within computer science. To this question cybernetics obviously could only respond in the affirmative, since it had already defined the activity of thinking as the property of a certain class of machines. It is important to see, however, that cybernetics represented not the anthropomorphization of the machine but rather the mechanization of the human. This is only one of many received ideas about cybernetics that needs to be stood on its head.

When the question "Can a machine think?" is posed today, one thinks above all of computers. Cognitivism—as the tendency that has long been dominant within cognitive science is known—is often thought of as dogmatically relying upon the computer metaphor: to think is to manipulate physical symbols by following rules after the fashion of a computer program. This definition is commonly—and altogether mistakenly—said to be due to cybernetics. The error has to do, first of all, with a matter of historical fact: when the cybernetics movement came into being, the computer did not yet exist. As we shall see, the computer was conceived by John von Neumann as a direct result of cybernetic ideas; it did not form the technological background against which these ideas developed. Here again the reversal of perspective that needs to be brought about is total. In this case, at least, the old "idealist" thesis—so denigrated by sociologists of science, who see themselves as resolute materialists—turns out to have been correct: it is not the physical world that determines the evolution of ideas, but rather ideas that generate scientific and technological development.

But the error committed by those who hold cybernetics responsible for identifying thinking with the functioning of a computer is above all a philosophical error, the nature of which it is important to grasp. The computations carried out by a computer are of a very special kind in that they involve symbols, which is to say representations. On the cognitivist view, symbols are objects that have three aspects: physical, syntactic, semantic. It is on the strength of these symbols that cognitivism claims to be able to span the gap that separates the physical world from the world of meaning. Computation may therefore be described as the central pier of the cognitivist bridge. Cognitivism also assumes that purely formal computations carried out at the syntactic level are materially embodied in the causal processes that occur within the computer insofar as it is a physical object, and are interpreted at the semantic level on the basis of elementary meanings assigned to the symbols. This solution to the problem posed by the presence of meaning in a world of physical facts that are linked by causal laws has been sharply attacked. As John Searle, one of the fiercest and most influential critics of cognitivism and artificial intelligence, has argued, "Syntax by itself is neither constitutive of nor sufficient for semantics,"[3] which is to say that the execution of a computer program cannot in principle enable the machine to understand what it does, to be conscious of what it does, or to give meaning to the world in which it functions. The cognitivists have replied by conceding that a computer program, being an abstract and purely syntactic object, naturally cannot claim to be equipped with a mind, much less claim to *be* a mind. They concede also that mind can arise in the physical world only from a causal dynamics. But cognitivism asserts that if a mind arises as a result of implementing a certain program in the physical world, then any implementation of the same program in a different hardware, no matter what it may be, would produce a mind endowed with the same properties. In other words, what is essential for the emergence of mind is not the concrete causal organization of this or that material system possessing a mind; what is essential is its *abstract* causal organization, which remains invariant when one passes from one material system to another.[4]

The fundamental concepts that allow cognitivism to advance this type of argument today are due to cybernetics. As it happens, however, cybernetics conceived and articulated these concepts in a very different manner that made no reference whatever to a computer—an object that had yet to be invented in the form in which we now know it. The three levels postulated by cognitive science—computation, causal physical laws, and meaning—were already developed in cybernetic thinking; but, in passing from cybernetics to cognitivism, both the character and the order of these levels came to be altered. How and why this transformation came about is another one of the questions that I will address in the course of this book.

First of all, computation as cybernetics conceived it is not symbolic computation; that is, computation involving representations. It is purely "mechanical," devoid of meaning. The objects on which cybernetic computation bears have no symbolic value, being carried out by a network of idealized neurons in which each neuron is an elementary calculator that computes zeroes and ones as a function of the signals it receives from the neurons with which it is in communication. This type of neuronal network, which mimics the anatomical structure and functional organization of the brain, is one of cybernetics' very greatest conceptual inventions. Under the name of "connectionism" it has since come to constitute within contemporary cognitive science, and in particular within the field of artificial intelligence, a fully fledged paradigm capable of competing with cognitivism and what is now called classical artificial intelligence. A history of cognitive science that omits mention of its cybernetic origins, as is often done, gives the impression that connectionism is a new paradigm, devised

relatively recently in order to rescue cognitive science from the impasses
into which cognitivism had led it. This again is a glaring error. Once cybernetics is reintegrated into the history of cognitive science, as it must be,
it becomes clear that computation was first introduced into the construction of a materialist and physicalist science of the mind not as symbolic
computation involving representations, but instead as a sort of blind computation having no meaning whatever, either with respect to its objects or
to its aims.

And if, in the cybernetic conception, meaning and mind happen to be
associated with matter, it is because they *arise from* it. Someone who subscribes to Searle's critique of cognitivism and who holds that symbolic
computation is incapable of giving rise to meaning, even though it concerns objects that already have a semantic value, may feel all the more
strongly tempted to conclude that a type of computation that is devoid of
any meaning whatsoever has still less chance of conjuring up meaning. But
this is just the point: the cyberneticians did not derive meaning from computation; they derived it from causal physical laws. This brings us to the
second of the basic convictions of cybernetics.

As we enter the twenty-first century, there is nothing in the least odd
about the idea of a physics of meaning.[5] An impressive series of scientific
and mathematical discoveries made during the second half of the twentieth century has completely changed the way in which we conceive of
dynamics, the branch of mechanics (formerly described as "rational")
that concerns the path of development or trajectory of a material system
subject to purely causal physical laws. It is well known today that complex
systems, made up of many elements interacting in nonlinear ways, possess
remarkable properties—so-called *emergent* properties—that justify their
description in terms that one should have thought had been forever banished from science in the wake of the Galilean-Newtonian revolution.
Thus it is said of these systems that they are endowed with "autonomy,"
that they are "self-organizing," that their paths "tend" toward "attractors," that they have "intentionality" and "directionality"—*as if* their
paths were guided by an end that gives meaning and direction to them
even though it has not yet been reached; as if, to borrow Aristotelian categories, purely efficient causes were capable of producing effects that mimic
the effects of a final cause.

The many physico-mathematical concepts and theories that have contributed to this upheaval fit together with each other in extremely complicated ways. One thinks of "catastrophes," attractors and bifurcations of
nonlinear dynamical systems, critical phenomena and symmetry break-
ings, self-organization and critical self-organizing states, nonlinear thermodynamics and dissipative structures, the physics of disordered systems,
deterministic chaos, and so on. The models of this new physics make it

possible to understand the mechanisms of morphogenesis, which is to say
the emergence of qualitative structures at a macroscopic level that organize themselves around the singularities—or qualitative discontinuities—
of underlying processes at the microscopic level. By studying and classify-
ing these singularities, which structure the way in which physical phenomena appear to us, it may be possible to construct a theory of meaning. As
the editors of a recent collection of articles on this topic put it, meaning "is
perfectly susceptible to a physicalist approach provided that we rely upon
the qualitative macrophysics of complex systems and no longer upon the
microphysics of elementary systems."[6] It is very telling in this respect that
the physics to which cognitivism refers when it undertakes to "naturalize"
and "physicalize" the mind remains precisely a microphysics of elementary systems. Indeed, it would not be unfair to say that by postulating
an ultimate microlevel of reality whose elements are subject to fundamental laws, the cognitivists' physics is essentially a physics of philosophers, evidence for which is nowhere to be found today in actual physics
laboratories.

What has cybernetics got to do with all of this? To be sure, the physical
and mathematical theories just mentioned did not yet exist in the early
days of cybernetics, or were then only in an embryonic stage. But the cyberneticians, most of them outstanding specialists in physics and mathematics, were armed with a battery of concepts that included not only the
notion—already classical at the time—of an attractor of a dynamical system, but also more revolutionary notions that they invented or at least
considerably developed, such as feedback, circular causality, systems, and
complexity. Above all they disposed of an incomparable theoretical instrument: the neural network. These things were quite enough to fortify the
cyberneticians in what I described at the outset as their second fundamental conviction. Eloquent testimony to this is the fact that before adopting
the name "cybernetics," the movement described its mission as the elaboration of a "theory of teleological mechanisms." Indeed the title the cyberneticians gave to their first meetings was just this: "Teleological Mechanisms"—an expression that is continually encountered in their writings
and speeches, whether these were intended for publication in technical
journals, for presentation at scientific conferences, or to sway financial
backers and the general public. It is almost impossible today to imagine
how very scandalous this formula seemed at the time. It appeared to be the
ultimate oxymoron, a pure contradiction in terms, for it seemed to conflate
two types of explanation: mechanical explanation by causes, the only kind
admitted by science, and explanation by ends (*telos*), utterly forbidden by
science. Naturally the cyberneticians did not think themselves guilty of
any such confusion; naturally, too, they yielded completely to scientific

discipline in recognizing only causal explanations. What the expression "teleological mechanisms" was meant to signify was the capacity of certain complex physical systems, through their behavior, to mimic—to *simulate*—the manifestations of what in everyday language, unpurified by scientific rigor, we call purposes and ends, even intention and finality. The cyberneticians believed that behind these manifestations there lay only a causal organization of a certain type, which it was their business to identify. In other words, no matter the hardware in which this type of causal organization is implemented—and, in particular, no matter whether the hardware is part of a natural physical system or an artificial physical system—this causal organization will give off the same effects of purpose and intentionality.

John Searle, in his critique of cognitivism, has asserted that its principal error consists in confusing simulation and duplication. To quote one of his favorite examples, it would be absurd—as everyone will readily agree—to try to digest a pizza by running a computer program that simulates the biochemical processes that occur in the stomach of someone who actually digests a pizza. How is it then, Searle asks, that cognitivists do not see that it would be just as absurd to claim to be able to duplicate the neurobiological functioning of the mind by running a computer program that simulates, or models, this functioning? Fair enough. But how much force would this argument have if the process in question, rather than being a physical process such as digesting a pizza, were already itself a simulation? Consider the attempt by certain theorists (notably French deconstructionists) to demystify the concept of money. Noting that in the form of fiat money—paper currency, for example—it is a pure sign, lacking intrinsic value, inconvertible into gold or other mineral treasure, they conclude that money by its very nature is counterfeit. The fact that money nonetheless remains the basis of commercial exchange is due, they argue, solely to the existence of a potentially infinite chain of shared gullibilities: if money (truly) possesses a positive value, this is only because everyone (falsely) believes that it possesses a positive value. Let us suppose that this theory is correct: it must then be concluded that there is no essential difference between a dollar bill printed by the Federal Reserve and a *simulated* dollar bill—a counterfeit dollar. This counterfeit dollar will be used in commercial exchange in the same way as the dollar that has officially been authorized as legal tender, so long as it is believed to have the same value; that is, so long as no one suspects that it is counterfeit. For the cyberneticians, meaning is by its very nature counterfeit: its essence is confused with its appearance. To simulate this essence, for example by means of a model, is to remain true to it, since simulation amounts actually to duplicating it. This argument is one that the cyberneticians, for their part, could have made in response to a critique of the sort that Searle brings against cognitivism; it is not, however, an argument that cognitivists can use to defend themselves against Searle's attacks.

Must it therefore be said that the cyberneticians reduced meaning and finality to a pure illusion produced by certain forms of causal organization? One might with equal justification hold that, to the contrary, they rescued phenomenality—appearance—by uncovering the mechanisms (the algorithms) that generate it. The cyberneticians themselves were divided between these two interpretations, depending on their sensibility. The most radical and uncompromising among them wholeheartedly embraced the project of demystifying appearance; others showed greater subtlety, implicitly adopting the strategy developed by Kant in the second part of his third Critique, the *Kritik der Urteilskraft*, entitled "Critique of Teleological Judgment." In a sense, the typically cybernetic expression "teleological mechanisms" constitutes a striking condensation of this strategy. Only explanations that ultimately appeal to causal mechanisms are considered adequate. Nonetheless, faced with the most surprising manifestations of complexity in nature (life for Kant, the mind for the cyberneticians), recourse to another "maxim of judgment"—teleological judgment—becomes inevitable. Concepts such as "internal finality" are indispensable, and perfectly legitimate, so long as one keeps in mind that they have only heuristic and descriptive relevance. Teleological judgment consists in treating them *as though*—the Kantian *als ob*—they have objective value. The role played by simulation in the history of cognitive science since the earliest days of cybernetics is in part a reflection of this doctrine of make-believe.

Until now I have spoken of the cyberneticians as though they were a homogenous group, while suggesting a moment ago that there were clear differences of temperament and viewpoint within the movement. These differences were, in fact, sometimes quite pronounced. The debates, controversies, and, indeed, conflicts that resulted from them were what gave this episode in the history of ideas its exceptional richness. Whatever unity cybernetics may have enjoyed was a complicated one. The work of the Cybernetics Group, which constitutes the main object of this book, produced a very considerable progeny. In particular, it is important to note that it gave birth to a second cybernetics, very different in style than the first. This offshoot, which called itself "second-order cybernetics," was founded by Heinz von Foerster, who in 1949 became the secretary of the Macy Conferences. From 1958 to 1976 its home was the Biological Computer Laboratory, established and directed by von Foerster on the campus of the University of Illinois at Urbana-Champaign. The place of the second cybernetics in the history of cognitive science is modest by contrast with the importance of the concepts it developed and with the influence that these concepts were to exercise upon a great number of researchers (the present author included) in a wide variety of fields. One of its chief topics of research, self-organization in complex systems, led to fascinating breakthroughs in the direction of giving a physical interpretation to meaning. Its great misfortune was to have been overshadowed by artificial intelligence and cognitivism, which experienced a boom during these same years. Because von Foerster and his collaborators had the audacity—or perhaps only because they were foolish enough—to adopt in their turn the label "cybernetics," which in the meantime had acquired a poor reputation, the leaders of these rival movements, now in the process of asserting their primacy, dismissed them as amateurs and nuisances. But the history of cognitive science is by no means finished. As a result of the success currently enjoyed by connectionism, one begins to see the first timid signs of renewed interest on the part of some researchers in the ideas of the second cybernetics. Although these ideas are not the main interest of the present book, I will refer to them frequently in trying to explain why the first cybernetics, confronted with the theories of self-organization and complexity that were to be dear to its successor, turned its back on them, and indeed sometimes—a cruel irony!—actually combatted them. In retrospect this appears to show an astonishing lack of lucidity on the part of the original cyberneticians. What is more, it suggests that the origins of cognitive science lie in a failure.

Cybernetics and Cognitivism

We are now in a position to draw up a preliminary list of those things that both united cognitivism with its cybernetic parent and led to the break between them. Three levels of analysis are present in each case: computation, physical causality, and meaning. But hidden behind the nominal identity of these terms lie great differences in interpretation. The physics of the cognitivists is a fictional physics, a philosopher's physics; the physics of the cyberneticians is a true physics, a physicist's physics. The computation of the cyberneticians is a pure computation, independent of any reference to meaning; the computation of the cognitivists is a symbolic, conceptual computation, closely linked to meaning. Finally, and perhaps most important, the meaning in which cognitivists are interested is rooted in the properties of beings endowed with intentionality, and possibly consciousness as well: human beings and societies, organized biological forms, living and complex artificial systems. The meaning with which the cyberneticians were concerned was much more universal and abstract— "structuralist," one is tempted to say—in that it was consubstantial with all sufficiently complex forms of organization in nature, not excluding inanimate forms, and untainted by any trace of subjectivity. An amusing indication of how far this universalism could be taken is that among the hard-line materialists who made up the Cybernetics Group there was one scientist who, without seeming to be too far out of step with his colleagues, saw mind everywhere in nature, or at least in every manifestation of circular organization, whether a whirlpool in a torrent of water, a colony of ants, or an oscillating electric circuit.[7]

It is because the idea of a physics of meaning remains foreign to it that cognitivism is led to make symbolic computation the central pier of the bridge that will enable it, or so it hopes, to bridge the gap that separates mind and meaning from matter. The problems it has encountered arise from the fact that each of the two leaps proves to be a perilous one. On the one hand, the attempt to move from symbolic computation to meaning is open to attacks of the sort made by Searle, as we have seen. With regard to the attempt to move from symbolic computation to the domain of causal physical laws, the difficulty arises from the fact that the semantic and conceptual aspect of computation is not directly given in nature. The cyberneticians did not in principle run into these problems. In the last analysis this was because they took both physics and computation much more seriously than the cognitivists, stripping each one of anything that might call attention to the end to be reached, namely, mind and meaning; but also because they redefined mind and meaning in terms that excluded all reference whatever to psychology and subjectivity. The passage from physics to meaning, thus redefined, is direct, as we have seen. As for the relation between computation and causal physical laws, the cyberneticians had no hesitation in asserting their identity. They held that the laws of physics are computable and therefore that computational models and formalisms are perfectly suited to describing and specifying physical phenomena. Conversely, they were convinced by their theories, whether it was a question of electric circuits or the brain, that logic is embodied in matter, in natural as well as in artificial systems.

Cognitivism resulted from an alliance between cognitive science and the philosophical psychology that is known as philosophy of mind, currently a very active branch of analytic philosophy. Here we have a marriage that never could have occurred with cybernetics, and it is important to understand why. Philosophy of mind set itself the task of rescuing ordinary (or "folk") psychology by giving it a naturalist and materialist foundation— the only foundation, according to its practitioners, that is capable of conferring scientific legitimacy on any field of research, philosophy included. By "folk psychology" is meant the manner in which people give meaning to the actions and beliefs of their fellow human beings, but also to their own actions and beliefs, explaining them and interpreting them in terms of *reasons*. These reasons for acting and believing are constituted in turn by the agent's other beliefs, desires, intentions, fears, and so forth, all of them being "mental states" endowed with semantic content. Accordingly, explanation in terms of reasons presupposes and reveals the rationality of individual agents, and therefore possesses a normative component. To "naturalize" this type of explanation requires that it be rooted in a physicalist context in which the ultimate explanations are explanations by causes. It may be thought that naturalizing mind and meaning in this manner is bound to lead to serious errors by confusing the natural and the normative, facts and norms, nature and freedom—in a word, by confusing "is" and "ought." Philosophers of mind believe they have found a way, however, looking to the intermediate computational level postulated by cognitivism, to leap over this obstacle or otherwise to get around it. The computation of the cognitivists, it will be recalled, is symbolic computation. The semantic objects with which it deals are therefore all at hand: they are the mental representations that are supposed to correspond to those beliefs, desires, and so forth, by means of which we interpret the acts of ourselves and others. Thinking amounts, then, to performing computations on these representations. Revising one's beliefs, for example, is a question of inferring a new set of beliefs on the basis of beliefs that one already has, together with an observation that partially disconfirms some of these; rational planning is a question of forming an intention to act on the basis of one's desires and beliefs; and so on. For cognitivism and the philosophical psychology associated with it, conceptual computation of this sort manages to square the circle. It creates an intermediate level between the interpretive level of understanding, where we give meaning to actions and beliefs by means of reasons, and the neurophysiological (ultimately, physical) level, where these actions and beliefs are produced by causal processes. This intermediate level is where "mental causes" are supposed to operate—a hybrid of causes and reasons, or rather reasons treated as causes.

This strategy found itself faced with two sorts of objection, each of which asserted the nonexistence and impossibility of this intermediate level. Cognitivism had no alternative but to fiercely defend itself, for the very heart of its system was under attack. To revert to the image of a bridge, the central pier turned out to be vulnerable, and this pier was none other than the computing machine—more precisely, the computer as a metaphor for thinking. What was called into question was the very wager of cognitive science itself, namely, that the mind could be mechanized and, in this way, made a part of nature. The first objection, due to Wittgenstein's followers, acknowledges the causal level of physical processes, on the one hand, and, on the other, the level of norms, interpretation, understanding, and justification, and declares them to be utterly irreducible to each other: no bridge can be thrown up between them. Understanding in terms of reasons constitutes a language game that is incommensurable with that of explanation in terms of causes. The second objection came from "eliminativist" materialists who recognize only a single level, that of physical and physiological causal processes. Folk psychology along with its reasons, which pretend to the same explanatory status as causes, is thus relegated to the trash heap of prescientific illusions. A great part of philosophical debate about cognitive science today may be summarized as a confrontation among these three positions.

It needs to be understood that cybernetics proposed another conceptual approach distinct from the three I have just described. Like eliminative materialism, it banished from its language all talk of reasons, all talk of mental representations having semantic content, and so on. A fortiori, then, it recognized no intermediate level of symbolic computation operating on representations. Even so, can cybernetics fairly be characterized as eliminativist? To be sure, it eliminated psychology completely. But what made its approach distinctive was that it did not thereby eliminate the question of meaning.[8] It redefined meaning by purging it of all traces of subjectivity. Having redefined meaning in this way, it was able to reach it from the far bank of physical causation in a single bound. Since physical causality is computable, and since computation can be implemented in matter, this leap also linked computation with meaning. Had cybernetics succeeded in realizing its ambitions, it would have successfully accomplished the very enterprise—the mechanization of the mind—that cognitivism, proceeding from entirely different assumptions, struggles with today.

In light of this discussion, we can begin to see the outlines emerge of one of the key arguments that this book tries to develop. The major role that analytical philosophy of mind came to play in cognitive science was the result of a historical accident—and surely an unhappy accident at that. How did it happen? Why did it happen? Can the damage be undone? It will be seen that I have only conjectures to offer. I do, however, defend the view that the other great philosophy of mind of the twentieth century, phenomenology, could—and should—have allied itself with cybernetics if, despite the convictions of its founder, Edmund Husserl, it had been interested in providing a natural basis for its doctrines. A whole series of recent works seems to show that this is a fruitful avenue of research.[9]

I have said enough, I trust, to justify the view that all thinking about cognitive science today, about its present state and its history, that does not take into account its origins in cybernetics—as is quite generally the case, given the disrepute into which cybernetics has fallen—will yield only a very biased view of its current situation and its chances of escaping the impasse into which cognitivism has led it. My chief aim in this book is to provide just such an account. The ideas of cybernetics were good ones. By this I do not mean they were true (in fact, as I say, I am convinced they were not)[10] but that they constituted a coherent model that was perfectly suited to the objective that cognitive science continues to share with cybernetics, which is to say the mechanization of the mind. Those who dedicate themselves to this purpose today may find it useful to immerse themselves once again in these pioneering debates. If any further reason is needed to convince them of this, it would be the following, which is only apparently paradoxical: cybernetics ended in failure. It was a historical failure, one that was all the more bitter as its advertised ambitions were enormous; a conceptual failure, all the less comprehensible in view of the fact that it had marshaled very great intellectual advantages on its side; and, finally, if we consider all that is owed to it and that has gone unacknowledged, it was perhaps an unjust failure as well. However this may be, if cybernetics failed, despite having had so many good ideas, the practitioners of cognitive science today, whose ideas are not necessarily better, would do well to meditate upon the causes and reasons for the failure of cybernetics. The present book ought to a certain extent help them in this.

The Question of Humanism

In addition to the philosophical issues already mentioned, the American reader of this work will perhaps be surprised also to find references both to the work of Heidegger and to the movement of his French followers known as deconstruction (which is to be understood as a shorthand for the "deconstruction of Western metaphysics"). To American academics it may seem altogether incongruous to find associated in the same book—even surreptitiously—von Neumann and Heidegger, cybernetic automata and Lacanian psychoanalysis, Jerry Fodor and Jacques Derrida. The very existence of this sense of incongruity furnishes a fine subject for reflection, as I have already suggested.[11] It is therefore necessary at the outset to say a few words about what lies behind this rapprochement of apparently irreconcilable traditions.

In the last analysis, many of the attacks aimed against the materialism of cognitive science are motivated by the desire to provide a defense of humanism. This is not always obvious, for most critics wish to avoid giving the impression of falling into dualism, with its lingering air of religiosity. It required some courage for Thomas Nagel, in criticizing the use made by Jerry Fodor, one of the high priests of cognitivism, of the paradoxical notion of "tacit knowledge"—a type of knowledge that cognitivism was led to postulate at the intermediate level of computation on mental representations—to recall our traditional way of looking at human beings:

> Both knowledge and action are ascribed to individual persons, and they definitely exclude much that the organism can do but that we do not ascribe to the person. Now it may be that these concepts and the distinctions they draw are not theoretically interesting. It may be (although I doubt it) that the idea of a person, with which these other concepts are bound up, is a dying notion, not likely to survive the advances of scientific psychology and neurophysiology.[12]

In raising this disturbing possibility in order then to dismiss it, Nagel poses a classic question: can the idea that we have of the human person, which is to say of ourselves, survive the forward march of scientific discovery? It is a commonplace that from Copernicus to molecular biology, and from Marx to Freud along the way, we have had steadily to abandon our proud view of ourselves as occupying a special place in the universe, and to admit that we are at the mercy of determinisms that leave little room for what we have been accustomed to consider our freedom and our reason. Is not cognitive science now in the process of completing this process of disillusionment and demystification by showing us that just where we believe we sense the workings of a mind, there is only the firing of neural networks, no different in principle than an ordinary electric circuit? The task in which I join with Nagel and others, faced with reductive interpretations of scientific advance of this sort, is to defend the values proper to the human person, or, to put it more bluntly, to defend humanism against the excesses of science and technology.

Heidegger completely inverted this way of posing the problem. For him it was no longer a question of defending humanism but rather of indicting it. As for science and technology, or rather "technoscience" (an expression meant to signify that science is subordinated to the practical ambition of achieving mastery over the world through technology), far from threatening human values, they are on Heidegger's view the most striking manifestation of them. This dual reversal is so remarkable that it deserves to be considered in some detail, even—or above all—in a book on the place of cybernetics in the history of ideas, for it is precisely cybernetics that found itself to be the principal object of Heidegger's attack.

In those places where Heideggerian thought has been influential, it became impossible to defend human values against the claims of science. This was particularly true in France, where structuralism—and then poststructuralism—reigned supreme over the intellectual landscape for several decades before taking refuge in the literature departments of American universities. Anchored in the thought of the three great Germanic "masters of suspicion"—Marx, Nietzsche, and Freud—against a common background of Heideggerianism,[13] the human sciences à la française made antihumanism their watchword, loudly celebrating exactly what Thomas Nagel and others dread: the death of man. This unfortunate creature, or rather a certain image that man created of himself, was reproached for being "metaphysical." With Heidegger, "metaphysics" acquired a new and quite special sense, opposite to its usual meaning. For positivists ever since Comte, the progress of science had been seen as forcing the retreat of metaphysics; for Heidegger, by contrast, technoscience represented the culmination of metaphysics. And the height of metaphysics was nothing other than cybernetics.

Let us try to unravel this tangled skein. For Heidegger, metaphysics is the search for an ultimate foundation for all reality, for a "primary being" in relation to which all other beings find their place and purpose. Where traditional metaphysics ("onto-theology") had placed God, modern metaphysics substituted man. This is why modern metaphysics is fundamentally humanist, and humanism fundamentally metaphysical. Man is a subject endowed with consciousness and will: his features were described at the dawn of modernity in the philosophy of Descartes and Leibniz. As a conscious being, he is present and transparent to himself; as a willing being, he causes things to happen as he intends. Subjectivity, both as theoretical presence to oneself and as practical mastery over the world, occupies center stage in this scheme—whence the Cartesian promise to make man "master and possessor of nature." In the metaphysical conception of the world, Heidegger holds, everything that exists is a slave to the purposes of man; everything becomes an object of his will, fashionable as a function of his ends and desires. The value of things depends solely on their capacity to help man realize his essence, which is to achieve mastery over being. It thus becomes clear why technoscience, and cybernetics in particular, may be said to represent the completion of metaphysics. To contemplative thought—thought that poses the question of meaning and of Being, understood as the sudden appearance of things, which escapes all attempts at grasping it—Heidegger opposes "calculating" thought. This latter type is characteristic of all forms of planning that seek to attain ends by taking circumstances into account. Technoscience, insofar as it constructs mathematical models to better establish its mastery over the causal organization of the world,[14] knows only calculating thought. Cybernetics is precisely that which calculates—computes—in order to govern, in the nautical sense (Wiener coined the term from the Greek χυβερνήτης, meaning "steersman"):[15] it is indeed the height of metaphysics.

Heidegger anticipated the objection that would be brought against him: "Because we are speaking against *humanism* people fear a defense of the inhuman and a glorification of barbaric brutality. For what is more *logical* than that for somebody who negates humanism nothing remains but the affirmation of inhumanity?"[16] Heidegger defended himself by attacking. Barbarism is not to be found where one usually looks for it. The true barbarians are the ones who are supposed to be humanists, who, in the name of the dignity that man accords himself, leave behind them a world devastated by technology, a desert in which no one can truly be said to dwell.

Let us for the sake of argument grant the justice of Heidegger's position. At once an additional enigma presents itself. If for him cybernetics really represented the apotheosis of metaphysical humanism, how are we to explain the fact that the human sciences in France, whose postwar development I have just said can be understood only against the background of Heidegger's philosophy, availed themselves of the conceptual toolkit of cybernetics in order to deconstruct the metaphysics of subjectivity? How is it that these sciences, in their utter determination to put man as subject to death, each seeking to outdo the other's radicalism, should have found in cybernetics the weapons for their assaults?

From the beginning of the 1950s—which is to say, from the end of the first cybernetics—through the 1960s and 1970s, when the second cybernetics was investigating theories of self-organization and cognitivism was on the rise, the enterprise of mechanizing the human world underwent a parallel development on each side of the Atlantic. This common destiny was rarely noticed, perhaps because the thought of any similarity seemed almost absurd: whereas cognitive science claimed to be the avant-garde of modern science, structuralism—followed by poststructuralism—covered itself in a pretentious and often incomprehensible philosophical jargon.[17] What is more, it was too tempting to accuse French deconstructionists of a fascination with mathematical concepts and models that they hardly understood.[18] But even if this way of looking at the matter is not entirely unjustified, it only scratches the surface. There were very good reasons, in fact, why the deconstruction of metaphysical humanism found in cybernetics an ally of the first order.

At the beginning of the 1940s, a philosopher of consciousness such as Sartre could write: "The inhuman is merely . . . the mechanical."[19] Structuralists hastened to adopt this definition as their own, while reversing the value assigned to its terms. Doing Heidegger one better, they made a great show of championing the inhuman—which is to say the mechanical.[20] Cybernetics, as it happened, was ready to hand, having come along at just the right moment to demystify the voluntary and conscious subject. The will? All its manifestations could apparently be simulated, and therefore duplicated, by a simple negative feedback mechanism. Consciousness? The Cybernetics Group had examined the Freudian unconscious, whose existence was defended by one of its members, Lawrence Kubie, and found it chimerical. If Kubie often found himself the butt of his colleagues' jokes, it was not, one suspects, because he was thought to be an enemy of human dignity. It was rather because the postulation of a hidden entity, located in the substructure of a purportedly conscious subject, manifesting itself only through symptoms while yet being endowed with the essential attributes of the subject (intentionality, desires, beliefs, presence to oneself, and so on), seemed to the cyberneticians nothing more than a poor conjuring trick aimed at keeping the structure of subjectivity intact.

It is remarkable, as we shall have occasion to note in some detail, that a few years later the French psychoanalyst Jacques Lacan, along with the anthropologist Claude Lévi-Strauss and the Marxist philosopher Louis Althusser one of the founders of structuralism, should have adopted the same critical attitude toward Freud as cybernetics. The father of psychoanalysis had been led to postulate an improbable "death wish"—"beyond the pleasure principle," as he put it—as if the subject actually desired the very thing that made him suffer, by voluntarily and repeatedly placing himself in situations from which he could only emerge battered and hurt. This compulsion (*Zwang*) to repeat failure Freud called *Wiederholungszwang*, an expression translated by Lacan as "automatisme de répétition," which is to say the *automatism* of repetition. In so doing he replaced the supposed unconscious death wish with the senseless functioning of a machine, the unconscious henceforth being identified with a cybernetic automaton. The alliance of psychoanalysis and cybernetics was neither anecdotal nor fortuitous: it corresponded to a radicalization of the critique of metaphysical humanism.

There was a deeper reason for the encounter between the French *sciences de l'homme* and cybernetics, however. What structuralism sought to conceive—in the anthropology of Lévi-Strauss, for example, and particularly in his study of systems of exchange in traditional societies—was a subjectless cognition, indeed cognition without mental content. Whence the project of making "symbolic thought" a mechanism peculiar not to individual brains but to "unconscious" linguistic structures that automatically operate behind the back, as it were, of unfortunate human "subjects," who are no more than a sort of afterthought. "It thinks" was destined to take the place once and for all of the Cartesian *cogito*. Now cognition without a subject was exactly the unlikely configuration that cybernetics seemed to have succeeded in conceiving. Here again, the encounter between cybernetics and structuralism was in no way accidental. It grew out of a new intellectual necessity whose sudden emergence appears in retrospect as an exceptional moment in the history of ideas.

It is time to come back to our enigma, which now may be formulated as a paradox. Was cybernetics the height of metaphysical humanism, as Heidegger maintained, or was it the height of its deconstruction, as certain of

Heidegger's followers believe? To this question I believe it is necessary to reply that cybernetics was both things at once, and that this is what made it not only the root of cognitive science, which finds itself faced with the same paradox, but also a turning point in the history of human conceptions of humanity. The title I have given to this introduction—the self-mechanized mind—appears to have the form of a self-referential statement, not unlike those strange loops the cyberneticians were so crazy about, especially the cyberneticians of the second phase. But this is only an appearance: the mind that carries out the mechanization and the one that is the object of it are two distinct (albeit closely related) entities, like the two ends of a seesaw, the one rising ever higher in the heavens of metaphysical humanism as the other descends further into the depths of its deconstruction. In mechanizing the mind, in treating it as an artifact, the mind presumes to exercise power over this artifact to a degree that no psychology claiming to be scientific has ever dreamed of attaining. The mind can now hope not only to manipulate this mechanized version of itself at will, but even to reproduce and manufacture it in accordance with its own wishes and intentions. Accordingly, the technologies of the mind, present and future, open up a vast continent upon which man now has to impose norms if he wishes to give them meaning and purpose. The human subject will therefore need to have recourse to a supplementary endowment of will and conscience in order to determine, not what he can do, but what he ought to do—or, rather, what he ought not to do. These new technologies will require a whole ethics to be elaborated, an ethics not less demanding than the one that is slowly being devised today in order to control the rapid development and unforeseen consequences of new biotechnologies. But to speak of ethics, conscience, the will—is this not to speak of the triumph of the subject?

The connection between the mechanization of life and the mechanization of the mind is plain. Even if the Cybernetics Group snubbed biology, to the great displeasure of John von Neumann as we shall see, it was of course a cybernetic metaphor that enabled molecular biology to formulate its central dogma: the genome operates like a computer program. This metaphor is surely not less false than the analogous metaphor that structures the cognitivist paradigm. The theory of biological self-organization, first opposed to the cybernetic paradigm during the Macy Conferences before later being adopted by the second cybernetics as its principal model, furnished then—and still furnishes today—decisive arguments against the legitimacy of identifying DNA with a "genetic program."[21] Nonetheless—and this is the crucial point—even though this identification is profoundly illegitimate from both a scientific and a philosophical point of view, its technological consequences have been considerable. Today, as a result, man may be inclined to believe that he is the master of his own genome. Never, one is tempted to say, has he been so near to realizing the Cartesian promise: he has become—or is close to becoming—the master and possessor of all of nature, up to and including himself.

Must we then salute this as yet another masterpiece of metaphysical humanism? It seems at first altogether astonishing, though after a moment's reflection perfectly comprehensible, that a German philosopher following in the tradition of Nietzsche and Heidegger should have recently come forward, determined to take issue with the liberal humanism of his country's philosophical establishment, and boldly affirmed that the new biotechnologies sound the death knell for the era of humanism.[22] Unleashing a debate the like of which is hardly imaginable in any other country, this philosopher ventured to assert: "The domestication of man by man is the great unimagined prospect in the face of which humanism has looked the other way from antiquity until the present day." And to prophesy:

> It suffices to clearly understand that the next long periods of history will be periods of choice as far as the [human] species is concerned. Then it will be seen if humanity, or at least its cultural elites, will succeed in establishing effective procedures for self-domestication. . . . It will be necessary, in the future, to forthrightly address the issue and formulate a code governing anthropological technologies. Such a code would modify, a posteriori, the meaning of classical humanism, for it would show that *humanitas* consists not only in the friendship of man with man, but that it also implies . . . , in increasingly obvious ways, that man represents the supreme power for man.

But why should this "superhuman" power of man over himself be seen, in Nietzschean fashion, as representing the death of humanism rather than its apotheosis? For man to be able, as subject, to exercise a power of this sort over himself, it is first necessary that he be reduced to the rank of an object, able to be reshaped to suit any purpose. No raising up can occur without a concomitant lowering, and vice versa.

Let us come back to cybernetics and, beyond that, to cognitive science. We need to consider more closely the paradox that an enterprise that sets itself the task of *naturalizing* the mind should have as its spearhead a discipline that calls itself *artificial* intelligence. To be sure, the desired naturalization proceeds via mechanization. Nothing about this is inconsistent with a conception of the world that treats nature as an immense computational machine. Within this world man is just another machine—no surprise there. But in the name of what, or of whom, will man, thus artificialized, exercise his increased power over himself? In the name of this very blind mechanism with which he is identified? In the name of a meaning that he claims is mere appearance or phenomenon? His will and capacity for choice are now left dangling over the abyss. The attempt to restore mind to the natural world that gave birth to it ends up exiling the mind from the world and from nature. This paradox is typical of what the sociologist Louis Dumont, in his magisterial study of the genesis of modern individualism, called

> the model of modern artificialism in general, the systematic application of an extrinsic, imposed value to the things of the world. Not a value drawn from our belonging to the world, from its harmony and our harmony with it, but a value rooted in our heterogeneity in relation to it: the identification of our will with the will of God (Descartes: man makes himself *master and possessor of nature*). The will thus applied to the world, the end sought, the motive and the profound impulse of the will are [all] foreign. In other words, they are extra-worldly. Extra-worldliness is now concentrated in the individual will.[23]

The paradox of the naturalization of the mind attempted by cybernetics, and today by cognitive science, then, is that the mind has been raised up as a demigod in relation to itself.

Many of the criticisms brought against the materialism of cognitive science from the point of view either of a philosophy of consciousness or a defense of humanism miss this paradox. Concentrating their (often justified) attacks on the weaknesses and naiveté of such a mechanist materialism, they fail to see that it invalidates itself by placing the human subject outside of the very world to which he is said to belong.[24] What is more, the recent interest shown by cognitive science in what it regards as the "mystery" of consciousness seems bound to accentuate this blindness.[25] The dialogue that the present book hopes to inaugurate between the analytic philosophy of mind underlying cognitive science and Continental philosophy, despite the deep-seated prejudices of those on both sides who want them to have nothing to say to each other, finds its justification in precisely this state of affairs.

History of Science vs. History of Ideas

The question of humanism is all the more crucial for a study of the origins of cognitive science since the socioeconomic, political, and cultural context of postwar America in which cybernetics developed is liable to lead the historian of science astray. Owing to circumstances that I shall go on to describe later in the book, cybernetics was obliged from the beginning to ally itself with a movement—a political lobby, actually, operating under the auspices of the Macy Foundation—that sought to assure world peace and universal mental health by means of a bizarre cocktail concocted from psychoanalysis, cultural anthropology, advanced physics, and the new thinking associated with the Cybernetics Group. If only this context is considered, it may seem as though cybernetics was part and parcel of an effort to place science and technology in the service of human well-being. This interpretation is all the more tempting since one of the most famous participants of the Macy Conferences, and the one who gave cybernetics its name, Norbert Wiener, made himself known to the general public through a series of works that were frankly humanist in tone, through his many stands on behalf of the social responsibility of the scientist, and through various inventions relying on cybernetic advances to help people with disabilities. It is nonetheless my contention that the system of ideas and values embodied by cybernetics can be understood only if one recognizes its purpose as having been fully "antihumanist" in the sense of the preceding discussion.

I have already mentioned in the preface that Steve Heims's book on the Macy Conferences, *The Cybernetics Group*, appeared before mine. I need to make clear at the outset what I owe to this work and in what respects my approach differs from it.

Heims is a German-born physicist whose family fled Nazism and settled in the United States. He later broke with physics on moral grounds, feeling that the general orientation of research in this field had made it an instrument of inhumanity. He therefore resolved to step back and devote himself to the history of twentieth-century science. He turned his attention first to the careers of two incomparable figures who profoundly influenced the science, technology, and society of their time, before, during, and after the Second World War: John von Neumann and Norbert Wiener. The result was a notable work that took the form of a parallel biography of the two great mathematicians, significantly entitled *John von Neumann and Norbert Wiener: From Mathematics to the Technologies of Life and Death* (1980). Heims's research led him in turn to undertake a thorough examination of what exactly the cybernetic project had involved, each of his two protagonists having played a crucial role in its creation. Determined to reconstruct as faithfully as possible the circumstances and events of this pioneering period, he decided to write an account of the Macy Conferences, which, despite their very great historical importance, had until then not been the object of systematic study. The result of this second phase of research was *The Cybernetics Group* (1991).

The question naturally arose whether a second work on the Macy Conferences could be justified. After long deliberation, I came to the conclusion that another look at them was in fact needed, for at least two reasons. The first reason is that, despite my great admiration for Heims's patience and persistence as a historian, I disagree with his approach to the subject. Placing cybernetics in the context of postwar America is, in and of itself, an interesting point of view; but to see it as a reflection of this context, and nothing else, as Heims does, seems to me much more problematic. As I have already indicated, I believe too strongly in the autonomy and the

power of ideas to subscribe to an "externalist" perspective in the sociology
of science. In the present instance, such a perspective seems to me to introduce a very serious bias. An essential part of the context of the period, as
we have noted, has to do with a movement on behalf of mental health and
world peace that was both scientistic and humanist—humanist because
scientistic. Heims takes violent issue with the naive individualist ideology
of this movement, which seems to him to obscure the social and political
dimension of the problems of the time, without seeing that it concealed a
philosophical and scientific project of a wholly different nature. The problem is that he devotes the main part of his book to those members of the
Cybernetics Group who belonged to the movement, which gives a highly
misleading idea of what cybernetics was actually trying to do. The aim of
the cyberneticians was nothing less than to bring about the apotheosis of
science by building a science of the mind. It is just this ambition that
makes it the parent of cognitive science. That cybernetics should have
flourished at this particular moment in history has much less to do, in my
view, with the social, political, and ideological atmosphere of the time
than with the fact that it was the product of a long evolution in Western
thinking about what it is to know. This, at least, is the thesis I defend in the
first chapter of the present book. That this thinking should suddenly have
crystalized when it did, in the 1940s, was because the shock of the great
discoveries in mathematical logic of the preceding decade was needed for
it to assume a definite form.

I had felt a similar uneasiness on reading Heims's first book in which,
to oversimplify somewhat, he contrasts a wicked von Neumann with a
good Wiener: whereas the former raised the temperature of the Cold War
by working to perfect the hydrogen bomb, the latter designed prostheses
for the hearing-impaired. The question of the circular relations between
science, technology, and society is certainly an important one. But I do not
believe it ought to hinder analysis of the internal dynamic that underlies
the development of ideas.

The second reason follows directly from the first. Heims is so concerned
to denounce capitalism and its ambition of exercising universal control
over beings and things that he neglects, or in any case pushes into the
background, the question that I have placed at the heart of my inquiry:
how far can cybernetics be seen as the womb from which issued what
today is called cognitive science? This question, as we shall see, is controversial, and I try to answer it through a series of arguments that jointly
constitute a preface to some fuller intellectual history of cognitive science
that remains to be written. This has led me frequently to go outside of the
period that is the direct object of my inquiry in order to consider the reaction to cybernetics of various figures who came after. I hope I have, for
the most part at least, avoided the traps that lay in wait for every historical

essayist; in any case I believe I have not yielded too far to the temptation to take the easy way out by regarding cybernetics as somehow incomplete or deficient by comparison with later research. My resolve in this respect has been strengthened by the feeling that the cybernetic phase exhibited a richness of debate and intuition that cognitive scientists today would do well to contemplate. I do not reproach cybernetics for not having known what was discovered only much later. I reproach cybernetics for not having taken advantage of ideas that were both relevant to its purpose and within its reach, if only it had wanted to take notice of their existence.

My interests are therefore very different than those of Heims, which is why I venture to hope this work may have a place next to his. The reservations that I have expressed with regard to his work do not prevent me from reemphasizing the debt I owe him: lacking the materials he meticulously assembled over a number of years, the foundations of my own inquiry would be far weaker.

What I attempt in this book is an intellectual history that takes the form of an "ecology of mind," to borrow a phrase from one of the members of the Cybernetics Group, Gregory Bateson. The author of such a history cannot remain wholly in the background. I have already, in the preface, described my motivations and certain of my philosophical positions. Here it is enough simply to say that throughout this book, faced with a particular idea or position, I have not been able to refrain from expressing my enthusiasm and admiration or, depending on the case, my irritation and exasperation. These reactions are unrelated to my opinion of the truth or soundness of the position in question. As I say, I deeply believe that the materialism of cognitive science is wrong. But I much prefer materialists who know what they are about, who seek to work out the most coherent and general theory possible, to ideologues or conceptual tinkerers. Why? Because the only way to prove the falsity of materialism is to give it every benefit of doubt, to allow it to push forward as far as it can, while remaining alert to its missteps, to the obstacles that it encounters, and, ultimately, to the limits it runs up against. Any other method—fixing its boundaries in advance, for example—is bound to fail. Champions of materialism are therefore to be welcomed. I believe I have found such a hero, one who, far more than either Wiener or von Neumann, was the soul of the Macy Conferences: Warren McCulloch. His imposing personality dominates the present work.

Steve Heims, at the end of his book, ranks me among the "happy few" who still today carry on the tradition inaugurated by the first cybernetics. This is a dubious honor, which I am not sure I deserve. The verdict I deliver on the events described in this book is rather harsh. It is offered as the history of a failure—a grandiose failure, if you like, and in any case a productive one full of lessons to be learned; but a failure nonetheless, if what was actually achieved in the end is set against what was hoped for at the beginning. I said a moment ago that I have taken care to avoid the traps of retrospective history. Instead I have dared to practice a new and rather hazardous genre: counterfactual history. For cognitive science in its earliest stages missed so many important rendezvous, so many important opportunities, that the historian—still less the philosopher—cannot resist asking, again and again, "What would have happened if only . . . ?" A pointless exercise, perhaps—too facile, certainly—but one that nonetheless conveys this philosopher's abiding sense of frustration.

The Fascination with Models

Geometrica demonstramus quia facimus; si physica
demonstrare possemus, faceremus.

—GIAMBATTISTA VICO[1]

HERBERT SIMON, winner of the Nobel Prize in economics, is generally
considered to be one of the founders of artificial intelligence. Economists
use his theory of "bounded rationality," decision theorists and professors
of business management apply his concept of "satisficing," and cognitive
scientists rely on the computer program that he devised with Alan Newell
to simulate the creative processes of human thought involved in grappling
with problems framed in terms of ends and means—a program aptly
named "General Problem Solver." Historians of ideas regard him as someone who had somehow stepped out of the Renaissance into the twentieth
century, a sort of Leonardo da Vinci for our time. Some indication of the
scope of his intellectual ambition is given by the title of one of his principal
works: *The Sciences of the Artificial*.

The complete list of his works includes a number of other titles conceived on the same model: *Models of Man*, *Models of Discovery*, *Models of
Thought*, and *Models of Bounded Rationality*. The title of his recently
published autobiography, *Models of My Life*, hardly comes as a surprise
then. Frankly, this is a rather curious book. It reveals a man who constructed his life in full accord with the principles that guided his thinking—a way of thinking that leaves no doubt about the identity of *its* favorite model: the digital computer. Like all scholars of his stature, Simon has
traveled widely. He claims, however, to have learned nothing from his
travels abroad that he could not have learned, or had not already learned,
more quickly, more easily, and less expensively from the collections of any
number of good libraries in the United States. His own experience he sen-
tentiously declared to hold equally for every "normal American adult," in
the form of a "Travel Theorem."[2] From his memoir we learn that the first
time Simon and his wife visited Europe, in 1965, already fully convinced

of the truth of this theorem, they arranged their itinerary so that they would see nothing that they did not already know through books or pictures. The two weeks that they passed in France were a sort of pilgrimage devoted to Proust and Cézanne. At Sainte-Victoire and Estaque they went to the exact spots ("within three feet exactly") where Cézanne had planted his easel: "We learned nothing new; we had already seen the paintings." Citing Oscar Wilde ("Where were the fogs of London before Turner painted them?"), Simon concludes, "Nature, as usual, imitating art."[3] On the very first page of his memoir, he announces his fascination with the works of Jorge Luis Borges, that virtuoso of labyrinths and mirror games, the author of "Theme of the Traitor and the Hero," for whom history is only a copy of literature.

The Virtue of Models

Anthologies of artificial intelligence typically cite Thomas Hobbes as the precursor of the discipline and offer as their first selection an excerpt from the *Leviathan* (1651). The imputation is far from being absurd or anachronistic. Hobbes conceived the State or Commonwealth on the model of *automata* or "engines that move themselves by springs and wheels as doth a watch." What is the Leviathan? An immense "artificial man" (or "animal").[4] Behind the Hobbesian formula "Reason is nothing but reckoning,"[5] in which cognitive science proudly sees its own reflection, there lies an entire philosophical ancestry.

Hobbes's system was animated by an idea that later would be famously formulated by Vico as *Verum et factum convertuntur* ("The true and the made are convertible"). This means that we can have rational knowledge only about that of which we are the cause, about what we ourselves have produced. The principle of *verum factum* was originally understood as implying a want or lack on the part of human beings: we can never know nature in the way that God does, for God created what we can only observe. Quickly, however, the principle acquired a positive sense more in keeping with the growing affirmation of modern subjectivism: what human beings make can be rationally—that is, demonstratively and deductively—known despite the finitude of human understanding. Among the branches of knowledge, ranked in descending order according to their degree of perfection, mathematics comes first by this criterion, followed, however, not by the natural sciences but by the moral and political sciences. It is thus that Hannah Arendt interpreted both the artificial conception of politics developed by Hobbes and Vico's turn "from natural science to history, which he thought to be the only sphere where one could obtain certain knowledge, precisely because he dealt here only with the products of human activity."[6]

But the first principle of the science of nature itself, according to Arendt, had to be that one can know only in making, or rather in remaking. Despite his or her human limitations, the scientist "nevertheless from the outset approached [nature] from the standpoint of the One who made it."[7] This explains not only the scientist's emphasis on the "how" of physical processes rather than on the being of things, but also—and above all—the considerable role assigned by science to experiment: "The use of the experiment for the purpose of knowledge was already the consequence of the conviction that one can know only what he has made himself, for this conviction meant that one might learn about those things man did not make by *figuring out* and imitating the processes through which they had come into being."[8]

Figuring out, imitating, repeating, reproducing: this, it is well recognized, is just what scientific experiment does. It is nonetheless striking that Arendt did not see there is a kind of *making* in scientific activity that is more universal than the kind found in experimentation and that splendidly confirms her analysis: the fabrication of *models*.

Science is the sole human activity in which the word "model" has a sense opposite to the one given it in everyday speech. Normally we speak of a model as someone or something one imitates, or that deserves to be imitated. But a scientific model is an imitation from the start. It bears the same type of relation to reality as a scale model does to its object, being a more readily manipulable reproduction of it. This inversion of meaning is striking and worth pondering. There is much debate in history and philosophy of science about the nature and foundations of scientific knowledge. Now the fact that science as an *activity* consists essentially in constructing objects in the form of models is incontestably true, even if it is not as well known among nonscientists as it should be. What is a model? Here Karl Popper's warning about not starting from definitions applies: it would be hard to give a definition that is not liable to be swept away by the incessant activity of scientific *creation*. Let us say simply that a model is an idealization, usually formalized in mathematical terms, that synthesizes a system of relations among "elements whose identity and even nature are, up to a certain point, a matter of indifference, and which can, as a result, be changed, replaced by other elements, analogous or not, without [the model's] being altered."[9]

A model is an abstract form, as it were, that is embodied or instantiated by phenomena. Very different domains of phenomenal reality—hydrodynamics and electricity, for instance, or light and sonic vibrations—can be represented by identical models, which establish an equivalence relation among them. A model is the corresponding equivalence class. It therefore enjoys a transcendent position, not unlike that of a platonic Idea of which reality is only a pale imitation. But the scientific model is manmade. It is at this juncture that the hierarchical relation between the imitator and the imitated comes to be inverted. Although the scientific model is a human imitation of nature, the scientist is inclined to regard it as a "model," in the ordinary sense, of nature. Thus nature is taken to imitate the very model by which man tries to imitate it.

If, as Arendt would have it, the scientist is a *Homo faber*, this is above all because the scientist is a designer and manufacturer of models. This activity confers upon scientists a mastery that they would not dare to claim over phenomena themselves. Their mastery over models is, in the first instance, explanatory and predictive. It is due to the power of mathematical tools, which lend the exploration of a model's properties (in the form of thought experiments) an efficiency and an elegance that could never be attained through experimentation on the phenomenal world alone. Above all, this mastery consists in exploiting the creative power of analogy. Given two domains that are postulated to be representable by the same model, what is known about the first one can be used to suggest new experiments to be carried out on the second, to develop novel hypotheses and to discover whatever interesting properties it may have. Thus "when Bohr had been led to the hypothesis of a similarity between the structure of the nucleus formed by nucleons (protons and neutrons) and that of a drop of water formed by molecules, the known laws of evaporation became translated into those of radioactive disintegration, and the conditions under which the droplet divides in two anticipated those under which fission occurs: from this work the atomic bomb was to emerge."[10]

The model *abstracts* from phenomenal reality the system of functional relations that it judges to be the sole pertinent ones, putting aside, so to speak, everything that does not fall within the scope of the system and, in particular, as we have already noted, the number, identity, and nature of the elements that are thus brought into relation with each other. In this way the same model can represent the structure of the solar system and that of Rutherford's atom. The role that the various forms of functionalism play in science (including cognitive science) has its source in the universal practice of modeling. It is also plain that a model, by its very nature, is capable of assuming a variety of physical forms and that, conversely, a single class of phenomena may be captured by different models that are unrelated to each other, except in the sense that they are perfectly equivalent with respect to the result of the calculations to which they lead. Surely one of the most famous examples of this in the history of science is furnished by the study of the motion of a physical point, or particle, in a field of forces: the system of differential equations of Newtonian mechanics provides one model, the Lagrangian or Hamiltonian formalization another. The former postulates remote forces acting in an empty and passive space; the latter, by contrast, supposes an active space, a "field" that exercises influence over the objects that are thrown into it. The Hamiltonian model, through a fairly straightforward (albeit at first rather unsuspected) generalization of the Newtonian model, was later shown to be capable of generating quantum mechanics, something the Newtonian model could never have done.[11]

Models therefore have a life of their own, an autonomous dynamic independent of phenomenal reality. In constructing models, scientists project their mind onto the world of things. The enormous successes of scientific modeling seem to show that the mind is both distinct from matter and of a piece with it. But there is a certain danger in such a conclusion. Because a model is so much purer, so much more readily mastered than the world of phenomena, there is a risk that it may become the exclusive object of the scientist's attention. Theories, indeed whole disciplines can be organized around the study of a model's properties: witness economics, which goes on endlessly exploring the (admittedly impressive) resources of the general equilibrium model bequeathed to it by Walras. It is not clear that the newborn "science of the mind" has avoided making the same mistake.

Manipulating Representations

Let us now turn to the mind. The doctrine of *verum factum*, having influenced the development of mathematics, the moral and political sciences (including history), and the natural and life sciences, could not help but affect our knowledge of the mind once science found itself in a position to lay claim to this last bastion of Creation. That moment arrived when science felt confident at last of being able to deliver an adequate answer to the ancient problem that it had long ago abandoned to philosophy, having to do with the relation between the soul and the body or, to use today's vocabulary, between mind and matter.

Mind is not a product of mind: consciousness is not made by itself. It was for this reason that Vico recognized a dimension of irreducible opacity in the *cogito* and even, as a consequence, in the sociohistorical domain.[12] The history of ideas is full of ironies. In order for the contrary conviction to be born, namely, that the human mind can know itself rationally by virtue of the fact that it can conceive and fabricate a replica of itself, it was necessary for the validity of *verum factum* to be undermined in the one field in which it had never been called into question: mathematics. Until the publication of certain results obtained by mathematical logicians in the 1930s, it was possible to repeat what Hobbes had written almost three hundred years earlier in *De homine* (1658): "Therefore, because of this fact (that is, that we ourselves create the figures), it happens that geometry hath been and is demonstrable."[13] But with the work of Gödel and Turing, it became necessary to renounce what had once seemed obvious. The Hobbesian notion of genetic definition—the idea that all the properties of an object can be derived from its definition—no longer applied systematically to mathematics: while we are the source of mathematical entities, some of these remain forever beyond our reach. This prodigious discovery, whose consequences for the history of thought have not yet ceased to make themselves felt, was the point of departure for the new science of mind. We shall come back to it.

It is often said that the classic paradigm of cognitive science is organized around the metaphor of the computer—much too often, however, for the metaphor was by no means inevitable. Cognitive science, as I will go on to show, began to take shape before the computer existed, or, more precisely, when the computer existed as a physical object but before a functionalist theory of this object had been worked out. The theory that has become so familiar to us in the years since, according to which "software" is distinguished from "hardware," was the product—rather than the source—of the conceptual revolution that marked the advent of cognitive science.

To know is to create a model of a phenomenon that is then manipulated in accordance with certain rules. All knowledge involves reproduction, representation, repetition, simulation. These things, as we have noted, are what characterize the rational, scientific mode of knowledge. Cognitive science makes this the unique mode by which knowledge may be acquired. For cognitive science, every "cognitive system" stands in the same relation to the world as do scientists to the object of their science. It comes as small surprise, then, that the notion of representation occupies a central place in this scheme. But the analogy is still more profound: what enables any physical cognitive system—whether an ordinary person or a scientist, an animal, organism, organ, or machine—to know by means of models and representations should in principle itself be able to be modeled, by abstracting from a particular physical substrate, depending on the case, the same system of functional relations responsible for the faculty of knowing. Functionalism in cognitive science is therefore located on (at least) two logically interlocking levels: elementary representation and representation of the faculty of representation. It is at this second level that a science of cognition can both declare itself materialist, or physicalist, and claim autonomy with respect to the natural sciences (including the life sciences). Thus the mind, understood as the model of the faculty of modeling, regains its place in the physical universe. To state the matter differently, using terms that are now more familiar, the physical world contains information—possibly meaning as well—and mental faculties are nothing more than properties of information-processing systems.

Knowing amounts, then, to manipulating representations according to well-defined rules. Although this proposition is faithful to the spirit of the dominant paradigm of cognitive science, it nonetheless lacks something essential. The essential thing that is missing has to do with the *logical* nature of the rules and manipulations in question. Scientific models are typically expressed in mathematical form, as we have observed; more precisely, as a system of differential equations expressing a relation among magnitudes. The years immediately preceding the the decade that witnessed the birth of cognitive science—the story we are about to recount—saw the creation of mathematical models of both the nervous system and electrical circuits. It nonetheless took the genius of McCulloch and Pitts, on the one hand, and of Shannon on the other, to see that another, more pertinent type of model was required, a logical model. Not only could the functioning of certain physical systems be described in logical terms; these physical systems could be represented as *embodying* logic, the highest form of thought.

The Turing Machine

To be sure, in the beginning was the Word—*logos*; but *logos* turned out to be a machine. When, in 1936–1937, Alan Turing published his famous article "On Computable Numbers, with an Application to the *Entscheidungsproblem*,"[14] he could hardly have known that he was announcing the birth of a new science of mind. His interest was in solving a problem of logic posed by Hilbert that had to do with decision (*Entscheidung*): given any formula of the predicate calculus, does there exist an effective, general, systematic procedure for deciding whether or not the formula is provable? Since 1931, when Kurt Gödel published his scarcely less famous paper, "On Formally Undecidable Propositions of *Principia Mathematica* and Related Systems,"[15] the question had acquired a new topicality. What Gödel had done was to establish a theorem of "incompleteness": any formal system in the logical sense (namely, one that provides a formal language—a set of formulas that are to be taken as axioms—as well as rules of inference) that is sufficiently rich to accommodate arithmetic has the following property: either the system is inconsistent (i.e., it generates contradictory theorems) or there exists at least one true proposition that is not provable within the system. In the latter case, therefore, the formula corresponding to this proposition is not a theorem, nor, quite obviously, is its negation, since this corresponds to a false proposition. Even if the entire set of theorems of the system were to be thoroughly unpacked, neither the formula nor its negation will ever be found. So long as one remains "within" the system, one will never arrive at the truth value of the formula, which is therefore called "undecidable."

In order to establish this result, Gödel made a key move. He showed that it was possible to use integers to code not only formulas but sequences of formulas, particularly those sequences that constitute proofs. A proposition asserting that a given formula is provable can thus be expressed in the form of an arithmetical proposition. This arithmeticization of logic gave a rigorous foundation to the maxim that reasoning consists in computing (with integers). The incompleteness theorem did not quite provide a solution to the problem posed by Hilbert, however. For the theorem's import to be fully appreciated, it was necessary to clarify what was implied by such notions as "effective computation" and "finite procedure," in view of the fact that what the theorem asserts is the nonexistence of decidable, constructible, operational procedures adequate to answer certain questions about formal systems that are posed within these systems. In other words, what was still lacking was a rigorous, mathematical definition of the *algorithm*. Without such a definition, there could be no definite response to Hilbert's problem.

Already by 1936 there had been several attempts to specify the notion of effective computability, including one suggestion from Gödel himself ("general recursivity," "lambda-definability," and so on). Remarkably, these various characterizations, despite being so different in spirit, define the same class of functions. They are equivalent, in the sense of being coextensive. It was therefore tempting to suppose that this unique class corresponded to the intuitive notion of effective computability. That very year, independently of Turing, Alonso Church made the crucial leap.[16] Quite obviously equivalence proved nothing by itself. It might perfectly well have been the case that, entirely coincidentally, each such characterization missed the mark—in this case, the formalization of the intuitive notion of an automatic procedure, governed by fixed rules and devoid of anything akin to meaning, interpretation, or creativity. The truth of the matter is that there was nothing to prove: the problem of squaring mathematical definitions with a pretheoretical sense of such an automatic procedure is not something that is amenable to formal demonstration. This is why Church cast his suggestion that every computable function (in the intuitive sense) is a recursive function (in the mathematical sense) in the form of a *thesis* rather than of a proved statement. It could not be proved, any more than the mathematical definition of a sphere could be proved to be identical with our intuitive concept of a round object.

This mix of ideas was still lacking a decisive ingredient—decisive, in particular, for the history of cognitive science. In retrospect it seems astonishing that this ingredient did not appear obvious at the time. It seems plain to us now that the notion of effective computability that was being sought, involving only blind, "automatic" execution procedures, was most clearly illustrated by the functioning of a *machine*. It is due to Turing that this mechanical metaphor was taken seriously. In his remarkable study of the development of the theory of automata, Jean Mosconi makes an interesting conjecture about the nature of the resistance that this idea met with in the 1930s:

> Considering the calculating machines that existed at the time—the perspectives opened up by Babbage having been forgotten in the meantime—, any reference to the computational possibilities of a machine was apt to be regarded as arbitrarily narrowing the idea of computability. . . . If for us the natural meaning of "mechanical computability" is "computability by a machine," it seems likely that until Turing came along "mechanical" was used in a rather metaphorical sense and meant nothing more than "servile" (indeed the term "mechanical" is still used in this sense today to describe the execution of an algorithm).[17]

By the time of the Macy Conferences, ten years later, these antimechanistic brakes were totally worn out.

In his 1936–1937 article, Turing proposed a mathematical formulation of the abstract notion of a machine. The model thus defined has come to be known as a "Turing machine." In a moment we shall take a look at what a Turing machine does and what it can do. Turing himself believed that by means of this concept he had succeeded in penetrating to the essence of mechanical procedure. The claim made in his paper is that every mechanical procedure can be modeled by a Turing machine. Given that such procedures are "functional" (in both senses of the word, the one having to do with functionalism in the sense described earlier, the other in the sense of a mathematical function) and that ultimately what is at issue is computation, the claim amounts to asserting that every mechanically computable function is computable by a Turing machine. But this claim, known as the "Turing thesis," is obviously no more provable than Church's. Whereas "Turing-computability" has a formal definition, mechanical computability remains a vague, intuitive notion.

What can be proved, on the other hand (as Turing showed a year later[18]), is the following remarkable result: the class of functions computable by a Turing machine coincides with the class of recursive functions, which in turn is equivalent to the class of lambda-definable functions. The last of the formal characterizations of the notion of computability to be devised thus turned out to be equivalent to the earlier ones. The force of this result was at once to bolster the Turing thesis, corroborate that of Church, lend plausibility to the suspicion that the two theses were in fact one and the same, and, above all, reveal the profound kinship between the notion of effective computability and that of mechanical procedure—the latter, being the more intuitive, furnishing the key to the former.

Turing had provided himself with the means, therefore, to answer the decision problem set by Hilbert. It now sufficed to translate the question "Does there exist an effective general procedure by which it would be possible to determine whether a particular formula of the predicate calculus is provable or not?" into the question "Does there exist a (Turing) machine capable of deciding whether or not such a formula is provable?" This new formulation amounted to treating a formal system in the logical sense (that is, a set of axioms and rules of inference) as a mechanical procedure capable of producing new formulas called theorems.

It will be helpful at this point to recall what a Turing machine involves. To some readers, this machine will seem complicated; to others, it will seem extraordinary that such a primitive machine could claim to represent in a synthetic way everything that we intuitively understand by the notion of an effective, decidable, finite procedure. A Turing machine is composed of three parts: the machine itself, which at any given moment (time being assumed to be discrete) finds itself in a state (called the "internal state") corresponding to one among a finite list of states; a linear tape, infinite in both directions, representing the machine's memory and divided into squares, each of which either bears a mark or is empty; and, finally, a head for reading and either writing or erasing. The head is capable of carrying out the following operations: placed in front of a particular square, it can scan the square to determine whether a mark has been written on it or not; it can erase a mark in case it finds one inscribed there; it can inscribe a mark if the square is empty; and it can change position by one (and only one) square at a time, moving either to the left or to the right.

The functioning of the machine is governed by an invariant table that represents an input-output function. The input is the "configuration" of the machine at a given moment, which is to say the pair constituted by its internal state and the content of the scanned square (i.e., the presence or absence of a mark). The output is completely determined by the input and consists in three moves that lead on to the next moment: changing or retaining the internal state; changing or retaining the content of the scanned square; shifting (or not) the position of the head to the right or the left. Last but not least, for some inputs the machine is instructed to halt.

Once adquately coded, any given Turing machine (as determined by its table) realizes or instantiates a particular numerical function. The integer that constitutes the input of the function is represented by the marks that appear on an initial stretch of the ribbon on which the machine works. Step by step, in accordance with its instructions, the machine updates the state of the tape; when the machine comes to a halt (if in fact it does), the tape is decoded, yielding the value of the function for its input (i.e., the initial integer). The Turing machine is therefore an arithmetic computer. Thanks to Gödel, however, we know this means it is much more than that. Since logic can be arithmetized, the Turing machine is also a symbolic computer. It constitutes the model of symbolic thought.

The reader will have noted that the Turing machine is not a finite object: its tape, which is to say its memory, is unlimited. This may seem odd, since the objective here is precisely to model an effective, and therefore finite, procedure. As Mosconi puts it, very well once again:

> Turing machines are surprising in two respects: in that structures this basic can do so many things; and in that so-called "infinite" machines cannot "do everything." In fact, Turing machines are only finite machines equipped with an infinite memory. If too great a place is allowed to the infinite, one risks doing away with the very notion of a machine and of computation, since these things by their very nature are to some extent finite. This would be the result, for example, of imagining a machine that could execute an infinite number of operations in a finite time. One may say that the Turing machine is interesting because it is in some sense manageably infinite.[19]

A corollary of this is that the performance of a machine endowed with merely finite memory would be much less "interesting." We shall have occasion to return to this point.

Let us return first to Hilbert's decision problem. Turing showed that it is equivalent, in the mechanistic formulation he proposed, to the "halting problem": given a Turing machine, and assuming an initial state for its tape, does there exist a mechanical procedure—which, as the Turing "thesis" requires, must be another Turing machine—capable of determining whether the first machine will halt or, to the contrary, continue to loop indefinitely? What one wants, then, is to be able to construct a machine that, starting from the same initial state, will answer "yes" (in coded form) if and only if this initial state causes the first machine to halt. Turing managed to prove that such a machine does not exist. He was thus able to reply to the question posed by Hilbert in the negative.

This discovery, like the others we have encountered so far, was unexpected and disconcerting. Take the set of outputs of a given Turing machine (that is, the set of values of the numerical function that it models for all numbers that cause it to halt): although this set is, by definition, mechanically generated (technically speaking, "recursively enumerable"), it cannot, however, be completely characterized in a mechanical way, since to the question "Does such and such a value belong to the set?" there may be no mechanical response. Figuratively speaking, what the machine is capable of generating lies beyond the mechanical. The best minds of the age were bowled over by this discovery. We shall return to it later as well.

All these results were to have a considerable impact, though of course not immediately on culture in the broad sense, nor even on the scientific or philosophical community as a whole. Only a few researchers, assuming they are utterly committed to a theoretical project, are needed to move mountains in the history of ideas. It was thus that cybernetics was born in the 1940s—and, in its wake, cognitive science. At the beginning these "happy few" consisted of a handful of mathematicians, engineers, and physiologists. Some of them were geniuses in their fields. But the project that they shared in common and that gave meaning and vigor to their various undertakings was at bottom, and from the beginning, a philosophical one.

Looking back across the years, it is tempting to say that this project consisted in giving a scientific, and therefore materialist, response to the old philosophical problem of the relation between mind and body. There is a great deal of truth in this interpretation, but one must be careful to guard against retrospective illusions. It was only much later that the conceptual revolution introduced by the Turing machine was to serve as the basis of a functionalist solution to the problem of the relation between matter and thought. The doctrine of "computational-representational functionalism," based on the work of Simon and Newell and other pioneers of artificial intelligence, and defended and promoted by such impassioned philosophers of mind as Fodor and Pylyshyn, amounted to taking the metaphor of the computer—a Turing machine embodied in the form of electronic circuits—literally. The mind, or rather each of the various faculties that make it up (for example, the capacity to form the general concept "triangle" and to subsume particular instances of triangularity under this concept), was conceived as a Turing machine operating on the formulas of a private, internal language analogous to a formal language in logic. The symbols—the marks written on the tape of the machine—enjoy a triple mode of existence: they are physical objects (being embodied in a neurophysiological system) and therefore subject to the laws of physics (in the first instance to those of neurophysiology, which is supposed to be reducible to physics); they have form, by virtue of which they are governed by syntactic rules (analogous to the rules of inference in a formal system in the logical sense); and, finally, they are meaningful, and therefore can be assigned a semantic value or interpretation.

The gap that would appear to separate the physical world from the world of meaning is able to be bridged thanks to the intermediate level constituted by syntax, which is to say the world of mechanical processes—precisely the world in which the abstraction described by the Turing machine operates. The parallelism between physical processes subject to causal laws and mechanical processes carrying out computations, or inferential or syntactical operations, ceases to seem mysterious once one comes round to the view that the material world contains physical versions of Turing machines: computers, of course, but also every natural process that can be regarded as recursive.[20] The parallelism between syntax and semantics is guaranteed for its part by the logical theorems of consistency and completeness: the mechanical processes by which syntactic rules are carried out preserve the internal coherence of symbolic representations, as well as their adequacy as representations of what they represent. Preservation is obviously not the same thing as creation, however, and one of the stumbling blocks the computer model faces is the problem of determining how symbols acquire meaning. Turing-style functionalism constitutes the heart of what is called "cognitivism," which remains today the dominant paradigm of the sciences of cognition. The doctrine has nonetheless been the object of a number of profound critiques, the most severe of which have tended to come from those who helped found it.[21]

But in the period that we will consider in this book, the Turing thesis captivated the most adventurous minds of the age above all for what it implied about the relation between thought and machine, rather than for what it implied about the relation between thought and matter. This, at least, is my reading of what motivated the pioneers of cognitive science: the notion that thought, mental activity, this faculty of mind that has knowledge as its object, is in the last analysis nothing other than a rule-governed mechanical process, a "blind"—might one go so far as to say "stupid"?—automatism. Did this amount to devaluing humanity? To elevating the machine? Or, to the contrary, did they see man as a demiurge, capable of creating an artificial brain or mind? No doubt there is some truth to each of these interpretations, more or less depending upon which individual scientists are considered and the times in which they worked.

As time went by, zealots and ideologues began to assert ever stronger and more imprecise versions of the Turing thesis. It came to be presented as something *proven*. "Logical discoveries prove that there is nothing inconceivable about the idea of a thinking machine, or matter that thinks": one was to find this kind of statement—which is literally false or else devoid of meaning (since, once again, it is not something that is provable)—made even by the best authors. It was also to be said that everything the human mind is capable of doing and that can be precisely and unambiguously described, in a finite number of words, is executable by a suitably programmed computer; indeed, as Herbert Simon himself said in 1965, "Machines will be capable, within twenty years, of any work that a man can do."[22]

It is easy to mock vain and presumptuous predictions of this sort, which were to be scathingly refuted during the intervening years. But we should not be too harsh. To achieve what was in fact accomplished, which is far from negligible, what Karl Popper called "a metaphysical program of research" was required, a sort of act of faith that furnished the principles—the framework—for thought and, above all, the impetus for scientific investigation. The Turing thesis, in spite (or rather because) of the ideological distortions to which it so readily lent itself, was what it took to rally the resources of energy and intelligence needed to bring about the birth of a mechanistic and materialistic science of mind.

From the strictly logical point of view, the discoveries of the 1930s can be given an entirely different interpretation, as the deepest thinkers of the period, such as John von Neumann, well understood. If Turing's *theorems* show anything, it is that thinking is not necessarily the same as computation. Consider the numerical function that, for a given Turing machine, takes the value 1 for every number such that the machine comes to a halt when its tape starts from that number, and 0 in the contrary case. One can *conceive* of this mathematical entity, in the sense of being able to form a clear and distinct concept of it, without it being computable, owing to the unsolvability of the halting problem. It therefore cannot be *known*, if knowledge is understood (in accordance with the principle of *verum factum*) as an act that consists in expressing the generative principle of the object. Turing's mechanical model was well suited to deepening the fundamental distinction between thinking and knowing developed by Kantian philosophy. It is a cause for regret that this model has so often served as a pretext for sterile confrontation between those who take the slogan "thinking is computation" (the modern version of Hobbes's "Reason is nothing but reckoning") as their rallying cry and those who are merely infuriated by it.

Knowing as Simulating

In the same 1937 article, Turing demonstrated the existence of a specific Turing machine (there are, in fact, an infinite number of such machines) that he called "universal," a machine capable of imitating, mimicking, reproducing, *simulating* the behavior of any other Turing machine. Since, thanks to Gödel, we know that a set of rules or instructions can be coded by a number—or a sequence of marks—in an effective way, it suffices to imprint on the tape of the universal Turing machine a set of marks that codes the table of the machine to be imitated: for every input imprinted on its tape, next to the code of the machine to be imitated, the universal Turing machine will produce the same output as that machine.

Every Turing machine imitates a particular faculty of mind: it is the model of this faculty. The universal Turing machine imitates any particular Turing machine: it constitutes the model of models. We noticed earlier that functionalism in cognitive science defines mind as the model of the faculty of modeling. The universal Turing machine is therefore the model of the mind. Or must we say that it *is* the mind?

There is another formula that better captures—better than "thinking is computation"—the spirit of cognitive science: "knowing is simulating." Like the word "model," "simulation" means something quite different depending on whether it is used in a scientific context or in its ordinary sense. In the first case, simulation is a particular form of modeling that consists in reproducing, typically by means of a computer, the functioning of a system; it therefore involves the activity of knowing. In the second, where "simulation" rhymes with "dissimulation," one enters into the realm of pretense, make-believe, playacting. In the sciences of cognition, appeal to the doctrine of *verum factum* has resulted in a confusion of these two senses.

In 1950 Turing published an article, "Computing Machinery and Intelligence," that was to become scarcely less famous than his 1937 article. In it he proposed an operational method for settling a question that occupied many researchers at the time: can machines think? The method he proposed takes the form of a game. Significantly, Turing called it an "imitation game."[23] It might have been presented as having the following form. There are three players: a machine, a human being, and an interrogator who, being unable to see or hear either of the other two, must try to determine which is which through conversation with them by means, for example, of a teleprinter. The machine's strategy is to try to mislead the interrogator into thinking that it is the human being, while the latter attempts to affirm his or her human identity. The machine will have sufficiently well *simulated* the behavior of the human player if in the end the interrogator cannot tell them apart. In this case one will have succeeded at the same time in isolating an autonomous level of representation and communication (autonomous, that is, with respect to the physical basis of cognitive systems) where intelligence, thought, knowledge, and the like, are located.

Turing's imitation game was in fact made much more interesting by the introduction of a preliminary stage. In this stage the interrogator has to try to tell a man and a woman apart, the man trying to pass for a woman. Only then did the question arise: what would happen if the man were replaced by a machine? The introduction of this supplementary element significantly affects the nature of the test: to mislead the interrogator, the machine now has not simply to simulate the behavior of a human being (in this case a woman[24]) but indeed the ability of a human being (in this case a man) to simulate the behavior of another human being (in this case a woman). In this form the Turing test thus embodies the functionalist definition of mind as the simulation of the faculty of simulation.

Will it be possible one day for a machine, protected in this fashion by what amounts to a "veil of ignorance,"[25] to fool a human observer? The

controversy has tended to bear less on this point than on the adequacy of
the test itself. More than one critic—notably the philosopher John Searle,
in his famous "Chinese Room" thought experiment[26]—has charged that a
machine could perfectly well succeed without our thereby being forced to
conclude that it thinks. Searle invites us to imagine that a man who does
not understand a word of Chinese is locked up in a room and provided
with a store of Chinese characters and a program (written in his native
language, say, English) for manipulating these characters, which he can
identify only by their form. Questions are passed to him from outside the
room in the form of sequences of characters: following the instructions
contained in the program, he composes replies consisting of different sequences and passes them back outside. The answers given by an input-
output system functioning in this way, hidden beneath the veil of the
imitation game, would be indistinguishable from the answers given by a
Chinese woman who *understood* the questions being posed to her. It is
clear, however, that a man who does not understand Chinese cannot claim
to understand what he is doing, any more than the whole system made
up by the person and the room, with its characters and instructions, can be
said to understand. At the most, such a person's rule-governed manipu-
lation of symbols can be said to *simulate* the production and communication of meaning—it can hardly be said to *realize* these things. As Searle
himself has written elsewhere, "The computational model of mental processes is no more real than the computational model of any other natural
phenomenon."[27]

What Searle rejects here is much more than simply the "Turing test."
He rejects the whole development of *verum factum* in the Western scientific tradition that led to the identification of thought with the production
of models. For if this much is admitted—namely, that thought is nothing
but simulation[28]—how then could the simulation of simulation be refused
the status of thought?

Searle does not see, or refuses to see, that the effect of the "Copernican
revolution" unleashed by the new science of mind was to bring about a
deconstruction of the metaphysics of subjectivity that goes much further
than the philosophical enterprise that goes under this name. As far as
chinoiseries are concerned, one might, everything considered, prefer those
contrived by Searle's adversary, Jacques Derrida.[29] As Vincent Descombes
recalls, Derrida once observed that "the only way of pretending to speak
Chinese when speaking to a Chinese citizen is to address him *in Chinese*.
Consequently, in this type of utterance, simulation is simulation of simulation (to pretend, I actually do the thing: I have therefore only pretended to
pretend)."[30]

CHAPTER **2**

A Poorly Loved Parent

A dynamic science has no need of its past, it forges ahead.

—MARVIN MINSKY[1]

T HE CONSEQUENCES of the revolution in logic that occurred during the
1930s for the history of thought were deep and varied. One was that at the
beginning of the 1940s a small group of mathematicians, engineers, and
neurobiologists determined to found a science of mind struck up a dialogue, operating from 1947 under the code name "cybernetics." I contend
that what we call today cognitive science had its origins in the cybernetic
movement.

This thesis is far from self-evident, for two reasons. First, cognitive science was not the only offspring of this prolific movement. There were
many others, but they have grown up in such dissimilar ways that one is
hard-pressed to see a family resemblance among them; what is more, they
themselves do not acknowledge their own kinship. In the meantime it has
been forgotten that, in its heyday, cybernetics aroused the most extrava-
gant enthusiasms and the wildest expectations. From the technical, ideological, and theoretical points of view, it has shaped our era to an un-
rivaled degree. It is hardly surprising, then, that its descendants should be
numerous and distinctively different. Among its many achievements—
which I list here in no particular order, and without any claim to exhaus-
tiveness—cybernetics is responsible for introducing the logico-mathematical style of formalism and conceptualization to the sciences of the brain
and the nervous system; for conceiving the design of information-processing machines and laying the foundations of artificial intelligence; for producing the "metascience" of systems theory, which has left its mark on all
the human and social sciences, from family therapy to cultural anthropology; for providing a major source of inspiration for conceptual innovations
in economics, operations research, game theory, decision and rational
choice theory, political science, sociology, and still other disciplines;
and, thanks to its fortunate timing, for providing several of the scientific

"revolutions" of the twentieth century (a diverse group of cases ranging from molecular biology to Lacan's reinterpretation of Freud) with the metaphors they needed to announce their break with established paradigms. Modestly settling for a place among this jumble of disciplines was not something cognitive science ever contemplated. Still today, animated by a spirit of conquest, it dreams of clearing away the conceptual confusion that reigns in the human sciences.

There is a second obstacle to sustaining the charge of paternity that I am asserting here: the unwillingness (to say the least) on the part of cognitive science to admit that it is the child of cybernetics. When it does admit that it has something in common with cybernetics, it seems ashamed of their association. I shall have a number of opportunities in what follows to point out this estrangement; indeed it is to be found in most of the other fields on which cybernetics exercised an influence as well. There is no need, then, to insist unduly on this point in advance of illustrating it. Nonetheless I should say at the outset that it was the realization that the history of cognitive science is the story of the rejection of parent by child that led me to undertake this study in the first place: young people who are ashamed of their parents are unlikely to have a happy time growing up, and there is no reason why it should be any different in the world of ideas. The will to forget one's own history, typical of scientistic optimism, is nonetheless the surest way of condemning oneself to repeat its mistakes. For cybernetics did make mistakes—serious ones, as its children, who wanted to hide the fact that they were descended from it, were the first to point out.

A *New* Scienza Nuova?

Our story begins in the middle of World War II. Fixing a starting date is always arbitrary to some degree, though less so in this case than in others. In 1943, the year that witnessed the birth of a science of mind, there appeared independently of each other two articles, whose five authors—three in the first case, two in the second—were to constitute the nucleus of the cybernetic movement. These two articles set out programs of research that, taken together, summarized the ambitions of the new discipline.

The first, entitled "Behavior, Purpose and Teleology," was signed by Arturo Rosenblueth, Norbert Wiener, and Julian Bigelow, and published in January of 1943.[2] Wiener, who was first and foremost an applied mathematician, a "model builder," had been working during the war with Bigelow, then a young engineer, on the theoretical problems posed by antiaircraft defense. This research was conducted at MIT under the direction of Warren Weaver, who a few years later co-authored with Claude Shannon the seminal work on the mathematical theory of communication.[3] Bigelow was later to be recommended by Wiener to John von Neumann, and became the chief engineer of the computer under construction from 1946 at the Institute of Advanced Study in Princeton (popularly known as the JONIAC), which was to play an essential role in the development of the hydrogen bomb.[4]

The central problem of anti-aircraft defense is that, the target being mobile, it is necessary to predict its future position on the basis of partial information about its prior trajectory. Wiener worked out a probabilistic theory of prediction relying on theorems of ergodicity that was to revolutionize techniques of signal processing. Along with what was to become known as information theory, solving the problems of anti-aircraft defense brought into play the other basic ingredient of the nascent cybernetics: the concept of a feedback loop, intrinsic to all systems regulation based on the observed gap between the actual behavior of a system (its "output") and the projected result (its "goal").

Wiener, a polymath in the manner of von Neumann who had long taken an interest in physiology, had since 1933 been a member of an evening discussion club at Harvard Medical School. There he came into contact with the Mexican physiologist Arturo Rosenblueth, who shared his interest in philosophy of science.[5] Rosenblueth worked in Walter Cannon's laboratory at Harvard and was influenced by the notion of homeostasis as Cannon had developed it in the course of his research. Its range of application was vast, from organisms to society. Wiener and Bigelow brought to Rosenblueth's attention the analogy they had noticed between the conceptualization of anti-aircraft defense and the processes at work in the voluntary movement of a human subject. Rosenblueth pointed out that the brain of a patient suffering from damage to the cerebellum (the part of the brain concerned with muscle coordination and bodily equilibrium) who tries to carry a glass on his lips communicates oscillatory motions of growing amplitude to the hand—movements that irresistibly suggested the overshooting behavior of an undamped feedback loop. The outcome of their joint reflection on this topic was the article of 1943.

All of this is very well known, of course, but the article nonetheless holds a number of surprises for the reader today. The first is the awkwardness of its technical vocabulary. As a result, key concepts such as information, communication, and organization remain obscure. Feedback, for example, is described as a return of the *energy* of the output to the input—an affront to the dignity of cybernetics even before it had a name! But more than anything else it is the air of behaviorism about the article that amazes the present-day reader: of all the schools of psychology, behaviorism was the one with which cybernetics was to have the least patience. The authors take as their first objective "to define the behavioristic study of natural events and to classify behavior." Behavior is defined as "any modification of an object, detectable externally." The method recommended for identifying behavior concerns itself only with the object's relationship to its environment and (contrary to the rival method of "functional analysis") "omits the specific structure and the intrinsic organization of the object."[6]

Cybernetics, in the form in which it was anticipated in the article of 1943, undeniably treated the objects it studied as devices transforming input messages into output messages. This definition is still to be found plainly stated in Wiener's last works, some twenty years later.[7] What prevents it from being reduced to simple behaviorism, however, to a crude stimulus-response scheme, is precisely the notion of feedback. Thanks to this device, the object is capable of changing the relationship that it has established between input and output, between stimulus and response. For the observer who chooses to remain outside the object, everything occurs as though the object has the capacity to modify its response to a given stimulus with a view to achieving a certain goal. It appears, then, that the object is capable of carrying out a given purpose, learning to adjust its behavior in the light of the errors that it commits. The founder of the neocybernetic movement known as second-order cybernetics, Heinz von Foerster, was later to emphasize the importance of this apparent departure from orthodox behaviorism, all the while reproaching the founders of the movement's first phase for having fallen far short of realizing the possibilities they had thus opened up. To the "trivial machines" of behaviorism equipped with a stimulus-response rule, fixed once and for all, he opposed the extremely rich range of behaviors of which a "nontrivial machine" was capable, one modeled after a Turing machine, which is to say a machine provided with an internal state that it is capable of modifying as a function of input and the internal state of the preceding period.[8] Now a nontrivial machine in von Foerster's sense is nothing other than what logicians call a "finite-state automaton," in which a relatively small number of possible internal states and inputs becomes translated, by a sort of combinatorial explosion, into an intractable complication in behavior. It was this degree of complication that led von Foerster to observe that his nontrivial machine processed *information*, whereas the trivial behaviorist machine merely reacted to a *signal*.

No matter: the reader today cannot help but be struck by the behaviorist tone of the 1943 article. Its refusal to take into account the internal organization of the object is what really comes as a surprise for those who know cybernetics only from its second phase, inaugurated by the work of von Foerster and Ross Ashby, and culminating in the theories of biological organization of Humberto Maturana and Francisco Varela.[9] Emphasis is placed instead on the internal coherence and "autonomy" of the object, whether organism or complex machine, whose relations with the environment are reduced to simple perturbations, which convey no information whatsoever.

The sources of this surprise are interesting to note. The image that cybernetics has left behind—as much for its supporters as for its detractors—is that of a conquering *scienza nuova* that set itself up as a rival to physics and set itself the goal, in substituting form for matter, of putting an end to physics' ancient domination of the sciences. Philippe Breton, along with a number of other commentators, has argued for an interpretation of the 1943 article along these lines. On their view, this article, one of the two founding texts of cybernetics, urged that "content"—that is, the *physical* nature of the constituent elements of the material system under consideration, and of the relations among them—be dispensed with in favor of abstracting their *form*. One should, for example, try to isolate a *formal* device of feedback common to both animal and machine, without regard for the fact that the first consists of proteins and the second of electronic tubes. Hence the article's conclusion that "a uniform behavioristic analysis is applicable to both machines and living organisms, regardless of the complexity of the behavior"; also that the category of "teleology," understood as "behavior controlled by negative feedback," can be applied to the first as well as to the second.[10] Interpreted in this way, Breton argues, it "marks an essential break with the concepts of modern science, a rupture whose effects are still being widely felt in contemporary thought."[11]

This is going too far. The founders of cybernetics did not at all see themselves as building a *scienza nuova*. The revolution in the history of thought brought about by Vico's new science had already occurred long before, as we saw in the last chapter. To abstract the formal properties of phenomena and in this way be able to identify isomorphisms between different domains of phenomena is precisely what modeling is all about—even science itself. The attempt to propose a unified theory of machines and living creatures with reference to the category of purpose, conceived in mechanistic terms and rebaptized as "teleology," represented a spectacular increase in the extension of science, hardly a rupture with it. The cyberneticians harbored no ambitions either to break with physics or to somehow go beyond it. To the contrary, it was within the very framework of physics that they had received their scientific training and that they intended to situate their new ideas.

The stated desire of the cyberneticians to remain outside the object they were analyzing, to ignore its internal "contents," in fact concealed a rather different ambition. Close examination of the transcripts of the Macy Conferences discloses much about the deepest convictions of the authors of the 1943 article and forces us to a different interpretation than Breton's, one

that better accords with a literal reading of this article. It finds support in
a number of heated exchanges between the cyberneticians and the sole
invited representative of psychoanalysis over the notion of the unconscious; but it is most clearly manifest in a clash that occurred at the eighth
conference, in 1951, when Rosenblueth, seconded by Bigelow, clashed with
Herbert Birch, a specialist in animal communication. Birch had just finished reviewing various cases of what was called "communication" among
insects and lower vertebrates. The point he was trying to get across in
every case was that these behaviors, whose apparent complexity was striking (and, at the time, still poorly understood), were to be seen as mere
behaviors and *nothing more*—stereotypical behaviors at that, which could
scarcely be considered as displaying the capacities for intelligence and
comprehension that are associated with "true" communication. To drive
home the point he took the following extreme example, for which he would
not be forgiven by the cyberneticians. The scallop is one of the starfish's
favorite dishes. The presence of a starfish in the vicinity of a scallop causes
the scallop to take flight. Must one therefore say that "communication"
takes place between the two? If so, would one wish to continue to assert as
much if the boiled extract of a starfish, which produces exactly the same
reaction in the scallop, were to be substituted for the starfish itself? Birch
concluded his presentation by examining the distinctive characteristics of
"true" communication, which on his view was to be observed only among
the higher mammals, culminating in human communication: it implied
anticipation, intentionality, and symbolization, and required the capacities of learning, perceiving, and engaging in social life.

Rosenblueth exploded. These distinctions, he said in effect, are meaningless: they rely on certain notions—intelligence, consciousness, memory,
learning, anticipation, intentionality, content—that refer to what goes on
in the minds of individual human beings and, being inherently unmeasur-
able, do not pertain in the least to the problem of communication. We are
able to interact with others only through their *behavior*: this is the only
thing that we can see, that we can judge, and that can in turn affect us.
Naturally, he conceded, when we describe the behavior of living creatures,
whether it be that of human beings or of less developed organisms, or
indeed of a machine, we are in the habit of availing ourselves (unavoidably in some cases) of a "mentalist" vocabulary that may seem to suggest
that we are attributing a "mind" to these creatures. There is nothing
wrong with this as long as we are aware of what we are doing—that is,
as long as we recognize that this is simply a manner of speaking, which has
no bearing on the question that interests us: communication. As long as
this condition is respected, we can perfectly well speak of a machine as
having a "memory" or being capable of "learning." This is of no conse-

quence, inasmuch as we are referring to something objective and measurable that has nothing to do with our inner experience.[12]

The notion that cybernetics represented a decisive break with behaviorism must therefore be very strongly qualified. The science of mind that cybernetics wished to construct was (to use today's vocabulary) resolutely "eliminativist." The mental states invoked by ordinary or "folk" psychology to account for behavior—beliefs, desires, will, intentions—were to be banned from scientific explanation. That the cybernetics of Wiener and Rosenblueth was fundamentally nonmentalist has not always been sufficiently appreciated, particularly in France, where cyberneticians became acquainted with the 1943 article through a translation published nearly twenty years later.[13] In this version the middle word of the original title "Behavior, Purpose and Teleology" was rendered as "*intention*"—a mistranslation, since intentionality was part and parcel of the very mentalism that the authors wished to do away with, replacing it with the notion of purpose, understood in a *non*intentional sense. In later years Heinz von Foerster would often reproach the first wave of cyberneticians, and the pioneers of artificial intelligence who followed in their wake, for having spoken of machines in anthropomorphic terms. It may be more to the point, however, to observe that if the early cyberneticians spoke in this way, it was because for them humanity was to be conceived in terms of the machine. Accordingly, the distinction between voluntary and reflex behaviors, so fundamental in the history of physiology, as well as the distinction between consciousness and unconsciousness, lost all meaning. But the important thing to see here is that the assimilation of man to machine was not intended as a reduction. For the machine was the *model* of humanity—in both senses of the word.

Mechanizing the Human

The second foundational article published in 1943 was signed by the neuropsychiatrist Warren McCulloch and the mathematician Walter Pitts. The philosophical ambition of this article is considerable, since it attempted nothing less than to give a purely neuroanatomical and neurophysiological basis for synthetic a priori judgments, and thus to ground a neurology of mind.

The article by McCulloch and Pitts radicalized the approach of Wiener and his collaborators on two levels. Whereas the latter (especially Rosenblueth) denied all reality to the mind and treated the customary evocation of its faculties in everyday terms simply as a linguistic convenience, McCulloch set off in search of the logical and material mechanisms that embodied mind.[14] It seemed natural to him to try to answer questions like "Why the Mind Is in the Head."[15] It may seem therefore that the "mentalism" of McCulloch and the behaviorist critique of mentalism developed by Wiener were sharply at odds with each other. In the course of his many confrontations with the Gestaltists, McCulloch was even to find himself accused of "dualism" (Wolfgang Köhler arguing that his approach led him, in spite of himself, to attribute an autonomy to a world of "apparitions," of mental facts—to a psychological world with its own determining characteristics).[16] What McCulloch was doing, in fact, was relocating the "behavioristic study of natural phenomena" promoted by Wiener, Rosenblueth, and Bigelow inside the brain. To be sure, the "contents" of the very thing that is responsible for behavior were now considered to be amenable to scientific investigation; but these contents were themselves described in terms of the behavior of smaller units, "inside" which there was no question of penetrating, and which were considered only with respect to their relation to the environment—considered, that is, as operators transforming inputs into outputs, as neurons. In view of the fact that McCulloch transposed Wiener's behavioristic and communicational approach to a logically lower level, it is not a matter so much of Wiener's and McCulloch's approaches being opposed to each other as of the radicalization of the one by the other.

The other element of this radicalization concerns the relation between organisms and machines. Cybernetics in the form in which Wiener later popularized it was presented as the science of detecting and elaborating *analogies* between organisms and machines.[17] McCulloch's position at the time is well summarized in an article published more than a decade later, in 1955: "Everything we learn of organisms leads us to conclude not merely that they are *analogous* to machines but that they *are* machines."[18] The difference is twofold. It is first of all a difference of point of view. For Wiener, reasoning as an applied mathematician, it was enough to establish a mathematical isomorphism in order to conclude that an analogical relation obtains. What McCulloch was defending, by contrast, was an ontological position. The second difference, obviously related to the first, is that the machines Wiener was talking about were "real" machines: artifacts, artificial machines, technological objects. For McCulloch, the machine was a logico-mathematical being embodied in the matter of the organism: it was, if you will, a "natural machine," or a "logic machine," nature and logic being here fully equivalent to each other. It is thus without any incoherence whatsoever that McCulloch frequently distanced himself from the analogies sometimes rather casually asserted by his colleagues between artificial and natural automata—analogies that would do so much to discredit cybernetics in the eyes of "serious" scientists, or what Max Weber called blinkered specialists.[19]

An important confrontation between McCulloch and von Neumann, about which we shall have more to say further on, occurred in Pasadena in September 1948 at the Hixon Symposium, a conference sponsored by the California Institute of Technology. There von Neumann read his famous paper, "The General and Logical Theory of Automata," taking great care to note the differences as well as the common features of natural and artificial automata. McCulloch's reaction was revealing: he retreated into the camp of the biologists and psychologists, as though he wished to isolate von Neumann among the applied mathematicians and engineers. McCulloch's distancing of himself from von Neumann was motivated by a strictly philosophical disagreement about the status of models. A model, for McCulloch, was not a simple instrument of calculation having a purely pragmatic value, determined by the answer to the question "Does it work?" It had an ontological reality.[20] It should be noted, moreover, that McCulloch's 1955 article, mentioned earlier, concludes on this note: "Man-made machines are not brains, but brains are a very ill-understood variety of computing machines. Cybernetics has helped pull down the wall between the great world of physics and the ghetto of the mind."[21] It is enough to cite this passage alone in order to dispel two widespread but false notions about cybernetics that we have already had occasion to mention. Cybernetics was not, contrary to the usual, mistaken view, concerned with making the machine human—it was concerned with mechanizing the human. Nor, just as plainly, did it regard physics as the rival needing to be challenged—it regarded physics as supplying the model needing to be imitated.

McCulloch often recalled the singular journey that led him, in the company of Walter Pitts, a mathematician and logician of genius, to conceive the 1943 article. Its point of departure was a philosophical question that gnawed at him his whole life: how do we know what we know, and how do we desire what we desire?—a question to which he was later to give the memorable formulation: "What is a Number, that a Man may know it, and a Man, that he may know a Number?"[22] McCulloch ranged over the most varied disciplines, perpetually unsatisfied with the answers they gave: from philosophy to psychology, from psychology to neuropsychiatry and thence to neurophysiology, and finally from there to mathematical logic. Beginning in the 1920s, while still a psychologist and under the influence of Whitehead and Russell (but also perhaps of Democritus), he attempted to construct a propositional calculus in which the atomic propositions were "psychic events," or "psychons," localized in time and having the following properties: each psychon is an all-or-nothing event (i.e., either it is produced, or it is not); each psychon implies its temporal antecedent and affects the determination of subsequent psychons; psychons can be compounded in such a way as to produce more complex propositions concerning their antecedents. In 1929 it occurred to him these mental atoms might be the "all-or-none" electric impulses transmitted (or not) by each neuron to its neighbors.

The idea that Boolean algebra (that is, a logical calculus of propositions) can be materialized in the form of electric circuits and relay switches has come to seem altogether familiar to us, living as we do in a world of computers. It is hard for us today to imagine the intellectual shock that this discovery held for those who experienced it. Herbert Simon, for one, has said that the course of his intellectual career was decided at that moment.[23] No one today is surprised in the least that the brain, which we suppose to be the source of our logical faculties, should be compared to a digital computer. There was, moreover, a time (is there anyone still left who can remember it?) when the computer was called an "electronic brain." Legend has it that cybernetics was responsible for inventing this double metaphor—somehow in the manner of Wiener's analogies between organisms and machines. Thus Jean-Pierre Changeux, comparing the brain (with certain qualifications) "to a cybernetic machine or a computer,"[24] can say in his historical study *Neuronal Man*, "With Norbert Wiener, cybernetics took up [La Mettrie's thesis that man is a machine]. The human brain was no longer comparable to the mechanism of an automaton or a clock; rather it *resembled*, and *functioned as*, a computer."[25]

It is therefore important to recall that things did not at all happen thus. The first confusion to be cleared up has to do with the number of actors: they are not two—the organism and the machine—but three: the organism considered in terms of its structure (the brain), the organism considered in terms of its function (mind), and the machine—the last being conceived in two ways, as logic machine (Turing's machine, for example, or that of McCulloch and Pitts) and material, artificial machine (the computer). This third actor, in the first of these two incarnations, plays the role of the model, and, like Yorick's skull, is at the center of the drama. The drama is comprised of three acts.

Brain/Mind/Machine

The first act consists in the assimilation of mind to machine—a logic machine, to begin with. In the previous chapter we saw how the development of science in the West led to this result, at the end of a long crescendo culminating in the logical revolution of the 1930s and punctuated by the theorems of Gödel and Turing and by the Church-Turing thesis. At this juncture yet another voice must be added to an already rich score, that of Claude Shannon, a future participant in the Macy Conferences. In an article that appeared in 1938 in a technical journal of electrical engineering, the man who was later to be recognized as one of the founders of information theory proposed a logical theory of electrical circuits or, to be more precise, impedance matching networks composed of relays or switches.

The novelty of this paper was twofold. On the one hand, of course, such networks had already been the object of various kinds of mathematical modeling, only these depended on a mathematics of quantities; Shannon's first innovation was his recourse to a logical tool, namely, the propositional calculus. On the other hand, there existed prior to Shannon's paper a long tradition of research aimed at resolving logical problems by means of mechanical, physical devices. One of the high points of this tradition, which can be traced back to the beginning of the nineteenth century, came in the 1870s with the development of Jevons's "logical piano."[26] Shannon's second innovation consisted in shedding an entirely new light on the relationship between machine and logic.[27] His approach was essentially a theoretical one, ridding itself of the pragmatic, problem-solving character of the earlier tradition. Even though Shannon's theory addressed itself to a technical problem—in this case, how to produce an electrical network capable of realizing a given behavior—it unavoidably opened up philosophical perspectives. The first step was to show that logic is capable of furnishing a *model* in the scientific sense of the functioning of such a network. As we saw in the first chapter, however, the notion of a model retains— even for scientists—the sense of something deserving to be imitated rather than something that simulates. Inevitably, then, the conclusion followed that logic can be incarnated in a physical mechanism. Logic embodied in a machine, like God incarnate in Jesus Christ, thus takes on the identity of an artificial, or physical, machine. Since, moreover, all the elements needed to become convinced that the mind is a logic machine were at hand by this time, Shannon would have been able to conclude, by transitivity, that the mind is a physically constructible machine and therefore replicable, perhaps, by human artifice. The engineer in him no doubt was reluctant to take such a step. Others were less hesitant, however.

We know very little about the impact of Shannon's work upon the development of the McCulloch-Pitts model. In the course of the Macy Conferences it is never referred to—the Shannon who participated in those discussions was essentially the theorist who, in the interval, had devised information theory. By contrast, it is obvious that the Turing thesis did exercise a considerable influence upon McCulloch and Pitts, as upon some of the other participants in the conferences. Their 1943 article would never have come about had it not been for the impetus it gave to the authors' thinking. Indeed, the transactions of the Macy Conferences, along with many other works written by cyberneticians at the time, make it clear that despite their scientific and logical training, they frequently committed the error, propagated by the ideologues, of presenting the Turing thesis as a result that could be, and in fact had been, proved. At the ninth conference, in March 1952, Pitts expounded his view of the pedagogical responsibility of the cybernetician. In designing mechanisms capable of carrying out certain functions that "various people" had interpreted as prerogatives of a mysterious "mind's substance" or "some other nonphysiological entity,"[28] the cybernetician played an educational role of inestimable importance. *For us*, Pitts added, referring to Turing's thesis as if it were a theorem, this is a question that has long been "decided," and decided once and for all; it is for "the rest of the world," who need to be convinced, that we have to go through this painstaking business of showing that psychological functions can be mechanically performed, function by function. This profession of faith is all the more remarkable for being one of the rare moments during the Macy Conferences when the word "we" was used to designate the cybernetic community. Reading Pitts almost fifty years later, and experiencing again his shudder of excitement, one is acutely aware that for him Turing's thesis was a sort of secret treasure, for which he and the other cyberneticians had taken personal responsibility—a precious gift, sent from above, that was not to be squandered lightly.

The second act of the drama begins with the 1943 article by McCulloch and Pitts, entitled "A Logical Calculus of the Ideas Immanent in Nervous Activity."[29] It demonstrates the existence in principle of a logic machine equivalent to Turing's machine (in the sense that everything that can be done by the one can be done by the other, and vice versa), which, in respect of its structure and its behavior, can be regarded as an idealization of the anatomy and physiology of the brain. This result, to McCulloch's way of thinking at least, constituted a decisive advance, since it was now possible to regard not only the function of the brain (mind) as a mechanism, more particularly as a Turing machine, but its structure (the biological, natural, physical brain) as well. Thus McCulloch imagined it was possible at last to resolve the old problem of the soul and the body—or, to use his phrase, the problem of the "embodiment of mind." The brain is a machine and the mind is a machine, and the machines in each case are the same: therefore, mind and brain are one and the same.

Knowledge of neuroanatomy and neurophysiology at the time was less precise than it is today, of course; but, more important, it was less self-assured. Recall that the introduction of electronic microscopy dates from the 1950s. Since the beginning of the century, to be sure, the work of the Spanish school, led first by Ramón y Cajal and then by Lorente de Nó (who was to play an important role in the development of cybernetics), lent powerful support to the idea that the functioning of the central nervous system could be treated as a communication network among neurons. But, until the time of the last Macy Conferences, the mechanisms of synaptic transmission had yet to be sorted out: it was only in 1952 that Hodgkin and Huxley succeeded in completely elucidating the ionic basis for synaptic release and propagation of the nerve impulse. More important still, the arguments of the "continuists," who conceived of the brain as a continuous field whose function could only be understood as an indivisible whole, were still being energetically pressed, and the cyberneticians were to find themselves confronted with these arguments in the person of the Gestaltist Wolfgang Köhler and also, though to a lesser degree, in the person of Karl Lashley, the great neurophysiologist of the epoch, for whom it is known the fiery McCulloch felt a great respect, tinged with fear.[30] It took a certain amount of courage, therefore, for McCulloch in 1943 to propose a model of the brain as a network of idealized (or "formal") neurons. In this model, each neuron can receive impulses at any instant from its neighbors, itself firing if and only if a weighted sum[31] of the ones and zeroes that code the existence or absence of an impulse in the afferent synapses exceeds a certain limit, called the "excitation threshold."[32] To use the language of the propositional calculus, each idealized neuron is an elementary arithmetic calculator that computes a logical (Boolean) function of its antecedents. The brain as a whole is taken to be a network of such calculators.

From 1943 to 1963, alone or in collaboration with Pitts, McCulloch continued to explore the possibilities of his logic machine, utterly convinced (owing to his belief in Turing's thesis) of its capacity for exhibiting all the faculties attributed to the mind: perception, thought, memory, concept formation, knowledge of universals and their recognition, will, and even consciousness (defining this, as Spinoza did, as idea of ideas). He was to take a particular interest in the properties resulting from the existence in the network of closed circuits, cycles and loops. Such loops had been postulated by the neurologist Lawrence Kubie in 1930 in an article that appeared in the British journal *Brain*.[33] At the time Kubie was working with Sherrington, whose studies of involuntary movements and reflexes were recognized as authoritative. In 1938 Lorente de Nó experimentally demonstrated the existence of cycles in the nervous system.[34] In 1941 Kubie, who had by now become a psychoanalyst, conjectured that the neurophysiological basis of neurosis was to be looked for in these reverberating closed circuits, where firing sequences came to be trapped in an endless circle.[35] Jacques Lacan, of whom we will have more to say later, was familiar with this cybernetic reading of the compulsion (or automatism) of repetition—the famous Freudian *Wiederholungszwang*. It is probable that his interest during the 1950s in cybernetics had its origins in Kubie's conjecture.

McCulloch, by his own account was strongly influenced by Kubie's 1930 article. This is a point that deserves all the more to be noted in view of the fact that the transactions of the Macy Conferences vividly record the many heated exchanges between McCulloch and Kubie, who, as a psychoanalyst—the sole representative at these conferences of a discipline despised by the cyberneticians—was their favorite whipping boy.[36] Neuronal cycles played an important role in McCulloch's thinking, and the theme of "circular causality" is obviously one of the things that drew him closer to Wiener and his collaborators. These cycles, McCulloch believed in 1943—on the condition that they were not considered in terms of the model of a reflex arc, which is a regulating negative feedback, but as "reverberating circuits" implying a positive feedback—are the very means by which the sequences of events that reach the nervous system through the sense organs are captured and placed beyond the reach of time. It is therefore on the basis of these cycles that a theory of memory and of the formation of general ideas is to be constructed. Remarking upon this point in the 1943 article, Jean Mosconi comments:

> The mechanism for preserving a trace of the past by reverberation in cycles of neurons amounts to snatching the event away from its precise temporal localization in order to place it in an indefinitely renewed present. Thus some light is thrown upon the old psychological quarrels over the relationship between abstraction and forgetting, not only by the reference to a physiological substrate but also to a rigorous and positive logical content: the phenomenon in question corresponds to the transition from simple formulas with constant terms (e.g., "such-and-such an event occurred at instant t_0") to quantified formulas (e.g., "there was an instant in the past at which such-and-such an event occurred"), and therefore to a higher level of logical complexity and expressive capacity.[37]

In the course of the Macy Conferences, McCulloch was led to recognize the inadequacy of the 1943 model in relation to one of his chief ambitions: to give an account of the capacity of the mind to form and to know universals. This did not cause him to turn his back on his logic machine—far from it: he tried everything he could think of to make it more complex. First he attempted to endow it with learning capacities so that traces of past events could be retained, both in the pattern of connections and in the excitation thresholds. Convinced more than ever of the need to remain close to biological reality, he and Pitts later introduced randomness into their networks so that they would be able to function in the presence of errors as well of the "noise" to which elementary calculators and their connections were liable. In October 1946, at the second Macy Conference, Pitts presented the results of his initial thinking about random networks. This was enough to start von Neumann on the road that would lead him to construct his probabilistic logic.[38] That same year McCulloch was to compare learning in random neural networks to the mechanisms of magnetization.[39]

Learning, the role of chance, inspiration from models of the physics of disordered systems—McCulloch saw intuitively that his model could, and should, be developed along these lines, and the credit for this must in all fairness be given to him, even if he and Pitts did not do more than take the first steps. This poses the quite controversial question of the meaning and value of this pioneering work and of what remains of it today. Those who wish to think well of Warren McCulloch now that he is gone prefer to remember among his achievements only the contributions to formal logic and the theory of computability. Among this group are two of his former associates, Marvin Minsky and Seymour Papert, better known as pioneers of artificial intelligence—the discipline that was to rekindle, for better or for worse, the extinguished flame of cybernetics. Their eagerness to protect their old mentor from the accusations frequently brought against cybernetics calls to mind Sartre's witticism, "To be dead is to be a prey for the living."

Logic does, of course, play an essential role in the McCulloch-Pitts model of idealized neurons. The connection with Shannon's approach is relevant in this regard.[40] An attempt had been made prior to McCulloch to extend to biology, and in particular to the theory of the nervous system, the method that had succeeded so well in physics: mathematical modeling. This took some doing, since the majority of neurophysiologists strongly resisted the project of a mathematized neurology. One of them, however, Nicholas Rashevsky, undertook in the 1930s to lay the groundwork for a "mathematical biophysics." Among his students by the end of the decade was Walter Pitts.[41] The influence of physics was so strong that the first models preserved the tools and the very spirit of physico-mathematical modeling. To account for a macroscopic phenomenon, in this case, the properties of the nervous system, one develops a system of differential equations that describes the quantitative interactions among constituent elements, in this case, neurons. That assumes, obviously, that the quantities can be treated as differentiable, and therefore continuous, magnitudes. The novelty introduced by McCulloch and Pitts was a result of taking seriously, as Shannon had in the domain of electrical circuits, the "all-or-none" character of neuronal firing, which led them to propose a logical type of model. Rashevsky perceived the revolutionary character of their article and accepted it for publication in the journal he edited, the *Bulletin of Mathematical Biophysics*.

Can it be said, for all that, that the work done by McCulloch and Pitts was essentially mathematical logic? If this were the case, it certainly was not of prizewinning quality. Their arguments, later shown to be false on critical points, were corrected by Kleene in 1956[42] and completed by Arbib in 1961.[43] But the main point to be made is that a McCulloch-Pitts-style neural network is not equivalent to a Turing machine, for the class of functions that such networks allow to be computed is a subset of the class of recursive functions, which as we have seen is equivalent to the class of functions computable by a Turing machine. As Papert remarked (not without second thoughts) in his introduction to *Embodiments of Mind* in 1965, what McCulloch and Pitts achieved from a strictly logico-mathematical point of view was to introduce a new concept of computability, which Kleene associated with the concept of a *finite* automaton. As McCulloch and Pitts themselves realized, for their networks to have the same computational capacities as Turing machines, they would have to be equipped with those two essential elements of every Turing machine: a mobile head capable of reading, writing, and erasing symbols; and, more important still, a potentially infinite tape or memory. The brain being a physical—and therefore finite—organ, it clearly cannot compute everything that Turing machines can. But McCulloch and Pitts and the other cyberneticians were the first ones to forget this cardinal limitation: throughout the Macy Conferences they went on repeating in assured tones the magic formula "Any behavior that can be logically, precisely, completely, and unambiguously described, in a finite number of symbols, is computable by a neural network." They themselves thus helped bring about the lapse into misstatement that we have already remarked upon in connection with Turing machines.

McCulloch's Neurons

McCulloch often joked about being mistaken for a logician. Toward the end of his life, however, he surveyed with dismay the growing abstraction of the field of research that his 1943 article with Pitts had opened up. By the middle of the 1960s he had come to bitterly regret that what he had conceived as a theory of automata—that is to say, a theory of those *real* objects, whether natural or artificial, called automata, that *embody* the faculties of mind—should little by little have become a disembodied mathematical theory: automata theory.[44] Perhaps no passage better expresses the true nature of his project and how he regarded it than the following:

> [E]ven Clerk Maxwell, who wanted nothing more than to know the relation between thoughts and the molecular motions of the brain, cut short his query with the memorable phrase, "but does not the way to it lie through the very den of the metaphysician, strewn with the bones of former explorers and abhored by every man of science?" Let us peacefully answer the first half of his question "Yes," the second half "No," and then proceed serenely.
>
> Our adventure is actually a great heresy. We are about to conceive of the knower as a computing machine.[45]

The oldest philosophical questions were henceforth within the reach of scientific investigation. This was the good news. To reduce McCulloch's work to logic, on the ground that it proposed a model of the mind and of the brain that employs a logical formalism, is to commit the same category mistake as believing that the meteorologist or the ecologist who resolves a system of differential equations is doing creative work in mathematics. Once again, this amounts to a misunderstanding of the status of a model in the scientific process. McCulloch intended to operate, as we have already observed, both as psychologist and biologist. More precisely, his ambition was to avoid doing psychology, or "speculative epistemology," by using biology to turn it into "experimental epistemology." In 1964 he spoke ironically of those who had failed to understand that the object of his research was "the embodiment of mind" and, referring to his 1943 model, added, "The postulated neurons, for all their oversimplifications, are still physical neurons as truly as the chemist's atoms are physical atoms."[46]

If the idealized neuron *is* the physical neuron and devising a theory of it is a matter for biology rather than logic, this is due to the fact that the features of the physical neuron not retained by the formal theory do not belong to its *essence*. To better grasp what this means, one may ask, for example, what McCulloch's attitude would have been if he had had at his disposal the knowledge we have today of the nervous system. If he had known then what we know now about the respective roles of electrical and chemical transmission in the synapses, about the atomic and molecular mechanisms of the propagation of the nerve impulse, would he have profited from this in order to refine (if not actually revise) his model, or would he have rejected it? What McCulloch was looking to do was to *abstract* from the central nervous system a level of organization and, at this level, certain features of it in order to be able to reconstruct the observed functions of the real system as economically as possible. In both these aims he succeeded: the level was that of the neuron; and the features were those of his idealized neurons. The dizzying descent of our knowledge into ever more elementary levels of organization would not have mattered to him, and he would not have regarded it as a decisive step forward in relation to the problem he had set for himself.

McCulloch's approach was therefore functionalist, though in a way that was quite removed, of course, from the later representational and computational functionalism of the mind as a Turing machine, which was to be the distinguishing mark of artificial intelligence and of the dominant mode of research in cognitive science in the years to come. We have already mentioned this in the preceding chapter, and we will come back to it later on. It explains why McCulloch insisted on the fact that the physical mechanisms that he proposed to account for the faculties of mind were *sufficient* but not at all *necessary*. They were both possible, as the anatomical and physiological knowledge of the period demonstrated, and capable of manifesting such faculties.[47] But other embodiments, or other theories of these embodiments, were nonetheless conceivable. Here we encounter the notion of "multiple realizability," which as we have seen is integral to the practice of modeling. It is this notion that brought about the emancipation of the model, which was now free to take flight on its own wings.

If anyone truly understood this at the time, it was von Neumann. As he remarked with reference to the McCulloch-Pitts article of 1943, "They wanted to discuss neurons. They took the position that they did not want to get tied up in the physiological and chemical complexities of what a neuron really is. They used what is known in mathematics as the axiomatic method, stating a few simple postulates and *not being concerned with how nature manages to achieve such a gadget.*"[48] Von Neumann went on to say:

> They went one step further. This has been emphasized very strongly by those who criticize their work, although it seems to me that the extent to which they went further can be justified. They said that they did not want to axiomatize the neuron as it actually exists, but they wanted to axiomatize an idealized neuron, which is much simpler than the real one. They believed that the extremely amputated, simplified, idealized object which they axiomatized possessed the *essential* traits of the neuron, and that all else are incidental complications, which in a first analysis are better forgotten. Now, I am quite sure that it will be a long time before this point is generally agreed to by everybody, if ever; namely, whether or not what one overlooks in this simplification had really better be forgotten or not.[49]

A good illustration of the preceding interpretation is provided by Jean-Pierre Changeux's *Neuronal Man*. Changeux proposes in this work to defend the reductionist approach in neurobiology, the achievements of which are all the more spectacular as the ultimate level of reduction descends further along the physical scale of matter.[50] Now, when it comes to providing grounds for the philosophical thesis that "Man no longer has a need for the 'Spirit'; it is enough for him to be Neuronal Man,"[51] we find ourselves exactly at the level where Warren McCulloch situated it, and in the same terms.

A more direct indication is supplied by the attitude of McCulloch and Pitts themselves, supported by Wiener, during the discussion (fascinating for the history of neurophysiology) that opened the sixth Macy Conference, in March 1949. Von Neumann, who was absent, had transmitted this message: "10^{10} neurons, used as simple relays, are utterly inadequate to account for human abilities."[52] He suggested that the missing degrees of freedom (or of complexity) would be found in the internal, proteinaceous organization of the soma, the cell body of the neuron. The physiologists present wholeheartedly agreed with this: they were only too happy to denounce the simplistic character of McCulloch's axiomatized neuron. Neither McCulloch nor Wiener dodged their arguments, which were highly technical on the biochemical and physiological levels. But reading the transactions of the conference, one has the clear sense that for McCulloch—who was never peremptory or dogmatic in these discussions—they could not possibly affect the relevance of his model. The debate ended with Pitts showing that the calculation on which von Neumann had based his objection was invalid.[53]

A comparison suggests itself that is all the more pertinent to the extent that von Neumann's work *Theory of Games and Economic Behavior*, written in collaboration with the Austrian economist Oscar Morgenstern the same year that the McCulloch-Pitts article appeared, and published the following year,[54] was to supply the cybernetic debate with an important element: the individual actor, or agent, of economic theory. A hard-core neoclassical economist may be interested for personal reasons in the results of psychological research into the depths of the human soul, but this will not in the least dispose him or her to renounce the model of *Homo oeconomicus*, of the economic agent as input-output calculator: this individual stands in the same relation to an actual human being as the formal neuron does to a real neuron. Because the spirit that animates cybernetic modeling is profoundly similar to that of the modeling employed in mathematical economics, it comes as no surprise that the various disciplines issuing from the first kind of modeling (systems theory, operations research, optimal control theory, decision theory, and so forth) should have provided the second with some of its chief tools.

It is therefore absurd to say or to write, as is too often done, that the model of idealized neurons is only the product of a "formal" or "fictitious" neurology. One might as well say, as McCulloch remarked, that Maxwell's theory of electromagnetism (or any other formalized physical theory) is fictitious because it deals with idealized entities. It is true that the neurobiological community has on the whole remained indifferent to McCulloch's work. Even those who adopt his central idea (that the determining characteristic of the nervous system has to do with its being a network of neurons), and who work with formalisms derived from the McCulloch-Pitts model, seem to ignore the existence of this model or attribute it to other authors.[55] Exceptions were very rare: the neurobiologist Jerome Lettvin (who, it is true, collaborated with the great cybernetician) considered Warren McCulloch to have erected what still today stands as the only *theory* of the nervous system that we have at our disposal and attributes the disdain, ignorance, and ostracism to which it has been subjected to the field's lack of philosophical and theoretical ambition. Physiological and anatomical data accumulate, but it hardly occurs to anyone to relate them to mental processes.[56]

It is both an irony and a ruse of history that the McCulloch-Pitts model was to engender a notable posterity neither in logic nor in neurobiology, but instead in artificial intelligence. The irony is that McCulloch, of all the cyberneticians, was the least preoccupied with engineering problems. The ruse—well, to appreciate this we would have to review the entire history of cognitive science, from cybernetics to the present day: this history remains to be written,[57] and it would no doubt be premature to attempt such a work just now, considering how swiftly the field continues to evolve. I will content myself here with a few brief suggestions.

Following the cybernetic phase, the chief subject of the present work, neural network research experienced a considerable boom, culminating in the work carried out between 1957 and 1961 by Frank Rosenblatt at Cornell University on behalf of the U.S. Navy, which was interested in modeling visual perception. Rosenblatt's model, known during its moment of glory by the name "Perceptron," was a particular type of McCulloch-Pitts network, arranged in multiple layers of neurons and capable of learning. The neurons of the input layer simulated the activity of the retina, the neurons of the output layer classified the features that the system "recognized" in the object presented to it, and the neurons of the layers in between (known as "hidden units") carried out the intervening computations. In the Perceptron, only the connections between the output layer and the outermost computation level were capable of learning.

In the work summarizing his research, first published in 1961,[58] Rosenblatt distinguished his approach from that of McCulloch and Pitts. According to Rosenblatt, theirs was "top-down" in the sense that they decided first what functions or tasks they wanted their machine to be able to perform and then derived a structure capable of realizing them. A constructivist (or artificialist) method of this sort—which Rosenblatt called a "monotypic model approach"—requires that the logical organization of the network be rigorously and fully defined. Ironically, Rosenblatt criticized the McCulloch-Pitts approach for having too much of an engineering spirit about it, for being insufficiently biological. As against this method, Rosenblatt proposed a "genotypic model approach"—a "bottom-up" method that consisted in exploring the functional properties of a class of networks whose structure is only partly specified, subject only to the requirement that it meet certain constraints and probability distributions.[59] All the while acknowledging his debt to McCulloch and Pitts, Rosenblatt cited two others as more immediate influences: Ross Ashby, a cybernetician of the second phase, and the economist and social philosopher Friedrich von Hayek, both of whom we discuss later. Although the Perceptron's inventor thus rather unjustly distanced himself from McCulloch, his criticism marked a turning point in the interpretation of neural networks. By now it was less a question of logical modeling and more a question of exploring the capabilities of a class of complex networks made up of simple interacting elements.

In the meantime the infant discipline of artificial intelligence had resolutely set off in other directions, as we have seen. While cybernetics in its second phase retained the ambition of modeling natural intelligence, and so remained in touch with advances in neurology, artificial intelligence was to free itself from this constraint, casting its lot instead with the development of computers. Although both traditions treated thought as computation, the first continued to locate the agents of computation at the neuronal level; the second, in assigning them to a presumptively autonomous psychological level of mental representations, created what was to become the distinctive style of orthodox cognitive science, or "cognitivism." The champions of artificial intelligence, exasperated by the overselling of the Perceptron, missed no opportunity to attack its mathematical formalization as insufficiently rigorous. A severe blow was delivered by Minksy and Papert in 1969 in their work *Perceptrons*.[60] By demonstrating its logical limitations, they were seen as trying to put an end to the wild hopes for the kind of modeling that the Perceptron had encouraged. In fact, these limitations affect mainly the simplest models—a two-layer network, for example, turns out to be incapable of "learning" a certain logical connective, the "exclusive *or*" (i.e., the Boolean function *XOR*: "either A or B but not A and B"); but Minsky and Papert, by arguing that more complicated models would rapidly become intractable, appeared to be sounding the knell for network modeling in general.[61]

The second wave of cybernetics, in the 1960s and 1970s, managed to get along by its own devices, developing a program of research into self-organizing systems. Most artificial intelligence researchers maintained that this work amounted to little or nothing. In another book published in 1969,[62] Minsky provided a historical analysis of the legacy of cybernetics. Cybernetics was represented as a tree whose trunk divided into three branches: "cognitive simulation," after the fashion of Newell and Simon; artificial intelligence proper; and, finally, a "dead branch," the second cybernetics (or the theory of self-organizing systems). Ten years later, even Hubert Dreyfus, that ferocious scourge of artificial intelligence, was to rely on Minsky's opinion, very sharply criticized though it had been in the interval, as an excuse for not taking cybernetics seriously, saying that it had produced no result worthy of interest.[63]

Connectionism vs. Cognitivism

As it turns out, there is justice in the world. The beginning of the 1980s were to witness a very powerful revival of research into neural networks, the neurons in question now being called "formal neurons" to make it clear that there was no intention of poaching on the territory of the neuro-biologists. This renewed interest arose from the discovery of new learning techniques involving the complete set of layers of "hidden" neurons, and above all the application to these networks of processing methods developed to handle the physics of disordered systems—specifically in connection with the theory of "spin glasses," which deals with the aggregate behavior of the magnetized atoms of a crystal that has been subjected to an external magnetic field. The wealth of properties that these techniques (some of them inspired by thermodynamics) have revealed about neural networks is beyond comparison with what was known about them in the 1940s and 1950s. These properties can be interpreted in cognitive terms: the networks are capable of learning, recognizing patterns, memorizing by association, and so on; so well, and to such a degree, in fact, that this line of research stands today as the principal rival of orthodox artificial intelligence, which in the meantime has become tired and winded, as if it had reached the limits of what it can do.

A good part of the disagreement that currently fuels debate in cognitive science is a result of the conflict between the two models, which in the meantime have been elevated to the rank of paradigms: orthodox cognitivism, for which thinking is the same as computing, as this is done by a serial computer (that is, sequential calculation using symbols that have both a physical reality and a semantic, representational value); and the neural network approach, according to which thinking is also the same as computing, only computing in the rather different way that such networks operate, which is to say in massively parallel fashion, with the interesting behaviors appearing only at the aggregate level, "emerging" from the system of interactions among simple elementary calculators.

Today the whole question has to do with whether these two paradigms fit together, and if so, how. Daniel Memmi has distinguished four possible positions or attitudes: first, what he calls *segregation*, which assigns different domains of competence to neural networks and to cognitivism, the former being confined mainly to tasks of pattern recognition and associative memory and the latter to modeling "higher" forms of cognition (reasoning and natural language, for example); second, *compilation* (in the sense in which this term is used in computer science), which relegates neural networks to the subordinate role of "realizing" cognitivist models at the lowest level, in the same way that in a computer the instructions given in a higher-level language are translated into a language that the machine can "understand"; third, *hybridization*, which conceives cognitive systems as combining and integrating the performances of both models, and so implies that each can be translated into the other; and, finally, *inclusion*, which accords the principal (indeed the only) role to neural networks, the challenge being to show that the logical rules governing computation with representations, which artificial intelligence (or cognitivism) takes as given, can emerge as regularities (or quasiregularities) from the functioning of the network, as a result of which the neural networks paradigm includes cognitivism as a particular, limiting case—just as general relativity "includes" Newtonian gravitation as a limiting case for bodies moving at speeds much lower than the speed of light.[64]

I have deliberately refrained up until this point from mentioning the name by which neural network modeling is known today: connectionism. This term had already in fact been used by Rosenblatt back in 1958.[65] For a certain time one spoke of "neoconnectionism." But since no one seemed to know to which "archeo-" (or "paleo-"[66]) connectionism this new version referred, the "neo" was dropped. The link with the model of McCulloch and Pitts had thus been lost: a dynamic science, after all, has no time to look back upon its past.

What might have turned out to be McCulloch's posthumous revenge wound up looking more like his second funeral. Reverting for a moment to the four theoretical positions described by Memmi, it is plain that the last two give pride of place to connectionism. But both of them imply that connectionism has had to make a decisive move in the direction of cognitivism—the better perhaps to swallow it whole, as may turn out to be the case. Whatever the outcome, connectionists today are led as a result to pose questions about their networks that are quite different from the ones McCulloch posed, foremost among them the problem of the symbolic representation of the "external world." We will take up this question in the next chapter.

Von Neumann's Machine

Let us go back to the 1940s, with which we are mainly concerned. We spoke earlier of a play with three acts. The first assimilated the mind to a logic machine. The second treated the brain as a machine as well. Since the machine was the same in each case, mind and brain were inferred to be one and the same. It remains to announce the third act of the drama. Only in this final act (rather than the first, as legend has it) did the physical, artificial machine make its entrance. The facts, however, are well known. Let us begin once again with dates, which eloquently frame the action of this decade. It was not until 1943—decidedly a propitious year for cybernetics—that construction began on the first ultrarapid electronic calculating machine, ENIAC, at the Moore School of Electrical Engineering at the University of Pennsylvania. As remarkable as it may seem to us today, this computer dinosaur managed to be built without benefit of the idea that the logical conception of a calculating machine was *separable* from the design of its circuitry—a design that found itself constrained by the current state of technology and the nature of physical components—or, as we would say today, that the "hardware" is distinct from the "software." It was due to the insight of John von Neumann, who had been called in as a consultant on the ENIAC project, that the hardware/software distinction came to be formulated, which would make it possible to lay the conceptual foundations for the second generation of computers. Where did he get the idea? From reading the 1943 article by McCulloch and Pitts. Finding himself confronted with the fact of a new addition to the world of physical objects, the computer, von Neumann was to adopt exactly the same strategy that McCulloch and Pitts had adopted, confronted with the reality of the biological brain: he *abstracted* from it a logic machine—and, what is more, the *same* one. It is sometimes said in jest that if Turing was the father of the computer, von Neumann was the obstetrician or midwife. Quite obviously a third element is missing: the womb. This, it needs at last to be recognized, was McCulloch's machine.

Without von Neumann's preparatory work on the logic of the artificial machine, the underlying idea of the modern computer almost surely could not have been given a physical embodiment. The underlying idea is that the rules or instructions governing the operation of a computer—the "program," as it would later be called—can be placed on the same level as the data upon which the computer operates. It was this deliberate bringing together of what elementary logic wants to keep separate, operator and operand, that enabled the computer to be seen as a universal machine in the Turing sense. The universal Turing machine had already managed to collapse the two, since its tape (or "memory") was imprinted with the code of the particular machine to be simulated (its "instructions") as well as the code of the data to be manipulated. There was no need for separate memories for the two sets of information. To work backwards, however, as von Neumann did, from the physical machine (the computer) to Turing's machine, an intermediary stage was required, and this was McCulloch's machine.

ENIAC was a parallel machine, as was McCulloch's. The machine conceived by von Neumann, which was to be called EDVAC, functioned sequentially. Von Neumann theorized this innovation in comparing natural automata with artificial automata. In the brain, neurons are extremely numerous and function slowly: it is the fact of their organization in parallel that optimizes the processing of information. The components of an artificial calculator, by contrast, are few in number but capable of very high speeds: they must be serially arranged. Still today, nearly all computers (sometimes called "von Neumann machines") are serial processors. Their domination is so complete that even connectionist neural networks, these highly parallel machines, are *simulated* on von Neumann machines—only one of the many surprising shifts and exchanges of position encountered in this checkered story, like so many *chassés-croisés* in a ballet.[67]

Norbert Wiener, Arturo Rosenblueth, Julian Bigelow, Warren McCulloch, and Walter Pitts: following Steve Heims, I will call these authors of the two foundational articles of 1943 the "cyberneticians."[68] But just as the Three Musketeers were actually four, so the Five Cyberneticians were actually six. I have already had occasion to say a great deal about the d'Artagnan of the group, John von Neumann—no matter that he was a Jew from Central Europe, he was every bit their d'Artagnan, endowed with the same loquacity, possessed of the same flamboyance as the dashing Gascon. The full personality of John von Neumann cannot be captured within the confines of cybernetics alone, of course. But his work, which, for better or for worse, opened up new avenues of research for science and technology in a remarkable number of fields,[69] intersected with cybernetics at least at two points: first, via his *Theory of Games and Economic Behavior* (written with Morgenstern, as we have noted, in the *annus mirabilis* of 1943 but not published until the following year); second, and more important, via his elaboration of a general theory of natural and artificial automata, the initial impetus for which, as we have seen, came from reading the McCulloch-Pitts article of 1943. We have also just noted the decisive role that von Neumann was to play in the design of the artificial automata that we know as computers today. Less well known, generally speaking, is his contribution to the very problem that tormented McCulloch: the circular relationship between logic and brain. Von Neumann must have managed to learn a great deal of neurophysiology to have been able to compare the brain to a computer in the systematic way that he did. The outlines of this theory were laid out in the historic paper ("The General and Logical Theory of Automata") he read to the Hixon Symposium at Caltech in September 1948.[70] Later he was to tackle the two problems that he judged essential to be solved in order to understand the logic of organisms: how a reliable automaton can be made out of unreliable components, and what principles of organization are sufficient to give an automaton the capacity for self-reproduction. His premature death in 1957, at the age of 54, was to cut short his investigations. But in 1948, while paying McCulloch and Pitts the hommage due them for their discovery, he was at pains to distance himself from it, and this in a most interesting way.[71]

He began by raising the question of how large a brain must be in order to embody this or that function or property of mind. We have already mentioned his conjecture at one of the Macy Conferences (as elsewhere) that there was a strong likelihood that the number of formal neurons necessary to produce these properties would be substantially greater than the number of real neurons in the human brain. Then came the core of his critique. He conceded to McCulloch—too quickly, as we saw in the last chapter—that to have shown that every behavior that is unambiguously describable in a finite number of words is computable by a network of formal neurons was indeed a remarkable result. However, he went on to ask, is it reasonable to assume as a practical matter that our most complex behaviors (and here von Neumann, good cybernetician that he was, took "behaviors" to mean faculties of the mind: thought, concept formation, memory, learning, and so forth) are describable completely and unambiguously using a finite number of words? In specific cases it is often possible. Our ability, for example, to recognize the same triangular form in two empirical triangles displaying differences in shape, size, and position can be so described. But would this still be possible if it were a matter of globally characterizing our capacity for establishing "visual analogies"? In that case, von Neumann conjectured, it may be that the simplest way to describe a behavior is to describe the structure that generates it; it may even be the case that it is infinitely simpler to describe the structure than to describe the behavior. It is meaningless, under these circumstances, to "discover" that such a behavior can be embodied in a neural network, since it is not possible to define the behavior other than by describing the network itself. The moral of the story was only hinted at by von Neumann at the 1948 conference. It was, after all, rather paradoxical for him, a mathematician, to be defending this position as against that of McCulloch, a neurophysiologist. For McCulloch, neurophysiology was to be explained in terms of logic; to von Neumann, it seemed more fruitful to try to enrich logic using neurophysiology as a model. He was often to say that formal logic in its current state was too rigid, too combinatorial to be considered as the sole logic of automata, whether natural or artificial. He himself was seeking to build a more complex logic, whose variables could take continuous values, drawing upon the methods of probability theory, thermodynamics, information theory, and the calculus.[72]

Von Neumann thus posed the question of *complexity*, foreseeing that it would become *the* great question for science in the future. Complexity implied for him in this case the futility of the constructivist approach of McCulloch and Pitts, which reduced a function to a structure—leaving unanswered the question what a complex structure is capable of doing. It is significant that Marvin Minsky, who wrote his doctoral thesis under von Neumann, regarded his teacher's attack on McCulloch's approach as an aberration, an admission of weakness, a lack of faith in what he had managed to accomplish.[73] The very man who had been instrumental in the development of the computer, and hence had made the field of artificial intelligence possible, seemed to Minsky, one of the founders of AI, to be wasting his time in a frivolous flirtation with biology.

It remains to be asked whether von Neumann's rather radical critique proved to be a fertile influence upon the cybernetic movement. We know that McCulloch was deeply affected by it (all the more so since, as we have seen, he himself put biology before logic in trying to make sense of his work) and that he devoted the last years of his life to research on alternative logics, though apparently without great success. Ross Ashby, Frank Rosenblatt, and, later, the neoconnectionists—moving in the opposite direction from orthodox artificial intelligence—posed the issue of complexity in von Neumann's terms, positing a class of only partially and statistically defined structures whose general (or "generic") possibilities they then set out to explore. As I have noted in the introduction, and as we shall see in greater detail in what follows, it was nonetheless the study of complex *natural* systems, rather than cybernetics (and sometimes directly in opposition to the cyberneticians themselves), that initially demonstrated the truth of von Neumann's prophesy; indeed, complexity was to become a major theme in certain branches of the natural and life sciences, such as embryology and the thermodynamics of irreversible, far-from-equilibrium processes. Whatever their differences, McCulloch, von Neumann, and Wiener each helped to shape the paradigm of the "new science" anticipated by Vico, which is to say a science of *design*. For a time the natural sciences managed to escape the hold of this paradigm, and so were able to conceive of the complexity of their objects with reference to models of their own devising. It took quite a long time for the distinction between nature and artifice to fade away. But by now it has disappeared.[74]

CHAPTER 3

The Limits of Interdisciplinarity

I think that cybernetics is the biggest bite out of the
fruit of the Tree of Knowledge that mankind has
taken in the last 2000 years.

—Gregory Bateson[1]

THE HISTORY that is being recounted here is essentially an intellectual
history. A few facts and dates are nonetheless necessary for setting the
ideas of this history in context. In May 1942 a conference on cerebral inhi-
bition was held in New York under the auspices of a philanthropic organization dedicated to the advance of medicine, the Josiah Macy, Jr. Foundation. It brought together two friends of long standing, the physiologists
Arturo Rosenblueth and Warren McCulloch. Present there as well, in addition to the medical director of the foundation, Frank Fremont-Smith, was
Lawrence Frank, a dilettantish sort of intellectual entrepreneur and formerly an administrator of the foundation, the psychoanalyst Lawrence
Kubie, and the (husband and wife) anthropologists Gregory Bateson and
Margaret Mead.[2] There was much talk of hypnosis, but Rosenblueth also
presented the basic ideas of the famous article with Wiener and Bigelow
that was to be published the following year.[3] Bateson admitted later that
they came as a shock to him. McCulloch, sensing the resonance between
these ideas and the ones that he was developing in concert with Pitts, proposed to Fremont-Smith that a cycle of conferences be organized around
what would only later be called cybernetics,[4] on the model of the conferences that the foundation sponsored on a wide variety of social and medical themes—themes that ran from blood pressure regulation to infancy
and childhood, from liver injury to metabolic interrelations, blood clot-
ting, the nerve impulse, and the problems of aging.[5] Fremont-Smith welcomed the suggestion. It was to be acted upon, but not until after the war.

In the aftermath of this conference, exchanges intensified between
McCulloch's group at Chicago and Wiener's group at MIT. A direct link
between the two was forged in 1943 with Pitts's departure (with McCul-

loch's blessing) to join Wiener. McCulloch, for his part, was hoping to get Rosenblueth to come to Chicago. Having lost his job at Harvard, Rosenblueth decided to return instead to his native Mexico, having been invited to set up a physiology laboratory at the National Institute of Cardiology in Mexico City.[6] As a result Pitts and Wiener were to become regular travelers along the Cambridge–Mexico City–Chicago triangle.

At the same time Wiener was engaged in a lively correspondence with von Neumann on the question of analogies between organisms and machines. They had come to the view that the time was now ripe for scientific investigation in this area to be given institutional form through the founding of a journal, a learned society, and even a research center. In January 1945 a meeting was organized at the Institute of Advanced Study in Princeton, where von Neumann was based.[7] Among those present, in addition to von Neumann and Wiener, were Pitts, Herman Goldstine (who was working on the ENIAC project at the time), McCulloch, and Lorente de Nó.[8] Wiener was to emerge from this meeting more convinced than ever that "the subject embracing both the engineering and neurology aspects is essentially one" and that plans to establish a "permanent program of research" should go forward.[9]

MIT was the ideal home for the research center Wiener had in mind. He arranged for an attractive offer to be made to von Neumann, who took advantage of it, however, to strengthen his hand in negotiations with the Institute of Advanced Study. The Institute, which had been rather reluctant to allow von Neumann to build his ultrarapid computer there, was now persuaded. Wiener, though naturally disappointed by von Neumann's decision to stay in Princeton, did not hold it against him, and even sent his favorite engineer, Bigelow, to join von Neumann's team there.[10] Thus it came about that cybernetics in its first incarnation never had a research center of its own. The Macy Conferences were to function as a sort of substitute.

The Macy Conferences

Once the war was over the Macy Foundation turned its attention to the suggestion made by McCulloch in 1942 and put him in charge of setting up a series of conferences on the new (and so far nameless) direction in research. In keeping with the policy of the foundation, meetings were to be held at regular intervals (usually every six months), bringing together a small group of some twenty scientists who, as official participants in the series, were authorized to extend invitations to five "guests" per session. Much greater emphasis was laid on spontaneous exchange and discussion than on formal presentations. The first meeting took place in March 1946 in New York. Its title, "Feedback Mechanisms and Circular Causal Systems in Biological and Social Systems," is usually taken as a reference to Wiener's work, but it can also be seen as echoing that of McCulloch, in view of the importance assigned by his theory to closed, reverberating circuits of neurons. The inclusion of "social systems" in the program was due to Bateson's initiative. He had become convinced, as a result of the 1942 meeting, of the pertinence of the new ideas to research in the social sciences, and he assisted McCulloch in selecting representatives of the "soft" disciplines to participate in the first round of conferences. Psychologists formed the strongest contingent among these: Gestaltists such as Molly Harrower, social psychologists such as Kurt Lewin, experimental psychologists such as Heinrich Klüver, and the psychoanalyst Lawrence Kubie.[11] The sociologist Paul Lazarsfeld and the mathematician Leonard J. Savage were also present,[12] along with, of course, Bateson and Mead, representing anthropology.

The fall of 1946 was a period of intense activity for the group. In response to a suggestion made by Lazarsfeld at the first conference, Bateson organized a special conference outside the current cycle[13] (but still under the auspices of the Macy Foundation), aimed at giving researchers in the social sciences the opportunity to enter into dialogue with Wiener and von Neumann. This conference, devoted to the topic "Teleological Mechanisms in Society," was held in September.[14] Among the participants were the sociologists Talcott Parsons and Robert Merton, as well as the anthropologist Clyde Kluckhohn.[15] The second conference of the series organized by McCulloch for the Macy Foundation took place in October, under the new title "Teleological Mechanisms and Circular Causal Systems,"[16] and then, immediately afterward, a symposium put together by Lawrence Frank for the New York Academy of Sciences was held on the theme "Teleological Mechanisms." Frank, who sought to create what he called a "climate of opinion," described the ideas of the group in lyrical terms, asserting that what was at stake was the construction of "a new conceptual frame of reference for scientific investigation in the life sciences."[17] It was at this meeting, whose spirit was clearly more "activist" than that of the Macy Conferences, that Norbert Wiener presented (probably for the first time, before a major scientific audience) a unified version of the theory emphasizing the key concepts of message, communication, information, feedback, automaton, and so on—terms that from now on were to be standard in cybernetic discourse. Note that here Wiener was developing his own views, and only to a rather smaller degree those of McCulloch, passing back and forth with little qualification between machine and organism and between organism and society.[18] It was left to McCulloch to close the symposium by presenting "a recapitulation of the theory" of teleological mechanisms and suggesting avenues for future research. Whether through adroitness, conviction, or deference, or some combination of these, he managed to present what amounted to a substantial exposition of his own ideas within the general framework erected by Wiener.

The third Macy Conference, bearing the same title as the second one, was held in March 1947.[19] This was also the year when Wiener coined the word "cybernetics" to unify the gathering movement of ideas under a single banner.[20] Wiener's work of the same name was to appear in 1948. The two final conferences of the first cycle were held in the fall of 1947 and the spring of 1948, both devoted to the topic of "Circular Causal and Feedback Mechanisms in Biological and Social Systems."[21] And in September 1948 the important symposium already mentioned that was organized at Caltech by the Hixon Fund Committee took place. At this symposium von Neumann and McCulloch found their views criticized by the greatest figures of the age in neurophysiology (Karl Lashley and Ralph Gerard), psychology (Wolfgang Köhler), and embryology (Paul Weiss)—criticism that was far livelier and more pointed than what they were used to encountering at the Macy Conferences, over which McCulloch was able to exercise a measure of influence and control. The atmosphere at the Hixon Symposium was stormy by comparison.

In February 1949 a young Austrian physicist specializing in electrical engineering named Heinz von Foerster left Vienna to come to the United States. In his pocket he carried a monograph on memory that relied on concepts used in quantum mechanics to model the "all-or-nothing" character of the nerve impulse. This manuscript made its way into McCulloch's hands, and von Foerster soon found himself invited to participate in the sixth Macy Conference, the first of the new cycle. At that time von Foerster's English was still a bit rough. In order to force him to improve his command of the language as quickly as possible, it was decided that he should be named secretary for the second round of five conferences, charged with responsibility for keeping the minutes. Thus von Foerster found himself submerged at once in the turbulent waters of cybernetics.[22] His first act was to secure the group's unanimous approval that henceforth the transactions of the Macy Conferences appear under the title "Cybernetics." The theme "Circular Causal and Feedback Mechanisms in Biological and Social Systems," employed since the fourth conference, was to be retained as a subtitle.

From 1949 to 1953, once a year, in March (in the case of the last meeting, April), the final five Macy Conferences on cybernetics took place, the only ones whose proceedings were published. Wiener and von Neumann were absent from the eighth, held in 1951; by the time of the ninth, their names had disappeared from the list of "members" of the group. The history of this period ended sadly. In 1952 Pitts convinced McCulloch to rejoin him at MIT. Shortly afterward, for reasons that are not clear, but which involved to one degree or another personal rivalries and a family scandal, Wiener broke off all relations with the group. This divorce was to leave a profound mark on McCulloch, Pitts, and their friends for the rest of their lives.[23]

Of the documents presently available to the historian of ideas, the transactions of the last five Macy Conferences must inevitably form the starting point. As von Foerster later noted, the fact that for many years it has been very difficult to obtain access to these transcripts has worked to give the Macy Conferences something of the sacred quality of a foundational myth. No record remains of the first five conferences. We do, however, dispose of a letter addressed by McCulloch beforehand to "the members of the fourth conference on teleological mechanisms" in 1947, which was intended to provide them with a detailed record of the first three meetings.[24] Similarly, the transcript of the tenth conference includes a summary of the first nine,[25] drawn up by McCulloch. The "Note by the Editors" that prefaces the transcripts of the eighth and ninth conferences contains useful information about the history of the whole series of meetings; and Wiener refers to the first three conferences in the introduction to his *Cybernetics*.

The careful research carried out over a good many years by Steve Heims, who, in addition to conducting interviews with still-living conference participants, scoured the personal archives of a number of the members of the group,[26] patiently going through their correspondence and other relevant documents, has made it possible to piece together a more exact picture of the first five conferences. Certainly these were more important than the second five in assisting the birth of cybernetics. Among other remarkable feats, Heims was able to reconstruct the confrontation between Köhler and the cyberneticians, one of the highlights of the fourth conference in October 1947.[27] This meeting, which was intended to illustrate the possibilities for collaboration between Gestalt psychology and the new physico-mathematical approach, turned out to be a failure—a failure that was to influence the course of the later conferences. A brief record exists of the fifth conference, which was given over to discussion of the structure of language (with Roman Jakobson participating as an invited guest).[28]

These details need to be kept in mind, to prevent the disparity between what we know about the first five meetings and the second five from skewing our sense of the conferences as a whole. This bias might be significant, particularly when it comes to comparing McCulloch's influence with that of Wiener, which, as we will see, turns out to be decisive in understanding what the cybernetic project actually amounted to. McCulloch, in effect the presiding officer of the conferences, did not miss a single one, whereas Wiener had disappeared by the time of the eighth, and so figures in only two volumes of the published transcripts. Unquestionably he played a key role along with von Neumann in the first round of meetings, which we know was more eventful than the second and which served to establish the identity of the group, its composition, and its program of discussion. But on the other hand, when Heims poses the question—the crucial question, really—of what enabled an interdisciplinary group having no common research agenda, united solely by a willingness to get together from time to time to discuss subjects of mutual interest, to last as long as it did,[29] and answers the question by attributing such stability to Wiener's "dominant" influence,[30] is this not yet further evidence of the injustice committed time and again against McCulloch? Is it fair that only Wiener's name should remain associated with cybernetics, considering that the conferences went on with the same verve even in his absence?

However this may be, the published transactions of the last five conferences constitute an irreplaceable document. Like the meetings themselves, of which they give us an extremely precise account, the heart of the transcripts consists not in the formal presentations they contain but in the informal, often quite lively discussions that are also recorded there, the rapid-fire exchanges, the brief asides, the constant interruptions—all of which reveal the character of the various participants, the points on which they differed as well as those on which they agreed, and the coalitions that formed among them as a result. This is exactly what the Macy Foundation had in mind when it conceived the conferences. It saw them as full-scale experiments designed, on the one hand, to bring out what is never apparent when scientists present their results—the prior processes of decision, selection, and exclusion that were involved in selecting the paths of research that led ultimately to the results obtained; and, on the other hand, to illustrate the various difficulties—psychological, semantic, and so forth—that hinder communication between specialists in different disciplines, and to suggest ways to break down these barriers. In other words, the Macy Conferences were meant to supply firsthand material for what would later be known as "Science-Technology-Society" studies.[31]

To this corpus of documentary evidence, let us add the proceedings of the New York Academy of Sciences conference on "Teleological Mechanisms" as well as those of the Hixon Symposium at Caltech. At this latter meeting, as we have already seen, the cyberneticians did not find themselves in a commanding position, and it is interesting to compare their performance on that occasion with the manner in which they debated among themselves at the Macy Conferences. A further (and invaluable) basis for comparison is provided by the proceedings of the 1968 Alpbach Symposium, organized by Arthur Koestler on the theme "Beyond Reductionism."[32] Participating in what was to be a major event in the history of systems theory were, among others, Paul Weiss, Ludwig von Bertalanffy,

Friedrich von Hayek, and C. H. Waddington.[33] On this occasion the notion of self-organization (the real theme of the conference, even if it was
not called by this name) was to be used as a weapon against cybernetics.
The comparison with the earlier conferences is all the more interesting
since Weiss, an embryologist, now at home in his natural environment,
had directly attacked the cyberneticians at the Hixon Symposium twenty
years before. Finally, let me make it clear that in what follows I shall
continue to take into account events that, like the Alpbach Symposium,
occurred in the years after the Macy Conferences, in particular the
achievements of the second cybernetics and the debates currently taking
place within cognitive science, in trying to assess the circumstances surrounding the birth of cybernetics.

The Cyberneticians in Debate

The Macy Conferences played host to such a stream of participants and
accommodated such a diversity of themes that any attempt to impose a
structure on them is to some extent bound to be arbitrary. I nonetheless
venture to propose the following reconstruction of the ten conferences,
fully aware that the relative lack of information about the first five increases the chance of error.

With regard to the participants themselves, let us limit our attention to
those whose interventions seem for one reason or another to represent key
moments in the debate.[34] In a first group we will put the six cyberneticians,
adding the names of three eminent future representatives of the second
generation, Heinz von Foerster, W. Ross Ashby, and W. Grey Walter, as
well as four important information theorists, Claude Shannon, Donald
MacKay, Yehoshua Bar-Hillel, and Henry Quastler. It would be by no
means unreasonable to add a final member to this group, thus bringing the
total to fourteen: the mathematician Leonard Savage, who throughout
the years of the conferences was working out the decision theory for which
he would be known.[35] Despite evident differences of opinion among the
members of this group regarding the promise of the nascent cybernetics
(Savage, in particular, did not take its interdisciplinary ambitions seriously), they all had in common a certain view of science that assigned a
privileged role to mathematical modeling.

Next come the anatomists, physiologists, physicians, and naturalists,
whose comparatively limited taste for abstraction led them to sound notes
of caution, warning, or criticism with regard to the passion for modeling
displayed by the members of the first group. From this second group we
will retain eight names: in addition to the great neurophysiologists whom
we have already mentioned, Rafael Lorente de Nó and Ralph Gerard, the

medical doctors Frank Fremont-Smith and Harold Abramson, the surgeon William Livingston, the anatomists Gerhardt von Bonin and John Z. Young, and the zoologist George Hutchinson.

The psychologists formed an impressive group by themselves: we list here fifteen, one more than the "mathematicians." They represented the continent to be conquered: some were content to see the conquest go forward and sometimes even led the way; some offered valiant resistance, actually defying the conquerors. Two of them, Wolfgang Köhler and Molly Harrower, were Gestaltists; two more were social psychologists with Gestaltist loyalties, Kurt Lewin and his former student Alex Bavelas. Additionally there were the experimentalists Heinrich Klüver, John Stroud, Joseph Licklider, Heinz Werner, Donald Marquis, and Hans Lukas Teuber; also the psychiatrist Henry Brosin (who was to preside over the Hixon Symposium) and the neuropsychiatrist Eilhard von Domarus; a psychoanalyst, Lawrence Kubie; and two comparativists specializing in animal behavior, Theodore Schneirla and Herbert Birch.

Finally we come to a small group of representatives of philosophy and the social sciences: the anthropologists Gregory Bateson and Margaret Mead, the sociologist Paul Lazarsfeld, the philosopher Filmer Northrop, and the eclectic Lawrence Frank. To their number may be added the linguist Roman Jakobson.

This would be no more than an arid accounting exercise were it not for at least one invaluable clue that it provides. Contrary to a certain impression that cybernetics itself was to encourage, it was not so much the life sciences that it set out to confront—in order first (as is usually supposed) to draw its inspiration from them, then to revolutionize and, finally, to conquer them. No doubt this picture developed as a result of Wiener's habit, and that of his disciples, of detecting analogies between organisms and machines everywhere they looked. But this is a false picture: the first target of cybernetics was the sciences of mind. This is all the more remarkable in view of the fact that at just the same time certain physicists, following the example of Niels Bohr, were turning their attention to biology. One thinks, of course, of Schrödinger's *What Is Life?* which appeared in 1944,[36] but the work of Max Delbrück (a student of Bohr) on bacteriophages— viruses that infect bacteria and are capable of self-reproduction—needs also to be recalled in this connection. Von Neumann, now more the "inside outsider" than ever,[37] was interested in Delbrück's research and had challenged Wiener to prove to him that it would not be more fruitful from the mathematical point of view to model bacteriophages than the brain.[38] Delbrück was therefore invited to become a regular member of the Macy Conferences. He attended the fifth and swore afterward never to return. The first day of that conference, as we have already noted, was given over to a discussion of language, with Roman Jakobson, Charles Morris, and

Dorothy Lee among the invited guests. The next day Wiener gave an analysis of candidate mechanisms for realizing Maxwell's "demon" and entertained the possibility that order might emerge from chaos, a theme that much later was to enjoy a certain vogue with second-order cybernetics and the physics of disordered systems. Pitts proposed a formal analogy, very much in the cybernetic style, between the collisions of molecules and the emergence of a hierarchical order among hens (the famous "pecking order"). Delbrück was to declare later that the whole meeting was "vacuous in the extreme and positively inane."[39] This judgment may be unduly severe, but one can make sense of it in the following way. With Delbrück's work, physics—mainstream physics, bringing to bear the full rigor of its orthodoxy, even if this was the orthodoxy of quantum mechanics—was taking over the problems of biology. Schrödinger, in his 1944 book, had in a sense given the green light for this enterprise, predicting that the mechanisms of heredity and genetics would one day be reduced to the known laws of physics. Now, there was no professional physicist among the cyberneticians. To be sure (as we have already pointed out, and as we will have reason again to strongly insist in what follows, for the point is too often ignored), the cyberneticians' battle was carried out in the name of physics. But it was a most unusual physics, one that courted danger in trying to move forward by leaping over the world of the living in order to link up directly with logic and the mind. A strict physicist like Delbrück was bound to suspect charlatanism in this.

We find ourselves in the presence here of one of the most striking ironies in the history of science. Some years later, the "phage group" directed by Delbrück invented molecular biology through its discovery of the genetic code. Must we therefore say that the declared ambition of reducing biology to physics had been crowned with success after all? It has not gone unremarked that molecular biology was obliged to resort to a quite strange (and strangely unphysicalist) vocabulary to describe the biochemical mechanisms responsible for the "teleonomy" of life—a notion popularized by the French team that worked on the project, teleonomy being conceived as still further removed from *intentional* finality or purpose than the "teleology" of the cyberneticians. "Program," "code," "information," "transcription," "message," "translation"—the whole vocabulary of molecular biology is imported directly from the description of communication among humans. Biology had thus been reduced to a physics repainted in the colors of psychology! In reality, we know that there was an intermediary and that this intermediary was cybernetics—the discipline that set for itself the objective of "pull[ing] down the wall between the great world of physics and the ghetto of the mind," to quote once more Warren McCulloch's lyrical phrase.[40] Cybernetics, it seems, has been condemned to enjoy only posthumous revenge.

There were therefore no biophysicists or biochemists present at the Macy Conferences. Their absence constitutes in any case additional evidence that the influence of McCulloch, who theorized the embodiment of mind in the machine, was not less than that of Wiener, who conceived of organism and machine as models of each other. A cursory study of the discussions that took place during the conferences, and the broad topics into which they break down, points to this conclusion as well. It is useful to define a "unit of discussion" very roughly as coinciding with a presentation of greater or shorter length followed by open debate (while acknowledging that there are a good many exceptions, since these exchanges sometimes went off in unforeseen directions). Using this measure we count seventeen units of discussion about whether or not the model of the logic machine applies to both brain and computer; of these, seven units were devoted more specifically to anatomical and physiological issues, and four to the problem of *Gestalten*.

With regard to the matter of analogies à la Wiener between organisms and machines, our tabulation shows only seven units, two of which concerned experimental psychology. To these however one might legitimately add four units specifically devoted to information theory, which gives a total of eleven units bearing the stamp of Wiener's influence—as against the seventeen that reflect the preoccupations of McCulloch and von Neumann (while admitting, again, that this way of dividing things up is unavoidably arbitrary to some degree and contrary to the announced objectives of the Macy Conferences). More surprising, perhaps, is the small number of units dealing with "cybernetic machines" (Shannon's "Rat" and Ashby's homeostat, for example), which together fashioned the image of the new discipline: a generous estimate yields only five units. But these, it could reasonably be held, signaled the themes of the second, rather than the first, wave of cybernetics.

Next we come to the important group of discussions on the neuroses and pathology of mental life (seven units); on human and social communication (eleven units, of which six had specifically to do with language and one with the theory of games); on abnormal communication (two units)—twenty units in total, then, on communication considered as behavior, one of the cyberneticians' favorite themes.

Finally, the very minor share of time given over to general epistemological discussion should be noted. One counts only a single unit devoted to a question that aroused the enthusiasm of second-generation cyberneticians but to which those of the first replied in a considerably more positivist way: the role of the observer. It surfaced at the sixth conference. The discussion involved Kubie, Wiener, Fremont-Smith, and Stroud.[41] Kubie had posed the problem of the observer in psychoanalysis, arguing that he or she had to be as "inhuman" and "detached" as possible. Wiener immediately came up with a physical analogy: the resonance effect that light produces on a particle that it allows to be observed. Stroud dreamed up psychological experiments in which the observer would be a machine—provoking scarcely a word of protest from Mead and Bateson. Von Foerster was later to display a curious amnesia when he claimed that the Macy Conferences had gradually brought the observers back into the realm of science from which they had been excluded.[42] This amounted to confusing what was to become one of the preoccupations of the second cybernetics with those of the first. Von Foerster himself would play a decisive role in identifying cybernetics with epistemology and in the construction of a "cybernetic epistemology." Under his influence, the new science was to become, as he would later say, a cybernetics of observing systems and no longer one of observed systems.[43] This is certainly the characteristic trait that most often comes to mind today when one thinks of cybernetics, due in part to the influence of the French neocybernetic school; nonetheless it would be a serious error of interpretation to project it back upon the spirit of first-generation cybernetics, which was more concerned with obtaining for the sciences of the mind the same degree of objectivity enjoyed by physics.

Unifying the Work of the Mind

Cybernetics is often regarded today as having attempted to radically transform the ways of thinking that are peculiar to the natural sciences, with the ambition of creating a "new science" whose object would be the relations among the elements of a whole rather than the elements themselves—a science of the totalities generated by these relations. In representing a holistic approach opposed to the reductionism of "orthodox" science, it is therefore seen as a desperate effort to go against the apparently irreversible tide of contemporary science, ever more professionalized and specialized, and to disprove Max Weber's stern warning about blinkered specialists in his 1919 essay "Science as Vocation."[44]

This image of cybernetics was in fact shaped by the influence of its second-generation practitioners, in the form of systems theory and various related theories of self-organization. Gregory Bateson's own work also did much to popularize this view, which, as Heims has rightly pointed out, is consonant with both the spirit and the letter of Wiener's work as well.[45] Heims suspects that there may have been serious philosophical differences between Wiener, on the one hand, and Rosenblueth and Bigelow, on the other, with regard to the proper interpretation of their joint 1943 article. He argues that the positivism reflected in many of Rosenblueth's remarks in the course of the Macy Conferences—one striking example of which we have already noted—would not have been endorsed in the least by Wiener.[46] Be this as it may, those who still today brandish the image of cybernetics as a new science bent on conquest are either hard-line but outmoded champions of an approach that has been marginalized in the interval or, more frequently, fierce opponents of cybernetics for whom the slightest reminder of its imperialistic ambitions is enough to justify the most complete condemnation. The question that interests us here is this: how far does the image correspond with the reality of the first generation of cybernetics, as manifested by the Macy Conferences?

At the beginning of each conference, Fremont-Smith (a physician who, it will be recalled, was also an official of the Macy Foundation), made a point of reminding the audience of the interdisciplinary purpose of these meetings. He hammered away at a single theme: whereas nature knows no boundaries, the progress of human knowledge was now threatened by the growing specialization, professionalization, and isolation of scientific disciplines. The marching orders issued to the participants were therefore to knock down the artificial barriers that stand in the way of specialists speaking to each other, in order to hasten the eventual unification of science.[47] Communication was not merely the object of the conferences—it was also their mode and their very reason for being. From the remarks of some of the participants, foremost among them Lawrence Frank, it is clear too that this effort was indissociable from a certain desire to break with the epistemology of "orthodox" science and to call into question the "analytic method." Frank, in his opening speech at the New York Academy of Sciences colloquium on teleological mechanisms, did not hesitate to lump together in a single indictment Galilean-Newtonian mechanistic and deterministic philosophy, linear causality (the familiar cause-and-effect—or stimulus-response—formula, accused of betraying an animistic belief in mysterious forces), and the reductionism of a style of science that sees only states or products and ignores processes. To these he opposed the neomechanism of cybernetics, allied with the concepts of the new physics, advocating a bold ecumenicism that brought together Einstein and the concept of a physical field, Irving Langmuir's notion of "divergent" phenomena (anticipating the notion of "sensitivity to initial conditions," which is to say the idea that an imperceptibly small event at one point in a system can perceptibly alter the behavior of the system as a whole, made famous forty years later by chaos theory), the uncertainty principle (wrongly attributed to Schrödinger) and, of course, the main ideas of cybernetics itself. All the ingredients necessary to formulate a theory of organized systems, essentially "organisms" and "personalities," were therefore at hand; a circumstance that ultimately would redound to the greater glory of biology, he suggested, recalling the words of the great biologist Haldane, reflecting some sixty years earlier on the physics of his time:

"That a meeting-point between biology and physical science may at some time be found there is no reason for doubting. But we may confidently predict that if that meeting-point is found, and one of the two sciences is swallowed up, that one will *not* be biology."[48]

The reader of the Macy Conference proceedings who confines his or her attention to the rhetoric of Fremont-Smith, Lawrence Frank, and Margaret Mead, three of the most dynamic, persistant, and activist participants at the conferences, will be quickly carried off on a false trail. To stay on track one needs to put the series of conferences back in the social and political context of the time, as Steve Heims has done in his book *The Cybernetics Group*. America in the years after the Second World War was traumatized by the collective madness that had just torn the world apart. The notion of "mental health" came to assume importance in private and government circles, where it was seen by many as the key that could unlock the door of a new world order, now that peace had finally been restored. The Macy Foundation was providing financial assistance to organizations that had been created or developed to promote this objective. Fremont-Smith, Frank, and Mead helped to set up the World Federation for Mental Health in 1948; and the board of directors of the International Committee on Mental Hygiene, which had already been established before the war, included several participants in the Macy Conferences: Fremont-Smith, Mead, Brosin, Harrower, and Kluckhohn. Lawrence Frank perfectly captured the spirit of these efforts in describing the society of his time as a "patient" that only science could cure.

Science, yes, but which one? The credo of the World Federation for Mental Health provides a first clue: "The sciences of man offer the hope of a new approach to the problem of war and a world community . . . it is the ultimate goal of mental health to help men to live with their fellows in one world. . . . The concept of mental health is co-extensive with world order and the world community that must be developed so that men can live together in peace with each other."[49]

It was therefore faith in the curative, liberating, and pacifying power of the human sciences that motivated these pioneers. But we need to be more precise. The human science that enjoyed their support was *psychiatry*—considered as a social science. Various currents or schools of thought combined to mark off a new field of investigation, known by the name of "personality and culture": the cultural anthropology of Franz Boas, for example, who along with Ruth Benedict had been Margaret Mead's teacher at Columbia; the Chicago school of social science, led by John Dewey and George Herbert Mead; the psychiatric school of Harry Stack Sullivan and the social anthropology of Edward Sapir, who had also been a student of Boas. The central notion common to these various approaches was that of a *circular causality* between personality and culture: the notion that the personality of individuals is shaped by the social and cultural milieu in which they live, and, conversely, that this milieu reflects the basic personality of those who inhabit it. Accordingly, it ought to be possible to act upon the psychology of individuals in order to bring about the changes desired in global society, on the condition that the inevitable feedback effects of such intervention are taken into account. Plainly the way had been cleared for acceptance of the new ideas of cybernetics, information theory, and game theory, which carried with them scientific and methodological credibility.[50]

A good idea of the militant zeal that animated those participants of the Macy Conferences who considered themselves part of the personality and culture movement in spreading the new credo can be had by reading Lawrence Frank's inaugural address at the New York Academy of Sciences conference, to which we have already referred:

> The concept of teleological mechanisms . . . may be viewed as an attempt to escape from these older mechanistic formulations that now appear inadequate, and to provide new and more fruitful conceptions and more effective methodologies for studying self-regulating processes, self-oriented systems and organisms, and self-directing personalities. . . . It is suggested that we look at this conference as an important, perhaps a major, step toward the new climate of opinion now emerging in scientific, philosophical, and even artistic activities. We are not only witnessing, but, by these meetings and discussions, actively participating in creating this new climate of opinion. . . . As I see it, we are engaged, today, in one of the major transitions or upheavals in the history of ideas. . . . When the social sciences accept these newer conceptions . . . and learn to think in terms of circular processes, they will probably make amazing advances. . . . Already, the fruitfulness of the newer approach has been shown in the psychocultural approach which has begun to illuminate the dual aspects of social-cultural regularities and of highly individualized personality activities and patterned expressions.[51]

The physician and foundation administrator Frank Fremont-Smith was not to be outdone. Bent on promoting a vision of interdisciplinary cooperation that would join physics and psychology, he stressed the urgency of finding a common language for the two that would guarantee world peace. Physicists, he explained at the sixth conference, in March 1949, specialize in developing weapons of hostility, whereas psychologists, and particularly psychoanalysts, specialize in understanding the motivations of hostility. Indeed, the constituent assembly of the World Federation for Mental Health at its meeting the previous year had adopted as its motto the phrase from the brand-new UNESCO constitution, "Since wars begin in the minds of men, it is in the minds of men that the defense of peace must be constructed." Physicists and psychologists must therefore collaborate, with the aim of enlisting the principles of science and of logic in the service of resolving the "problems of social behavior and world peace." This could be done only if psychoanalysts agreed to keep abreast of developments in basic science and if physicists, chemists, engineers, and mathematicians agreed to undergo psychoanalysis.[52]

Fremont-Smith saw another reason for collaboration between the exact sciences and psychoanalysis, having to do with the mechanisms of scientific invention. Logic is necessary to organize knowledge and to devise ways for testing it. At the same time, no advance is possible in science without creativity. But because the creative process involves the other part of the human mind, that realm of shadows where the unconscious and the irrational lurk, the workings of the mind as a whole can only be glimpsed if the talents of the mathematician are united with those of the psychoanalyst.[53] Margaret Mead was often to take a similar line, arguing that the separation and isolation in Western culture of what remained unified in other cultures was a source of weakness: our dark side divided from our bright side, the "grammar of dreams" divorced from that type of thinking that Walter Pitts, by contrast, believed to be the only "normal" kind—rational thought.[54]

The Physicalist Temptation

Here we should perhaps pause for a moment and take a step back to see where the argument up until this point has led us. The first two chapters attempted to reconstruct what was involved in trying to establish a physicalist science of mind based on a new conception of the machine. It was unavoidable, under the circumstances, that the mathematical and physical sciences would have to deal with the traditional sciences of the mind, which is to say with the various psychological sciences. This was just as the cyberneticians intended it should be. Biology itself was pertinent only to the extent that it already furnished a biology of mind, but not, as I have insisted, insofar as it posed the question "What is life?" If the cyberneticians felt the need to confront psychologists, it was therefore for reasons quite removed from the ones that motivated their host, Fremont-Smith. Their view of psychology was more straightforward: they saw it above all as a territory to be conquered, as a rival to be vanquished, as a source of information to be stockpiled and of challenges to be welcomed and met. Wiener had his own psychologist, Edwin Boring, who had supplied him with a list of psychological functions described from the behaviorist point of view, asking for their electrical or electronic "equivalents" (in the sense of being capable of producing the same input-output transformations.)[55]

Thus too Heinrich Klüver, at the first Macy Conference, challenged Mc-Culloch and Pitts to account for the brain's capacity to perceive and recognize *Gestalten* by means of their network of idealized neurons,[56]—a challenge that the two cyberneticians wasted scarcely any time in taking up.[57] Paradoxically, the battle that took longest to fight was over a question that the cyberneticians had assumed would be the easiest to dispose of, having to do with the seat of the unconscious, but which they found raised time and again—in virtually every conference, in fact—by the indefatigable Kubie. From their point of view, the notion of the unconscious was utterly inconsistent: as Rosenblueth tried to explain at the eighth conference, either a mental event occurs or it does not; either a train of nerve impulses is registered or it is not. To say that one has been registered, only "unconsciously," is nonsense.[58] The cyberneticians did not seem at all willing to engage in the sort of collegial give-and-take with psychoanalysis that Fremont-Smith was hoping for. For them, psychoanalysis was only an obstacle to be swept away.

The encounter between cyberneticians and psychologists, which was the raison d'être of the Macy Conferences, rested on a huge misunderstanding. The promoters of the personality and culture movement wanted to create a relationship of reciprocal dependence between the mathematical and physical sciences, on the one hand, and the established psychological sciences (psychoanalysis, developmental psychology, Gestalt, phenomenology, and even behaviorism) on the other; the cyberneticians meant to wage a battle against these sciences in the name of mathematics and physics. Far from being identified with a search for a general synthesis in which everything is related to everything else, the interdisciplinarity practiced by the cyberneticians was very sharply focused and, it is not going too far to say, used as a weapon—to reverse Haldane's prediction, cited by Lawrence Frank, if there was a science that risked being "swallowed up" by cybernetics, that science was certainly *not* physics.

When one rereads the conference proceedings with this misunderstanding in mind, a half-century later, the many instances of mutual incomprehension that pepper the exchanges, often comically, gradually become clear. At the sixth conference, for example, the "dialogue" between Norbert Wiener and the physician Harold Abramson, a colleague and friend of Fremont-Smith, can now be savored for its somewhat surreal quality: Wiener expounding the usefulness of dimensional analysis for the unification of science while Abramson, playing in counterpoint, as it were, goes on about the need for physicists and psychologists to communicate with each other to assure world peace—Fremont-Smith having previously explained to the group that the unification of all scientific disciplines presumed the creation of a science of man.[59] Still more comical was the way in which several of the representatives of the human sciences actually delivered themselves up as willing victims to the ferocious appetite of the cyberneticians. The unfortunate Kubie—who, it is true, was a psychoanalyst of a rather particular kind, having limited himself to the first stage of Freud's categorization (the conscious, the preconscious, and the unconscious) while ignoring the second stage (ego, id, superego) and sharing Freud's belief in the biological roots of psychoanalytic concepts (having been trained as a neurophysiologist)—frequently displayed a remarkably conciliatory, not to say submissive, attitude, despite his stubborn determination to defend psychoanalysis against the attacks of the cyberneticians.

It was thus that, in the exchange with Rosenblueth that we mentioned earlier, Kubie granted that "psychiatry" must be practiced as an "objective scientific process," as a "natural science" relying on "operational" concepts, and that the technique of psychoanalysis ought to exhibit the same qualities of reproducibility as the experiments of the exact sciences.[60] Rosenblueth went even further, saying that there is nothing in the language and approach of the natural sciences that renders them inadequate to deal with the problems that psychiatry is concerned with.[61] Pitts, for his part, added heatedly, "If the methods which the psychoanalyst uses in dealing with this material are not scientific, it is up to him to make them so, not for us to admit that his methods or modes of dealing with them are just as good as ours, if we are scientists."[62]

Even Fremont-Smith and Frank, the most ideological members of the personality and culture movement, rendered homage at every opportunity to the superiority of the mathematical and physical sciences. At the sixth conference, Fremont-Smith expressed the hope that "the knowledge, extraordinary ingenuity and wisdom, coming from the mathematicians, physicists, and engineers" might be brought "to bear on the human problem." Accordingly he demanded that the social sciences speak a language that made sense to physicists and engineers.[63] Frank went still further in acknowledging the subordinate role of the human sciences in relation to the "true" sciences. At the ninth conference, he described the desired "reciprocity" between the social sciences and the sciences of the nervous system in the following terms: the former ask of the latter, "Are the assumptions that you make such that we can adopt them when we deal with the social sciences?" whereas the latter asks of the former, "Are the assumptions you are making in social science compatible with the kind of assumptions and knowledge we have about the nervous system?" The logic of this would appear to be of the "heads I win, tails you lose" variety.[64] As the neurophysiologist Lashley had previously declared at the Hixon Symposium, almost four years earlier, seemingly to the approval of almost everyone present, "Our common meeting ground is the faith to which we all subscribe, I believe, that the phenomena of behavior and of mind are ultimately describable in the concepts of the mathematical and physical sciences."[65]

The physiologists, for their part, were treated as counselors, guarantors, and informants. Not all of them, of course, accepted this subordinate role. The neurophysiologist Ralph Gerard is a case in point. At the seventh conference he solemnly warned the group against the dangers of adopting a mathematical formalization that ran too far ahead of what observation and experimentation could supply in the way of evidence. It is interesting to note that, on at least two occasions, Gerard gave the impression of wishing to defend biology against a takeover bid by physics: first, at the beginning of his talking paper "Some of the Problems Concerning Digital Notions in the Central Nervous System," when he referred to young physicists rushing forth to the hunting grounds of biology; and later in his ironic reply to a statement made by Bigelow that unmistakeably betrayed the cyberneticians' desire to perpetrate a physicalist seizure of control over the study of the nervous system.[66]

It may be that Gerard misread the situation. The cyberneticians were not physicists, and their target was not biology. At the same time it is true that they themselves did not really see things differently, at least not with regard to the identity of the conqueror. Far from imagining itself as causing a rupture with "orthodox" science, cybernetics saw itself as its vanguard, intent on occupying the upper regions of Creation. To repeat one more time: the battle it fought was not fought in the name of some "new science"—it was fought in the name of mathematics and physics.

Cybernetics, if the truth be told, thought of itself as the apotheosis of physics. This conviction was best expressed by McCulloch. "[L]et us now compel our physicist to account for himself as part of the physical world," his statement to the Hixon Symposium began. "In all fairness, he must stick to his own rules and show in terms of mass, energy, space, and time how it comes about that he creates theoretical physics. He must then become a neurophysiologist (that is what happened to me), but in so doing he will be compelled to answer whether theoretical physics is something which he can discuss in terms of neurophysiology (and *that* is what happened to me). To answer 'no' is to remain a physicist undefiled. To answer 'yes' is to become a metaphysician—or so I am told. But is that just?"[67] It is clear that for McCulloch, to oblige physics to give an account of itself was not to cause it to sink into "metaphysics" but to help it put the finishing touches on its masterpiece, which obviously, albeit in a different sense of the word than the one McCulloch attributes to it, *is* the height of metaphysics. The second cybernetics was to make itself the champion of metaphysics in this other sense, with the work of von Foerster, Ashby, Bateson, and their disciples, which asserted that science, in the form of cybernetics, had finally succeeded in raising itself to the level of self-consciousness, and so in becoming *epistemology*.[68]

This confused attempt to join a project of social renovation through science to an enterprise of scientific conquest may lead some readers to suppose that the Macy Conferences were utterly awash in ideology. In fact, the main part of the discussions bore on highly specialized subjects involving neurophysiology and experimental psychology. As von Foerster explained in his introductory note to the eighth volume of Macy Conference proceedings, the cyberneticians' effort at unification was not located at the level of solutions but at the level of *problems*. Certain classes of problems, each defined by a single logical structure, cut across the most varied disciplines. Cybernetics was built principally around two of these classes: the problems of communication, on the one hand, and the problems posed by the study of self-integrating mechanisms on the other.[69] Confining its attention to problems enabled the group to avoid drifting off into awkward and unproductive ideological discussions. In the same note, von Foerster thus emphasized that after six years of association the cyberneticians had not yet developed any sort of private lingo. Cybernetic jargon was limited to a handful of terms: "digital/analogical," "feedback," "servo-mechanism," "circular causality"; and even these terms, von Foerster observed, were used much less frequently by the members of the group than by partisan outsiders.

The cyberneticians showed no reservation about entering into technical discussion with the widest variety of specialists, examining with equal ease the results of a psychoacoustic experiment and a theory of the conditions under which the words of a language acquire a specific individual meaning. The few generalists present, the most notable of whom was Gregory Bateson, often found themselves lost. In their frustration at being unable to follow the discussion, they were apt to beg their colleagues not to lose sight of the universalist vocation of cybernetics. Careful examination of the transactions of the conferences makes it painfully clear how "out of it" Bateson actually was. Ignorant of the most elementary logical concepts, he was liable, for example, to confuse the ordinary sense of the word "quantification" with the interpretation given it in logic,[70] with the result that he often misunderstood what was being said.[71] The many admirers of his work may shrug this off, saying that his flawed grasp of cybernetics was exactly what enabled him to develop his own thought, unhindered by scientistic prejudices. One wonders.

If there was little ideology produced within the group itself, were the cyberneticians nonetheless concerned to send a message to the outside world? The question came up at the beginning of the seventh conference. A series of splashy articles had recently been published in leading magazines about the group's activities, the upshot of which was that since the brain had been shown to be a machine, one could now look forward to the construction of intelligent machines. Certain conference participants saw in these articles a reason to lament the credulity, intellectual laziness, and low average IQ of the general public, accusing it (not without some measure of hypocrisy) of showing an enthusiasm—amounting to a "national fad," in Ralph Gerard's phrase—that the group could well do without. Whereas Gerard was more prone than the others to unfavorable comment about the public's intellectual abilities, with Stroud being the most harsh-spoken of the group, Wiener was the only one to display a certain tolerance toward the articles that had appeared in *Life*, *Time*, and *Newsweek*— remarking that he did not find totally reprehensible their use of the adjective "thinking" in relation to such machines.[72]

It was, at bottom, a perfectly ordinary situation, in which scientists blamed nonscientists for taking them at their word. Having planted the idea in the public mind that thinking machines were just around the corner, the cyberneticians hastened to dissociate themselves from anyone gullible enough to believe such a thing. Perhaps the most galling example of this disingenuousness occurred at the ninth conference, when a mathematician (in this case the engineer Bigelow) scolded representatives of the "soft" sciences for falling into the trap of succumbing to the fascination of mathematics. . . .[73]

Philosophy and Cognition

Cybernetics is the metaphysics of the atomic age.
—MARTIN HEIDEGGER[1]

WHAT GIVES COHERENCE to the many different research programs that go under the name of cognitive science today is the philosophical work being done in connection with them. Without cognitive philosophy there would be work in psychology, in linguistics, in neurobiology, in artificial intelligence; but there would be no science of cognition. It is philosophers (and not psychologists, or linguists, or neurobiologists, or computer scientists) who have reflected upon and systematized the basic attitude shared by workers in the various disciplines that make up the field. The existence of such a joint outlook—the only thing, in fact, that holds these disciplines together—in no way implies the existence of a single paradigm. There are, as we have seen, at least two paradigms: classical (or "orthodox") cognitivism and connectionism. But the conflict between the two is itself the source of common ground. Ultimately, those who find themselves on opposing sides in the controversies that have punctuated the history of the field see themselves less as adversaries than as members of a single extended, quarrelsome family. It is philosophy that lays down and enforces the rules governing these family arguments, and that ultimately decides their outcome.

In this circumstance, as in others we have examined, there is no shortage of irony. Cognitive science likes to represent itself as having reclaimed for science all the most ancient questions posed by philosophy about the human mind, its nature and organization, and its relations with the body (which is to say the brain), with other minds, and with the world. But the identity of this self-proclaimed science of mind remains profoundly philosophical. The science that speaks on behalf of the various disciplines that make up the field (mainly neuroscience, artificial intelligence, cognitive psychology, and linguistics), that provides these *sciences d'esprit* with the soul that ironically they would otherwise lack, is in reality none other than philosophy. But it is a peculiar kind of philosophy—a philosophy that crept into the Trojan horse of these sciences, as it were, in order to assert dominion over the realm of the mind and to chase out from it the intruders still to be found there: rival philosophies (especially the philosophies of consciousness, phenomenology and existentialism), rival psychologies (chief among them behaviorism and psychoanalysis), and rival sciences (the social sciences, particularly structuralist anthropology).

Naturalizing Epistemology

What, then, is cognitive philosophy? Better known as "philosophy of mind," it stands today as the most active and flourishing branch of analytical philosophy. But to say this is to state a paradox, which rests in large part on what must seem an enigma to analytic philosophers themselves when they look back over the history of their own field.

It is generally agreed that the decisive achievement of the founders of what is now called analytical philosophy was the break with "psychologism." Let us note first off that it was by virtue of the same break that another great tradition of contemporary philosophy, phenomenology, came into existence. This parallel development was not accidental for, as we shall see, philosophy of mind shares a fundamental concept with phenomenology. Whether one thinks of the formalism of Hilbert; or the logicism of Frege, Russell, and Carnap, for all of whom the essential thing was to cut all ties between logic and psychology, the objectivity of the former needing to be founded on something other than the contingency or facticity of the latter; or of the logical positivism of the Vienna Circle, of which Carnap, again, was a prominent member and which conceived of philosophy as an activity aimed at purifying the language of science by eliminating from it all "metaphysics"; or of Wittgenstein and the Oxford school of ordinary language philosophy, for whom there was no such thing as a "private language," which meant that the sole access to thought is through the analysis of language, so far as this is a public activity subject to norms recognized by an intersubjective community—in all these cases there was a determined refusal to base philosophy on psychology and, at the same time, an insistence on assigning priority to the study of language. From the first, analytic philosophy was a philosophy of language through and through.

According to the standard account, this "linguistic turn" at the beginning of the century was, however, to be followed by a "cognitive" turn. Paradoxically, the rejection of psychologism would therefore ultimately wind up giving birth to a cognitive philosophy that purported to be philosophical psychology. Although it is true that analytic philosophy is not much given to reviewing its past (something its counterpart, Continental philosophy, does endlessly), it cannot help but wonder about this singular reversal. The types of reasons it gives, when it does think about it, are varied. The first type relates to the internal evolution of philosophy of language. Both the Chomskyan program of generative grammar and the pragmatic current stemming from the work of Paul Grice imply that as speakers and interlocutors we "get inside the heads" of others: without appeal to certain cognitive capacities that subjects must be assumed to possess (combinatory in the one case, inferential in the other), there would be no way on either view to account for the nature and properties of language and of verbal communication. A second set of reasons draws upon the development and progress of cognitive science itself. Thanks to this research, it is maintained, it is now possible to successfully carry out the program fervently advocated by Quine: the "naturalization of epistemology." Henceforth the questions traditionally posed by philosophy concerning the objective foundations of our knowledge can be given answers based on research in the empirical sciences—answers involving causal processes, reducible in principle to the laws of physics, that explain how we obtain knowledge (in the sense of justified belief) and, more generally, why our "mental states" are adapted to the external world.[2]

A moment's reflection suffices to show that these reasons explain nothing. Philosophy moved to cut itself off from psychology, as from the natural sciences as a whole, in order to conduct its own inquiry into the objective validity of knowledge and the very *legitimacy* of a science of nature—an inquiry inaugurated by Kant, which he christened "transcendental"—for reasons of principle that were perfectly independent of the progress of the empirical sciences. A transcendental inquiry into the truth content of knowledge is not to be imagined as the limit of a factual inquiry into the actual genesis of knowledge as the precision and reliability of this inquiry approach the infinite. In other words: the *quid juris* is not the limit of a *quid facti*, since a normative question can never be given the same type of answer as a factual question—that is, "ought" is not reducible to "is."

These Kantian distinctions were the very source of Frege's antipsychologism, just as they were of Husserl's. To attempt to justify the cognitive turn of analytical philosophy by the progress made recently by the sciences of cognition is therefore utterly futile. It would be truer to say that the change brought about by the emergence of a cognitive branch within analytical philosophy is much less radical than it seems, and this for two reasons: first, even if it is not as conscious of the fact as it should be, cognitive philosophy preserves still today something of its Kantian heritage and so continues to keep its distance from psychologism; second, it has not wholly managed to free itself from the priority initially given to language.

The first point has been argued in an important article by Joëlle Proust, above all with regard to what she calls the "implicit philosophy" of artificial intelligence.[3] Proust urges us not to be fooled by the way in which its leading practitioners, particularly Allen Newell and Herbert Simon, conceived of their work, and especially the way in which they presented it to the public and to their sponsors when it became necessary to defend and illustrate the ambitions of the new discipline. For Newell and Simon it was important to persuade people that artificial intelligence was a respectable science—one that, though it was a science of the "artificial," nonetheless contributed to the empirical understanding of nature. On their view, to construct a machine that embodies a hypothesis about reality or constitutes a model of it, and to test this hypothesis or model by running the machine, was to be faithful to the predominant experimental method of the natural sciences.

The truth of the matter, as Proust shows, is quite different. The very concern for universality exhibited by artificial intelligence makes it possible to regard this enterprise in an entirely new light, seeing artificial intelligence as a philosophy—and a philosophy of a transcendental type at that. It was intended as a search for the formal conditions of cognitive activity common to all systems that are capable of such activity, whether they may be human subjects, animals, or machines. It set itself the task of exploring all the possible modes of intelligence, beyond those particular ones that human beings are capable of displaying. The purpose of this inquiry was ultimately to discover the a priori, necessary and sufficient conditions that both made knowledge possible and grounded the objectivity, which is to say the universality, of this knowledge.

Of course the solution proposed by artificial intelligence to this problem was not the same as the Kantian solution. The transcendental subject was replaced by the "physical symbol system" and the universality of the synthetic a priori by the universality of the Turing machine. But in both cases the distinction between psychology and the critique of knowledge, between the contingent laws of cognition and necessary rules, was carefully made. It might be said that, in naturalizing and mechanizing its transcendental inquiry, artificial intelligence deprived it of all meaning. But let us not forget that what guarantees the universality of the Turing machine is only a thesis—a metaphysical thesis, in the same sense that Popper spoke of a "metaphysical program of research." Kantian metaphysics, as the science of the a priori powers of the knowing subject, is not so very far removed from this.

I have not forgotten that the object of my own inquiry is the cybernetic phase of the genesis of cognitive science. The present detour through the

history of philosophy of mind is not, however, without a point. What Joëlle
Proust says about artificial intelligence applies equally to its predecessor,
and in particular to the undertaking advocated by Warren McCulloch.
One notices in McCulloch the same tension between a desire to enlarge the
scope of natural science so as to include the empirical study of mind, on
the one hand, and a concern for philosophical inquiry on the other. On the
one hand, there is his ambition to build an "experimental epistemology,"
of which the idealized neural model was to constitute the finest flower; on
the other, there is the insistent reference to Kant, for it was McCulloch's
intention to take up the challenge of providing a physical basis for synthetic a priori judgments. He was the first, as we saw earlier, to stress that
the *material* mechanisms represented by the neural model were sufficient
but hardly necessary conditions for giving an account of the faculties of
mind. This does not mean, however, that it was not a matter *at the formal
level* of searching for necessary *and* sufficient conditions. Seymour Papert,
to whom we have already referred, a former student of McCulloch and
himself a pioneer of artificial intelligence, makes it clear in his preface to
Embodiments of Mind that this is indeed what was at issue.[4] As Jean Mosconi has commented with reference to this preface,

> There is more to [McCulloch's approach] than [simply] a certain attitude that
> can be observed in anyone who constructs "models" of nervous activity. As
> against those who contented themselves with ensuring the adequacy of "prag-
> matic tests," McCulloch insisted (in Papert's words) on "a rationalist quest
> for necessity and comprehension," revealed especially by his interest in con-
> structing a theoretical structure indifferent to the various contingent choices
> that can be made regarding the characterization of formal neurons. That this
> study sometimes limited itself to particular cases did not detract from the
> generality of the project, according to Papert: it was rather a question of style,
> or of a lack of [suitable] mathematical tools.[5]

To which it might be added that McCulloch, emboldened by his equivalence theorem, was imbued with the universalist spirit of the Turing machine—and so, as a consequence, of his own machine.

The Obstacle of Intentionality

Let us come back to analytical philosophy. It will be recalled that the
second reason that led us to strongly qualify the importance of its "cognitive turn" was that the philosophy of mind that resulted from it remains
profoundly marked by the philosophy of language. Here we find ouselves
faced with the question of representation.

In one of the rare studies that compares what today has become known as connectionism with the McCulloch-Pitts model, Daniel Andler takes McCulloch and Pitts to task for having utterly ignored the problem of representation.[6] Andler defends the thesis, mentioned earlier, that the advantage—and opportunity—of contemporary connectionism consists in its ability to link itself up with the cognitivist mainstream (even if only, as I suggested, to be in a better position to devour it), mainly by borrowing from it the notion of representation. Nothing in principle prevents present-day neural networks of the parallel distributed processing type,[7] for example, from exhibiting those higher cognitive properties that until now have been the privileged possession of classical artificial intelligence—thus avoiding the ghetto of perception in which research of the Perceptron variety seemed to have gotten stuck. In particular, it may be hoped that connectionism will soon be able to account for the capacity of a network to "produce" logic, taking this capacity to be an *emergent* property of the network as a whole—which means that it cannot be localized at some lower level, and in particular not at the level of its elements. "But," it may be protested, "how can that be? Didn't McCulloch long ago provide a demonstration that each neuron can be interpreted as a logical calculator, as embodying, for example, one of the connectives that make up the set of logical connectives (*and, or, not,* and so on); and that the network in its entirety can be treated as a universal symbolic calculator?" No, Andler forcefully replies, nothing of the sort can be said to have been demonstrated. That logic may serve to model the network does not imply that the network is to be regarded as a model of logical thought. What McCulloch's argument fails to do, but must do if it is to be philosophically sound, is to show how the signal transmitted by a given neuron is able to represent a proposition about the world—that is, show how the coding that allows an equivalence to be established between some thought content and a computation effected by the network can be assigned a meaning in terms of representation.

Andler's argument is powerful and convincing. Note, however, that it takes two things for granted, namely, that knowing subjects *have* representations and that a representation's mode of being corresponds to the idea of representation found in cognitive philosophy. On the latter point of view, a "mental state" represents something to the extent that it has a content and that this content concerns the world. Cognitive philosophy resorts to a technical term to designate this representative capacity of mental states: they are said to be "intentional." The intentionality of mental states is bound up with their "aboutness"—the fact that they are *about* certain objects. These objects are heterogeneous with respect to mental states; that is, they are things (or properties of things, or else relations among several things) that stand outside the mind. One might immediately object that this shows cognitive philosophy is at odds with the general movement to which cognitive science belongs, as described in the first chapter of this book. If to think is to simulate, then, as Proust points out, pushing her Kantian reading of artificial intelligence à la Newell and Simon a step further, "to refer, for a physical symbol system, is necessarily to *simulate* symbolically the structure and the properties of an object. The main presupposition of simulation is that it preserves the structure of reality. However the notion of 'reality' must in its turn be contained in the terms of the system. . . . The idea of a fact [that is] radically heterogenous with the 'knowing' system has . . . simply no meaning."[8] In Kantian terms: the object of a representation (the object for the subject) is not the thing itself; it is the appearance of this thing within the representation in the form of a phenomenon, which thereby acquires an objective validity.

If, by contrast, one posits that the object of a representation is the thing-in-itself, as cognitive philosophy does, then this thing certainly cannot be said to constitute its *content*. When I think that I may have forgotten to lock my bicycle, for example, the actual object made out of metal and leather and rubber is not contained in my mind. The thing-in-itself does not exist in the representation: by its very nature, it is "constitutively" absent from the representation. What, then, is the nature of the content of a representation? The answer that philosophy of mind provides to this question is what continues to make it a philosophy of language, however much it may wish it were not. The answer it gives is a linguistic one, on two levels. Take the mental states that have long occupied the attention of cognitive science[9] and that, since Bertrand Russell gave them their name, have been known as "propositional attitudes." As the name indicates, they are supposed to connect a (psychological) attitude of the type "to believe that," "to desire that," "to fear that," "to have the intention of," and so on, with a proposition about the world. In the functionalist, computational, and representational version of philosophy of mind defended today by Jerry Fodor or Zenon Pylyshyn, this proposition is expressed in a sentence of the "language of thought," a private language whose symbols are inscribed in the material substrate of the brain.

To be sure, this hypothesis of a language of thought is not shared by all philosophers of mind—far from it. Nonetheless all of them, or almost all, accept that the criterion of mental "intentionality" is linguistic at a second level: the sentences of the public language that we use to attribute mental states endowed with content to others possess the property of being *intensional*. By that it is meant that they violate the rules of logical extensionality, the first of which concerns existential generalization. From the truth of the statement "Maurice's cow grazes in the meadow," for example, it may be inferred that there necessarily exists a meadow in which Maurice's cow grazes; by contrast, neither the truth nor the falsity of the statement "Maurice believes that the boozoos are fatter in Savoy than in the Dolomites" permits us to conclude the existence or nonexistence of boozoos.

The second rule violated by an intensional expression concerns the substitutability of terms having the same reference. My son, who just turned twelve years old, does not know that Tegucigalpa is the capital of Honduras; on the other hand, despite his lack of interest in logic, he knows that the capital of Honduras is the capital of Honduras. However, the sentence "The capital of Honduras is the capital of Honduras" becomes "Tegucigalpa is the capital of Honduras" when one substitutes for "the capital of Honduras" the term "Tegucigalpa," which refers to the same entity. It is this property that Willard Van Orman Quine made famous as the quality of "referential opacity." But it was in fact Roderick Chisholm who, in a book published in 1957, first proposed this linguistic interpretation of intentionality.[10] There he gave the following example: "Most of us knew in 1944 that Eisenhower was the one in command; but although he was identical with the man who was to succeed Truman, it is not true that we knew in 1944 that the man who was to succeed Truman was the one in command."[11]

The difficulties that philosophy of mind meets with today arise in large part from its initial commitment to the linguistic interpretation of intentionality. Many of its practitioners accept this interpretation while trying at the same time to "naturalize" it—that is, to supply an analysis of it founded ultimately on the laws of physics. The problem is that they want this physicalist enterprise to preserve something that ordinary psychology takes for granted, namely, that the contents of mental states have causal relevance in the explanation of our behavior. If Maurice went to Savoy rather than to the Dolomites to hunt boozoos, it is *because* he believed that he would find plumper animals there. For a long time the obstacle seemed insurmountable, because philosophy of mind had convinced itself that the semantic content of a mental state, as described by its conditions of truth and of reference, depends on the entire physical and social environment of the subject; but if this content is supposed to have causal power in the physicist's sense, it can only be conceived in terms of the intrinsic properties of the mental state. It therefore appeared that the theory of knowledge could be naturalized only at the cost of depriving mental properties and mental states of all causal efficacy insofar as they are mental—thus making them pure "epiphenomena."[12]

One of the most original theoretical proposals for overcoming this obstacle is the "anomalous monism" advocated by Donald Davidson in a famous 1970 article called "Mental Events."[13] Davidson postulated that every mental event is identical to a physical event; nonetheless there is no identity relation between classes or types of mental events and classes or types of physical events. In holding that properties, whether mental or physical, are just such classes of singular events, this philosophical position combined an ontological monism—the view that ultimately "there are" only physical events—with a dualism of concepts and properties— the view that mental concepts cannot be reduced to physical concepts. Such a nonreductionist monism is "anomalous" in the following sense: whereas mental events cause other mental events as well as physical events, the *relation* of causality connects events with one another only insofar as they are events of the world, independently of whatever description, mental or physical, that we may give of them. The causal relation is therefore extensional, and underlying it is a law of physics. By contrast, an *explanation* that involves properties or mental concepts, after the fashion of the explanations furnished by ordinary psychology, can only be intensional, for which very reason it instantiates no strictly deterministic law in the physicist's sense—whence its non-nomological, or anomalous, character. In short, though mental or psychological concepts enjoy an explanatory autonomy, ontologically the relation of causality does not involve the mental insofar as it is mental. The mental remains an epiphenomenon (one hardly dares say "superstructure").

Reviewing various attempts that have been made to give substance to a naturalistic materialism, notably functionalism and anomalous monism, Pascal Engel comments:

> This dual concern with the reduction of mental concepts to concepts acceptable from the point of view of a scientific psychology and with support for the autonomy of such concepts well illustrates the permanent dilemma of a materialist theory of mind. Indeed, the more successful the reduction (which is to say, the more one manages to "explain" mental concepts in "physicalist" or "naturalist" terms), the less correct our usual mental concepts (those of common-sense psychology and of our pretheoretical conception of the mind) seem—and the more one is tempted to "eliminate" [mental concepts] in favor of [physical concepts], to hold that there simply are no such things as beliefs, desires, sensations, and so on. In other words, materialism ceaselessly oscillates between its "eliminativist" and "non-reductionist" versions. The project of a "naturalized" philosophy of mind similarly oscillates between these two tendencies.[14]

To this one might add that the nonreductionist versions flirt rather often with disguised forms of dualism, and that the instability emphasized by Engel is still stronger than he claims. John Searle has stressed this point in connection with artificial intelligence and functionalism:

> Indeed, strong Artificial Intelligence only makes sense given the dualistic assumption that, where the mind is concerned, the brain doesn't matter. In strong AI (and in functionalism, as well) what matters are programs, and

> programs are independent of their realization in machines. . . . Unless you
> believe that the mind is separable from the brain both conceptually and em-
> pirically—dualism in its strong form—you cannot hope to reproduce the
> mental by writing and running programs since programs must be indepen-
> dent of brains or any other particular forms of instantiation.[15]

Quine, who for his part subscribes to Davidson's anomalous monism despite a personal philosophy that is close to eliminative materialism, em-
phasizes that this "monism" owes a great deal to dualism: "The age-old
mind-body dualism goes on, then, transmuted and transplanted as a dualism of concepts or language. As such, it remains irreducible."[16]

Once again we encounter an irony of history. Looking back, one may
say that the naturalization of transcendental philosophy was paradoxically perhaps easier to carry through to a successful conclusion than the
naturalization of a psycholinguistic philosophy of mind; and that although the first task was within the power of cybernetics to accomplish,
cybernetics had no idea how to go about doing it.

Brentano Betrayed

To illustrate these two claims, it is necessary to make a brief foray into that
other great current of twentieth-century philosophy, phenomenology. The
decisive role played in its development by the concept of intentionality is
well recognized, of course, and one suspects that its relation with what the
same term stands for in cognitive philosophy is distant at best, since in
Husserl it is "mental acts" that enjoy the property of being "intentional,"
this property constituting the "essence of the concept of consciousness."
What is less generally realized is that the intentionality that figures in philosophy of mind shares a common ancestor with Husserlian intentionality
in the philosophical psychology of Franz Brentano. Husserl studied with
Brentano in Vienna from 1884 to 1886, an experience that was to prove
decisive in shaping his later work, particularly the *Logical Investigations*
(1900–1901).[17] The great Austrian philosopher's legacy to philosophy of
mind was to be conveyed through the efforts of Roderick Chisholm, whom
we have already mentioned in connection with his invention of the linguistic version of intentionality; earlier Chisholm had been responsible for introducing Brentano's thought to America, publishing translations as well
as commentaries of several of his works, on the strength of which he came
to be regarded as a leading authority on Brentano. One of the two, however, must have betrayed his master. Was it Husserl, or was it Chisholm?

"All consciousness is consciousness of something": Husserl found the
inspiration for this formula (famous in France for the use that was later
made of it by Sartre in that variant of phenomenology known as existen-

tialism) in Brentano's thought; more precisely, in the following passage that he cites from his teacher's *Psychology from an Empirical Standpoint* (1874): "Every mental phenomenon is characterized by what the mediaeval schoolmen called the intentional (or mental) inexistence of an object, and by what we, not without ambiguity, call the relation to a content, the direction to an object (by which a reality is not to be understood) or an immanent objectivity."[18]

Every word here is potentially a trap. "Intentional," Brentano reminds us, is a scholastic term used by Thomas Aquinas, for example, in the sense of "mental" (as opposed to "real"). Form is united with matter in the real object, which is to say outside the mind; the "intentional" object is present only in its form. "Inexistence" (*Inexistenz*) comes from the Latin *inesse*, meaning "to be inside of": here, quite obviously, taking "inexistent" to mean "nonexistent" would be a serious mistranslation. The object *toward* which the mind *tends* (i.e., its *intention*) is located *inside* the mind: hence the reason its presence is said to be "immanent."

Mental life, according to Brentano, is above all an activity, a dynamic process. This activity is "presentation." "By 'presentation,'" Brentano adds, "[I] do not mean that which is presented, but rather the presenting of it."[19] This activity has a content, or more precisely an "object." The object is that very thing that is presented to the mind: the sound that we hear, the color that we see, the cold that we feel. Further confusing matters is the fact that Brentano calls these objects of presentation "physical phenomena"—by contrast with the previously defined mental activity. But he goes on to say, in order to dispel any possible ambiguity, that these "physical" phenomena are part of the "data of our consciousness."[20]

Mental activity is intrinsically conscious of itself. When we think, we have an immediate perception of the fact that we are thinking, and this perception of the thinking activity is simultaneously a perception of the object of thought. The act of internal perception cannot be an observation, Brentano notes, for that would imply an infinite regression of mental activities, each one pointing to a further one. It is by means of a global and unique act of apprehension that thought as activity is related both to itself and to its intentional object:

> Do we *perceive* the mental phenomena which exist within us? The question must be answered with an emphatic "yes" for where would we have got the concepts of presentation and thought without such perception? On the other hand, it is obvious that we are not able to *observe* our present mental phenomena. . . . This suggests that there is a special connection between the object of inner presentation and the presentation itself and that both belong to one and the same mental act. The presentation of a sound and the presentation of a presentation of a sound belong to one and the same mental phenom-

enon; it is only by considering it in its relation to two different objects, one of which is a physical phenomenon and the other a mental phenomenon that we divide it conceptually into two presentations. . . . In the same mental phenomenon in which the sound is present to our mind we simultaneously apprehend the mental phenomenon itself.[21]

We know what Husserl was to make of this idea. He used it to derive the classic phenomenological gesture, the *epochē* or "reduction," which amounts to deciding to see in the object of representation only the correlate (*noēma*) of mental activity (*noēsis*)—putting to one side the problem of the relation between the object of representation (the intentional object) and the thing-in-itself. Construed in this way, intentionality was to become Husserl's principal weapon in his critique of psychologism, as Alain Renaut has shown:

> To say that, for there to be consciousness, the object and the subject must link up in such a way that the object comes to "intentionally in-exist" for the subject (that is, to assume the form of the object of representation, as distinct from what is outside consciousness), was in effect also to designate a relation between object and subject that was no longer a question for psychology. . . . There exists, with regard to our representations, a level of questioning more radical than that of psychology: where the latter now and always presupposes the fact that we have representations, in order to limit itself to showing the role played by perception, memory, attention, and feelings, [phenomenology] is interested in posing the pre-psychological question of whether *in fact* there are representations and, if so, what is the *mode of being* of the object of representation—an *ontological* question, if you like, in the sense that the existence and the essence of representations are at stake; or, if you prefer, a *transcendental* question, in the sense that it is a matter of determining under what conditions representation is possible.[22]

Let us now imagine an ungifted first-year philosophy student who, having been asked to read the passages of Brentano cited here, systematically gets the meaning of the key terms wrong. On this misreading of Brentano, the object toward which representation tends is a *nonexistent physical object.* Accordingly, it must be the thing-in-itself. When I think of a cow or a boozoo, what in fact is absent from my representation? In the case of the boozoo, the physical flesh-and-bones beast is missing, for the reason that boozoos do not exist; in the case of the cow, the physical cow with its udders and milk and the rest is likewise missing but for the reason that, although cows do exist (unlike boozoos), they exist only outside of my mind. Intentionality is therefore no longer the mental *act* that goes beyond itself while remaining within itself, in the direction of an object that also remains internal to it—that "transcendance in immanence" that Husserl sought to detect; it now becomes a mental *state* endowed with a content, which in turn is related to an object whose existence is not guaranteed by the fact that the mental state itself exists. Therefore the content can only be intensional, and hence linguistic.

As enormous and as obvious as this interpretive trap may seem to us, it is the one that, consciously or unconsciously, Roderick Chisholm fell into: and, in any event, the trap into which he caused his readers—an entire generation of analytic philosophers—to fall. Unquestionably the most celebrated of these was Willard Van Orman Quine.[23] In a famous passage in *Word and Object* (1960), a work that strongly influenced many younger philosophers, some of whom were later to become influential in their own right, Quine relies on "a thesis of Brentano's, illuminatingly developed of late by Chisholm,"[24] with which he pronounces himself in agreement, since, as he says, it is identical with his own thesis of the radical indeterminacy of translation between languages, or of the mental states that a listener attributes to a speaker. "Brentano's thesis" is in fact none other than Chisholm's thesis. It asserts that mental states (and mental states alone) are endowed with the property of intentionality, understood as a linguistic relation to objects or states of affairs of the external world—external to the mind. Intentional expressions are irreducible to the terms that we use to describe "physical" phenomena. "One may accept the Brentano thesis either as showing the indispensability of intentional idioms and the importance of an autonomous science of intention," Quine concludes, "or as showing the baselessness of intentional idioms and the emptiness of a science of intention. My attitude, unlike Brentano's, is the second."[25] That was all the encouragement that his followers needed. Some, less inclined toward eliminativism than Quine and more conscious of the limits to any attempt to "naturalize epistemology," were to go on to propose "nonreductionist monisms" capable of reconciling "Brentano's thesis" with a relative physicalism. The rest of the story is in any case well known.

One may be tempted to deplore this misreading. That would be a mistake. Even if the history of philosophy well justifies the charge that philosophers are their own worst readers, it is equally true that from time to time their blunders and misinterpretations occasion rich works of great originality whose arguments come to gain wide acceptance. This is the only thing that should matter to the historian of ideas.

The Missed Encounter with Phenomenology

Daniel Andler is right to emphasize that it would be hard to find in cybernetics a notion of representation that prefigures in the least the psycholinguistic theory that today constitutes the conceptual core of cognitive science. Is this to say that the transcendental question "whether *in fact* there are representations and, if so, what is the *mode of being* of the object of representation" therefore slipped out of the cyberneticians' grasp as well?

With hindsight, it seems fair to say that if there existed a possibility of scientifically modeling—and therefore, if you will, of "naturalizing"—intentionality as it was first conceived by Brentano and then developed by Husserl, this lay in the study of networks as conceived and developed by Warren McCulloch. For cybernetics to have been able to come up with a feasible plan for research, however, it would have had to regard an idealized neural network from an entirely different point of view than McCulloch's.

It bears repeating that McCulloch and Pitts saw their networks as logic machines. Inspired by the revolutionary spirit of Turing's thesis, and armed with the equivalence theorem identifying their machine with his, they set themselves the pedagogical task of showing that one could conceive of a network capable of reproducing each of the principal faculties of mind. Now in Turing's scheme, a mental function was interpreted as a function in the mathematical sense: as an operator transforming inputs (stimuli) into outputs (responses). For many years this perspective—at bottom, a behaviorist perspective—constituted an obstacle to the Gestalt switch that would have permitted researchers to see the network as an "autonomous" dynamic system, informationally and organizationally closed, with neither input nor output. The alternative approach came to command attention only much later with the confluence of several new movements or schools of research. One of these, an offspring of the second cybernetics, grew out of the various attempts made during the 1970s and 1980s to formalize self-organization in biological systems using Boolean automata networks; in France this work was conducted chiefly by a team directed by Henri Atlan and including Françoise Fogelman-Soulié, Gérard Weisbuch, and Maurice Milgram;[26] in the United States, by Stuart Kauffman,[27] a former student of Warren McCulloch, and others at the Santa Fe Institute for the Study of Complex Systems. Another, also springing from the second cybernetics, was the Chilean school of autopoiesis, which went so far in its conception of informational closure as to deny the existence of representations altogether; this tradition of research was founded, with the blessing of Gregory Bateson, by Humberto Maturana and Francisco Varela, the latter exploiting various formalisms familiar from the theory of automata networks.[28] A third movement, which grew up in the very heart of neoconnectionism (though it is to be distinguished from the PDP school mentioned previously, whose interest is in extending and enriching Perceptron-style research), was the Attractor Neural Network (ANN) school, led by physicists studying the emergent properties of (almost) completely connected networks in which information is propagated in all directions; founded by John Hopfield at Caltech,[29] this movement has enjoyed remarkable development due to the work of Daniel Amit[30] in Israel, as well as the related research being done in France by Jean Petitot[31] applying dynamical systems theory to the study of automata networks.

All of this work, despite its profusion and variety, has one thing in common. All of it treats a complex network of interacting elementary calculators as an "autonomous" entity, as it were—autonomous in the sense that, being endowed with a spontaneity of its own, it is the source of its own determining characteristics and not a simple transducer converting input messages into output messages. From the McCulloch-Pitts model to that of Daniel Amit, the model as a mathematical creature has not changed: it remains, at bottom, a threshold automaton. What has completely changed is the way one looks at it: one is no longer interested in its computational capacities, only in its "self-behaviors" (or *eigenbehaviors*, to use the hybrid English-German phrase of quantum mechanics, from which systems theory borrowed this concept). What does this imply? Like every automaton having internal states, a network calculates its state in the next period as a function of its state during the current period. Now, a very general property of such networks is that, after a transition period (often quite a short one), its collective behavior stabilizes to a "limit cycle"—that is, a periodic spatiotemporal configuration—of weak periodicity: where the period is equal to one, as may be the case, the corresponding state is said to be "stationary," or "fixed-point." Everything occurs as though this stable collective behavior were *self*-reproducing, as though it were produced by itself—hence the term "self-behavior"—when in fact it is produced by the network. Let us take, for example, the case of an elementary automaton, or neuron, that happens never to be fired in the course of the limit cycle. It would thus appear to have no causal effect upon the outcome of the cycle. But this is an illusion: one needs only to remove the neuron, along with its synapses, from the structure of the network to realize that the collective behavior of the latter is affected by the absence of the former.

A given network usually possesses a multiplicity of self-behaviors (or, as they are sometimes called, "attractors"—a term borrowed from dynamical systems theory) and converges toward one or another of them depending on the initial conditions of the network. The "life" of a network can thus be conceived as a trajectory through a "landscape" of attractors, passing from one to another as a result of perturbations or shocks from the external world. Note that these external events come to acquire meaning in the context of the network as a result of the network's own activity: the *content*—the meaning—that the network attributes to them is precisely the self-behavior, or attractor, that results from them. Obviously, then, this content is purely endogenous and not the reflection of some external "transcendent" objectivity.

It should be obvious, too, that this line of argument will take us where we want to go, for it provides us with at least the germ of a very satisfactory model of what Brentano called "immanent objectivity." A few philosophers have already set to work on the problem. The attractor is an entity that both fully participates in the activity of the network and yet in some sense, by virtue of the fact that it results from a higher level of logical complexity, transcends the activity of the network. The dynamics of the network may therefore be said to *tend toward* an attractor, although the latter is only a product of these dynamics. The network is thus an *intentional* creature in Brentano's and Husserl's sense. Systems theory was to coin another term to describe this paradoxical relationship between the dynamics of a system and its attractor, referring to it as "autotranscendence." This is not very different, really, from Husserl's notion of "transcendence within immanence." It is not surprising, then, that certain cognitive scientists who rely upon automata networks in their research should more or less explicitly invoke the authority of some kind of transcendental phenomenology, nor that their work should be considered marginal by their peers on this account: in France, one thinks of Atlan,[32] Petitot,[33] and Varela.[34]

Was there any chance, at the time of the Macy Conferences, that cybernetics might have taken this road? I have already called attention to the ideological obstacle constituted by the Turing paradigm. But other circumstances intervened as well, particularly as a consequence of the training and philosophical interests of the conference participants. The sole professional philosopher to take part in the Macy Conferences was Filmer Northrop, a Yale professor who enjoyed a certain reputation during the period. In the 1930s he conducted a seminar for scientists interested in philosophical issues that brought together several people who would later participate in these conferences, among them McCulloch. But Northrop's own style of philosophy was scientistic: he looked to science for a way to reconcile the world's various philosophical systems, past and present—and particularly, once he discovered them, to the Rosenblueth-Wiener-Bigelow and McCulloch-Pitts models. His influence on the group was negligible. The philosophical training of the cyberneticians was restricted for the most part to philosophical logics: Wiener had studied with Russell at Cambridge, von Neumann with Hilbert at Göttingen, and Pitts with Carnap at Chicago. McCulloch, for his part, was a great admirer of Russell, G. E. Moore, Peirce, and the Wittgenstein of the *Tractatus*.

An encounter with Husserlian phenomenology, or rather with one of its offshoots, did nonetheless take place, though in the form of a confrontation—and a failed one at that—with *Gestalt* psychology. This school, a

product of the intellectual life of Weimar Germany, had come to the
United States as part of the wave of immigration accompanying the rise of
Nazism. Wolfgang Köhler had been one of the founders of the movement
in the 1920s, at the Psychological Institute of Berlin, where he had taken
over the directorship from his teacher Carl Stumpf, who himself had been
a student of Brentano and close to Husserl. The project of his research
team at the Institute, which included Kurt Koffka, Max Wertheimer, and
Kurt Lewin, was to resolve the problems posed by Husserlian phenomenology by means of an experimental type of scientific psychology that
drew upon the concepts of quantum mechanics (Köhler had studied physics with Planck as well), particularly that of a field. Their ambition was to
discover the laws (in the sense in which the term is understood in the
natural sciences) governing perception and the immediate experience that
we have of things, with the aim, above all, of preserving their "holistic"
character as organized wholes.

In the early 1920s Köhler had postulated a "psycho-physical isomorphism" between the physical events occurring in the brain and the facts of
psychological experience. The isomorphism he sought to detect experimentally was topological in character: the content of an internal perception of a figure, for example, ought to have, he believed, a corresponding
geometric pattern in the brain. Once settled in the United States, Köhler
was to undertake neurophysiological experiments in the hope of discovering a physical correlate to the phenomena of perception in the form of
continuous electric fields in cerebral tissue. When the cyberneticians invited him to the fourth Macy Conference, in October 1947, they expected
(as their experience with other advocates of a continualist model of cerebral function had led them to anticipate) that the discussion would concern the relative merits of this model as against the idealized neural model.
In the event, Köhler delivered a speech that his listeners judged to be
purely ideological, devoid of any reference to "concrete neurophysiological data," and the discussion abruptly came to a halt.[35] This missed opportunity was partially made up for the following year, at the Hixon Symposium, though there the confrontation between McCulloch's mechanism
and Köhler's holism took on something of the quality of a religious war.

When all is said and done, the one who came closest to naturalizing the
transcendental inquiry was not, paradoxically, the phenomenologist
Köhler but the logical atomist McCulloch. Köhler believed in a geometrical
parallelism obtaining between perception and its material substrate; Mc-
Culloch inquired into the formal and material conditions under which
knowledge was possible at all. One of his most remarkable successes in
this regard was the experimental work he carried out much later on the
frog with Pitts, Jerome Lettvin, and Humberto Maturana (out of which, by
the way, came the Chilean school of autopoietic systems). This research,

published under the memorable title "What the Frog's Eye Tells the Frog's Brain,"[36] drew attention to the existence of receptors in the visual system responding selectively to certain features of the stimulus, such as convexity, and interpreted them as the material equivalents of the categories of synthetic a priori judgment. Shortly thereafter, Hubel and Wiesel were to confirm these results in the cat, which won them the Nobel Prize for Medicine.

A Subjectless Philosophy of Mind

Kantianism, yes, but without the transcendental subject—as Paul Ricoeur said about the structuralism of Claude Lévi-Strauss.[37] This formula applies wonderfully well to cybernetics. The neural network of McCulloch and Pitts neither was, nor pretended to be, a model of the subject—any more than Newell and Simon's physical symbol system did. A model of the mind, yes; of the subject, no. Thus we are led to consider perhaps the most significant contribution of cybernetics to philosophy: mind minus the subject. The connection with Lévi-Strauss is all the more irresistible considering that the great anthropologist explicitly referred to cybernetics in his introduction to the work of Marcel Mauss, widely regarded as the first manifesto of French structuralism. The task of social anthropology, he asserted, was to reveal the "unconscious mental structures" at work behind such practices as the exchange of gifts in "archaic" societies. These structures, which play the role of a synthetic a priori, are manifested in the phenomena of communication, with "symbolic thought" being structured in the way that language is structured.[38] The year was 1950: Lévi-Strauss had just turned toward semiotics, under the influence of Roman Jakobson; he was also influenced by the recent publication of Wiener's *Cybernetics* (1948) and Shannon and Weaver's *Theory of Communication* (1949). Lévi-Strauss quickly came around to the view that a mathematical theory of communication introduced into anthropology by linguistics was the way of the future for the social sciences.

In inventing a type of transcendental inquiry that did away with the subject, cybernetics was to greatly assist the deconstruction of the metaphysics of the subject. This is a crucial point, one that is too rarely recognized. In a well-known interview given in 1966 but not published until a few days after his death, in 1976, Heidegger pronounced the anathema quoted at the head of this chapter: "Cybernetics is the metaphysics of the atomic age."[39] For most of his followers, but for many other philosophers as well, cybernetics seemed to raise the "philosophy of the *cogito*" to its greatest height, the final outcome of a misguided metaphysics that assigned to man the task of making himself master and possessor of all things. On this view, cybernetics, as the highest form of the will to power and of the will to will, was responsible for our missing "the essence of technology"—which, for Heidegger, lies outside technology in the mode of revelation and unveiling of Being that goes under the neologistic name *Gestell* (literally, "frame"). "So long as we represent technology as an instrument," Heidegger declared in his famous paper on the essence of technology, first presented in 1949, "we remain transfixed in the will to mastery."[40] This instrumental and anthropological definition of technology was to receive its fullest expression, on the Heideggerian view, with the advent of cybernetics.

Those who go on repeating this condemnation appear never to have pondered the following, troubling point. When, at the beginning of the 1950s, French practitioners of the human sciences (structuralists and, in the decades that followed, poststructuralists, whose intellectual debt to Heidegger's thought was no less indisputable) were looking for a way to say something about the mystery of Being, its unveiling, and so forth, they turned in their search for metaphors—poetic language not being their strong suit—to cybernetics. In the interest of showing that man is not his own master, that, far from mastering language, it is language that masters man, and that "symbolic order" is irreducible to human experience, it was the vocabulary of cybernetics and information theory that they systematically drew upon. The most typical case was that of Jacques Lacan. Cybernetics was the main topic of his seminar during the academic year 1954–1955, the culmination of which was the reading of Edgar Allan Poe's *Purloined Letter* in terms of automata theory.[41] Lacan was later to begin his *Écrits* by revisiting this analysis of Poe's story, the key to which he claimed to furnish in a text that took the form of cybernetic variations on the game of odd or even intended to illustrate "how a formal language determines the subject." Even if this part of his teaching seems to have passed over the head of more than one student, one cannot conclude from this that Lacan did not take cybernetics seriously. His lecture on psychoanalysis and cybernetics ("Psychanalyse et cybernétique, ou de la nature du langage"), given in June 1955, testifies further to his interest in the topic. Later the new literary criticism, caught up in its turn by the excitement of detecting the autonomy of signifiers and their infinite drift, was to display great dexterity in operating various types of "textual machines," desiring or other. Even the vogue of *mise en abyme*—schemes of infinite repetition and other forms of literary self-reference—looked to cybernetic concepts for inspiration.[42]

It is good form today to say that this interest was superficial, an intellectual fashion of the period. In the case of Lacan, this was assuredly not true: in certain areas his knowledge of cybernetics was quite detailed. He took an interest, as we have already seen, in the theory of closed reverberating circuits that Lawrence Kubie's work in the 1930s had led McCulloch to take up, and he was familiar with the work of the British neuroanatomist John Z. Young,[43] discussed at the ninth Macy Conference, in March 1952, testing this theory in the octopus. He followed the work of the second generation of cyberneticians as well and grasped at least the general thrust of Ross Ashby's formal results regarding the differentiating properties of computation.[44]

What one discovers in the cybernetic project, in reality, is exactly the ambiguity that Heidegger spoke of in connection with the essence of technology.[45] Technology reveals truth (the Heideggerian truth) about Being, a truth that involves the deconstruction of the metaphysical view of the subject; at the same time, the particular way in which technology unveils truth—by a process of framing (*Gestell*)—forces both humanity and the world to run the risk of being swallowed up in a frenetic quest after power and mastery. This is the same ambiguity noted by Philippe Breton, one of the few historians of the fate of cybernetics in France: "Cybernetics has been one of the principal destabilizing instruments of the anthropocentric conception of man. . . . Cybernetics therefore assumes [the form of] a terrible paradox: it affirms humanity while at the same time depriving man of it. In this sense, it rather openly expresses a fundamental characteristic of contemporary technical and scientific knowledge, by virtue of which the benefits of progress seem irrevocably associated with the rational portrayal of the death of man."[46] Jean-Claude Beaune also expresses a Heideggerian view in commenting on the ambiguity of technology: "[An] ambiguity that recalls the mythic essence of automatic technicity: the more faithful the technical imitation of the model (man), the more complete the rule of anthropocentrism [and] the more the human purposes of the object need to be clearly and bluntly stated, for the object tends more and more to slip out of the control of its maker. The more the products of man are made in his own image, the more this image slips away from him."[47] With cybernetic automata, "a new Copernican revolution is underway: the world's center of gravity is no longer man, but the machine."[48] Gilbert Hottois, for his part, revives the notion of the "automatization" of technique first developed by Jacques Ellul, seeing in it a way to discover "the non-anthropological essence of technique," its "fundamentally *ab-human* nature."[49]

There is no question that the ambiguity of the cybernetic enterprise appears most clearly in the interpretation given to research on automata. On the one hand, such research can be seen as the height of the anthropomorphization of technology. This was certainly the aspect to which the public was most sensitive; but it was also the source of one of Heinz von Foerster's most persistent criticisms of cybernetics in its original form (and of the artificial intelligence that followed in its wake), namely, that it spoke of machines in anthropomorphic terms. One can, however, just as easily regard the cybernetic automaton as the mechanization of the human, as the unveiling of what is not human in man—thus Lacan's remark to his students in the 1954–1955 seminar: "The question of knowing whether [the machine] is human or not is obviously completely settled—it is not. But there is the question too of knowing whether the human, in the sense in which you understand it, is as human as [you suppose]."[50]

Marc Jeannerod perfectly captures the spirit of cybernetics (even if he does so negatively and in a reproving sort of way) when he alludes to the demonstrated existence of nerve cells, which, like biochemical clocks, exhibit spontaneous rhythmic activity: these spontaneous oscillation generators, he says, "allowed one to compare the function of the nervous system to that of a machine that 'worked by itself' once prompted or, at the extreme, could trigger itself. However, such a physiology of spontaneity gives a singularly limited explanation of behavior. If it explains the automatic aspects quite well, it cannot, by comparison, be generalized to the other aspects of behavior without producing a *behavior without a subject*."[51] But this was precisely the objective of the cyberneticians. In their own way, they too contributed to the critique of the metaphysics of subjectivity.

As for the French Heideggerians, it is precisely because they were sensitive (and quite rightly so) to this aspect of cybernetics that they appealed to it to say what they had to say; and what they had to say, they said coherently. When Vincent Descombes, in his otherwise excellent study of French postwar philosophy, reproaches structuralism for incoherence in claiming to struggle against the "philosophy of consciousness" while drawing its concepts from "an engineering style of thought," he only betrays an ignorance of cybernetics that is widely shared—and which the unfortunate choice of the very name "cybernetics" (from the Greek word meaning "steersman," implying a theory of command, governance, and mastery) cannot excuse.[52]

McCulloch vs. Wiener

I would like to conclude this inquiry into the philosophical dimension of cybernetics with a brief comparison of the styles of thought of Norbert Wiener and Warren McCulloch.

Wiener remains even now a familiar figure. He gave cybernetics its name, and fashioned his own distinctive public image with the back-to-back publication of two books that enjoyed great public success: *Cybernetics* (1948) and the even more successful *Human Use of Human Beings* (1950). It was Wiener as well who laid down the basic vocabulary of cyber-

netics ("information," "message," "communication," "control," "feedback," and so forth) and who provided it with a certain style, which today
would be called "ecological" for its emphasis on respecting the interde-
pendence of phenomena. By contrast, McCulloch seems almost to have
faded from view: even in the fields in which he made lasting contributions,
many of the heirs to his legacy are unaware even of his name. Any serious
history of cybernetics owes it to itself first of all to redress the balance
between these two men, especially if it is based, as this book is, on a study
of the Macy Conferences, which from beginning to end were conceived,
organized, and presided over by McCulloch.

Wiener's carelessness as a thinker and his propensity for abusing metaphors and analogies were matched only by McCulloch's rigor in stubbornly pursuing what he solemnly regarded as a philosophical quest. The
contrast between the two men is clearly apparent in their approach to
logic. Wiener, even though he acknowledged Russell's great influence
upon the development of his thought,[53] was never an unconditional partisan of the methods of formal logic. Very early on, under the influence of
what Steve Heims calls a certain "romanticism typical of the 19th century," he had become convinced that any attempt to fit the phenomenal
world into a perfectly logical system of knowledge closed in upon itself,
was doomed to failure. Our knowledge of the world, he believed, must
allow room for paradox, incompleteness, and chance. The publication of
Gödel's theorem in 1931 therefore came as no surprise to him.[54] By contrast, McCulloch's intellectual journey was to take him, as we have seen,
deeper and deeper into the universe of logic.

Both men seemed marginal figures in the eyes of the scientific community of their time, but for quite different reasons. In Wiener's case, it was
his eclecticism that disconcerted his colleagues: armed with his cybernetic
toolbox, he could analyze any mechanism in terms of behavior or communication.[55] No doubt this was the source of his image as a mere "engineer,"
an image that gives only a very approximate sense of his way of tackling
problems. McCulloch, on the other hand, was a man possessed by a single
idea, which depended on holding together brain, mind, and machine at
any cost; but it was too "philosophical" an idea to be understood by the
physiologists of his time.[56] He did not, however, consider himself a philosopher. His aim was to build a natural—which for him meant logical—
science of mind, and it was within the framework of scientific method that
he looked for an answer to the ancient philosophical questions that tormented him. To this science, as we have seen, gave the name "experimental epistemology."

Certainly neither rigor nor eclecticism is a decisive factor in the influence that a thinker exercises. If nonetheless it is fair to say that McCulloch,
by the force of both his personality and his work, embodied what was at

stake in the cybernetic project in a way that Wiener did not, this is because one finds in McCulloch, though not in Wiener, a profound coherence between the ideological commitment of the man and the scientific work itself. In the final analysis, both of them did much to bring about the "deconstruction" of the Leibnizian and Cartesian conception of the subject: Wiener in arguing that the will is essentially mechanical, McCulloch in doing the same for perception, thought, and consciousness. Thanks to them, it was henceforth possible to give a rigorous formulation of the notion of a *subjectless process*, whether it is a process of behavior or of thought. McCulloch, however, even if he did not resort to this Heideggerian terminology, knew what he was about. This was manifestly not the case with Wiener. In the aftermath of his open break with the scientific and military-industrial establishment,[57] he began to devote himself to the role of public intellectual that was to occupy an increasing portion of his later years. The message he delivered was a humanistic one: a generous and somewhat naive philosophy of technology in which figured the themes of the neutrality of technical knowledge, the evil it can do if not adequately supervised by human beings, the responsibility of the scientist and the engineer, the decisive role that machines can play in helping bring about the emergence of a rational society[58]—in short, a discourse of control and mastery, according to which technology is an *instrument* that can and must be dominated; a discourse that misses the "essence of technology." Wiener's research during the period, which he freely discussed with his colleagues at the Macy Conferences, perfectly symbolized this message, devoted as it was to devising medical prostheses to aid people with disabilities through the use of new techniques of signal processing. If the true philosophical nature of cybernetics has been misunderstood by many, surely this is because they have limited themselves to Wiener's characterization of it, failing to see that this was contradicted by the implications of the scientific work that had actually been carried out—yet another reason to restore Warren McCulloch to his rightful position as the leading figure of the cybernetics movement.[59]

CHAPTER 5

From Information to Complexity

Warren McCulloch: "Like most all Scots, I fall in love with machines
and particular machines, and I am a sailor, and I know that
almost every sailor falls in love with a ship. . . ."
Margaret Mead: "But the ship does not fall in love with you!"
Warren McCulloch: "I'm not so sure!"[1]

Those who cast cybernetics as a science that brought about a rupture
with physics, whether they wished to praise or to blame it for having done
so, have generally characterized the relation between the two by this formula: physics is the science of matter and energy, cybernetics is the science
of *forms*. Opposing the two in this way is inadmissible. It depends, as we
have seen, on a complete misunderstanding of the essential role played by
mathematical modeling in modern science. Physics abstracts forms from
the phenomena it studies, thus providing itself with the means to establish
isomorphisms between different physical phenomena—detecting, for example, the same wavelike structure in the motion of the tides, the vibration of a string, and the dynamics of an electron. If cybernetics can be
credited with an innovation, it consisted not in any new approach to modeling but in extending this approach to new domains, which previously
had seemed resistant to modeling of any sort: the nervous system, faculties
of mind, and the like. The confusion on this point probably had another
source as well, however, deriving from the importance attached by the
cyberneticians to the question of *information*. The mistake here was to
identify information with form.

Information and Physicalism

Let us note first that the notion of information, in the minds of the cyberneticians—in any case in Wiener's mind—belonged to the realm of
physics, more precisely, to thermodynamics. At the 1946 symposium on

teleological mechanisms, Wiener proposed that information be considered as negative entropy. This idea had been advanced by Leo Szilard in 1929[2] and was later to be developed in a rigorous fashion by Léon Brillouin in 1956.[3] "In fact," Wiener added, "it is not surprising that entropy and information are negatives of one another. Information measures order and entropy measures disorder. It is indeed possible to conceive all order in terms of message."[4] By virtue of the very fact that he treated information as a physical concept, Wiener immediately took it out of the domain of communications engineering proper, to which it was to be confined by Shannon, to make it part of the study of organized systems, whether these were biological, technical, or social systems. What he was aiming at was a *physics of information*.[5] He saw the concept of information as supplying the means by which biological or even social questions could be reduced to problems of physics. Thus he could say, "The most important characteristic of a living organism is its awareness of the outer world. This means that it is furnished with organs of coupling to pick up messages from the outer world that condition its future conduct. To consider this in the light of thermodynamics and statistical mechanics is instructive."[6]

The "physicalism" of Wiener's position on the issue of information comes out particularly in the many discussions at the Macy Conferences concerning two categories dear to the cyberneticians: "digital" and "analog" (or, as the cyberneticians said, "analogical"). Other conference participants seemed to have a great deal of trouble grasping the distinction, which they nonetheless concurred in judging fundamental, in part because many of them believed that digital devices, being discontinuous, were capable of conveying more information than analog devices or that, in any case, they transmitted a nobler sort of information—nobler because "coded." Pitts conjectured that the nervous system became digital only at a late stage of evolution, "probably for the purpose of handling larger quantities of information."[7] Von Neumann distinguished between discrete ("coded") messages, such as nerve impulses, and continuous messages, such as hormonal transmissions. He conjectured that the first type of message, unlike the second, was propagated along quite well-defined and specific pathways.[8] A few—McCulloch among them—doubted that analog (equated with continuous) variables could be said to code information at all, except in the uninformative sense that the voltage delivered by a battery to a radio codes information.[9] If the debates on this subject were heated, it was because they involved the perennial question of which is the more productive approach to the study of the nervous system: a "discontinuist" approach, which looks at it in terms of neuronal networks and nerve impulses, or a "continuist" approach, which looks at it in terms of electric fields and continuous variables of a chemical and hormonal character. The neurobiologist Ralph Gerard came to be a persistent advocate of the "holist" or "Gestaltist" position associated with the continuist approach, going even so far as to argue that the discrete nature of the nerve impulse might only be an "accidental fact."[10]

It was in this context that Wiener was led to propose the hypothesis that the contrast between digital and analog represented a difference merely of degree rather than of kind. He did this in a very modern way, using the language of dynamical systems theory—language that prefigured that of bifurcation theory (better known as "catastrophe theory"). Consider, for example, a physical system whose equilibrium states are few in number and whose basins of attraction[11]—that is, the regions of initial conditions that lead to a particular given equilibrium—are neatly separated. Most of the time the system will find itself in one or another of its equilibrium states. In this case the underlying dynamic is continuous, but the phenomenology is discrete. In general, a small variation in the initial conditions has no effect on the equilibrium that is reached, unless the system finds itself at a bifurcation point, in which case it is liable to jump abruptly—"catastrophically"—from one equilibrium state to another, amplifying the small variation in initial conditions. Now, Wiener continued, the greater the attraction of the equilibria of the system, the less time it passes outside its equilibrium states and the more it behaves like a "digital" device. A system is therefore *more or less* digital, more or less analog. If its identity, and therefore the "landscape" of its attractors, is liable to vary regularly as a function of certain parameters, it can actually be made to pass through all the intermediate stages between a "pure" digital and a "pure" analog device. Wiener concluded his remarkable analysis by affirming the necessity of elaborating a "*physics* of digital devices."[12]

These speculations led Wiener to judge it futile to take sides in the quarrel that pitted Gerard against McCulloch and, in fact, to dismiss them both in turn. As against Gerard, he asserted that the channeling of messages along specific pathways is an essential characteristic of the nervous system; as against McCulloch, he surmised that continuous variables of a chemical and hormonal nature are indeed bearers of information. To reconcile these two positions it was enough to posit that these "analogical" variables continually modify the excitation thresholds of the neurons, which amounts to conceiving of the nervous system as an analogically controlled digital system. This kind of complexity, Wiener thought, was required if the system was to be able to learn.[13] As Jean-Pierre Changeux points out, the subsequent course of research was to prove Wiener right:

> The hypothesis of a chemical coding [was] confirmed, but this in no way eliminate[d] the two forms of coding already mentioned: one based on the geometry of connections, the other on the temporal succession of nerve impulses. Chemical coding complements the others. First, it permits a type of

additional signaling, one that involves not the propagation of impulses along cables, but the diffusion of chemical signals over long distances using, for instance, the bloodstream. Above all, it creates a diversity in connections that otherwise have a similar geometry. . . . Chemical labeling creates diversity.[14]

Moreover, this diversity "produces a 'signal-combining device' with possibilities for calculations that a strictly 'electrical' neuron would handle differently or not at all."[15]

Wiener also regarded hormonal messages (which he jokingly called messages "to whom it may concern") as the physiological substrate of emotion and affectivity, and he wondered whether a theory of the unconscious not terribly unlike a theory of communication might not be erected on the basis of this hypothesis.[16] This particular example reveals once again how different the scientific styles of McCulloch and Wiener were. McCulloch, the inventor of the neural network model, was so much the captive of this idée fixe, which with him came to border on a fanatical obsession, that he found it difficult to see the desirability of modifying it; in the case of Wiener, what I have called his eclecticism permitted him to mold his thinking to that of others, all the while preserving a certain distance from it, and so a welcome degree of flexibility. In this respect, among the group of cyberneticians and their friends, Wiener was certainly exceptional.[17]

"Information theory," in the sense in which it was used throughout the Macy Conferences, seems much less the key to a new vision of the world than a familiar tool, a simple *means* for arriving at a number of very different ends, which the cyberneticians taught the others how to use. In the first conference, the psychoanalyst Kubie was lectured for having spoken (as Freud did) of psychic "energy": henceforth he was to distinguish energy from information.[18] Later he was instructed to speak of neuroses in terms of a reduction of the quantity of information that the nervous system can process on account of the unavailability of certain circuits.[19] When he ran into trouble defending his thesis that symbolic communication began with the human species and its language, he was shown how to define symbols as "the products of information-preserving transformations, products that have the special property of not looking like the things of which they are transforms."[20]

Information theory served also to call attention to the capacity of the nervous system for recognizing and identifying a single abstract pattern underlying different stimuli, where one stimulus is obtained from another by means of controlled distortions. The psychoacoustician Joseph Licklider, whose expertise combined electrical engineering and psychology, reported to the group on a series of fascinating experiments he had conducted on "the manner in which and extent to which speech can be distorted and remain intelligible."[21] These in fact were part of military research he had begun during the war at Harvard, motivated by the need to ensure the accurate comprehension by subordinates of orders issued by a commanding officer and received by soldiers in a disturbed or disrupted environment. The mathematical analysis that Licklider performed to measure the "intelligibility" of a message led him to propose a formula similar to Shannon's. On the strength of this he conjectured that "the listener is indeed receiving information when he understands speech."[22]

Information theory was additionally used by the cyberneticians to evaluate the redundancy of natural languages such as English and to investigate whether such redundancy might have a functional purpose.[23] They were constantly computing quantities of information, in a quite matter-of-fact way, often in order to challenge or disconfirm a hypothesis. At one point von Neumann, as we saw earlier, expressed doubt as to whether the quantity of information at the neuronal level was sufficient to account for the capacities of human memory; Pitts, in an equally matter-of-fact way, came back with a more complete calculation. In his talk at the Hixon Symposium, McCulloch estimated (citing Wiener) that the information contained in our chromosomes could specify connections between ten thousand neurons at most, whereas the number we actually possess is on the order of 10^{10}. From this he concluded that the structure of the brain was genetically determined only in its broad outlines, the rest being left to chance—which is to say, to experience and learning.[24] This was a remarkable conjecture: current theories of the "genetic envelope" and of "epigenesis by selective stabilization" in the case of developing neurons and synapses now lend it support.[25] McCulloch made reference as well to Ramón y Cajal's suggestion that learning may correspond to the establishment of new connections. At the ninth Macy Conference, Henry Quastler presented his estimates of the "complexity" of organisms, defined in terms of the quantity of information they contain, and speculated that adaptation may not be the last word in evolution, since it is unable to explain the process by which living beings *become more complex.*[26]

Does this imply, then, that Raymond Ruyer was justified in saying in his 1954 book on cybernetics and the origins of information that "the theoreticians as well as the technicians of cybernetics are at bottom uninterested in anything that is not an immediate technical problem" and that they "believe that they do not have to be more philosophical than behavioral psychologists"?[27] This opinion seems to me entirely misguided and unjust. Ruyer reproaches the cyberneticians for never having posed the problem of the *origins* of information—in his view because, as prisoners of their own mechanist postulates, they were utterly incapable of facing up to it.[28]

It is true that the problem scarcely preoccupied the cyberneticians, but this is precisely because from the beginning, as far as Wiener was concerned at least, as well as for those who sided with him at the Macy Conferences, information was to be interpreted as a *physical* variable common to all natural systems rather than as an exclusive feature of the world of *human* signal transmissions. If every organism is surrounded by information, this is simply because it is everywhere surrounded by organization, which itself, by the very fact of being differentiated, *contains* information. Information, because it *is part of* nature, is therefore independent of human interpreters who assign meaning to it. Such considerations have led the American philosopher Fred Dretske, an engineer by training, to propose a naturalist and physicalist theory of intentionality that, of all the accounts put forth so far, certainly pushes Quine's project of a "naturalized epistemology" to its furthest extent[29]—but which therefore also raises Quine's error regarding Brentano's doctrine of intentionality to its highest level.

The problem that preoccupied the cyberneticians was rather the opposite: the enormous "waste" of information that is the price of passing from sensation to perception. McCulloch observed that the eye transmits to the brain only a hundredth of the information that it receives. He speculated that there is a reason for this: an enormous excess of information is required if we are to be assured that a given event impinging upon our sense organs at a given point is not due to noise, but actually corresponds to an external object. On this view, we pay in information for the certainty that there exists a world outside of us.[30] At the seventh Macy Conference, during the discussion that followed Shannon's presentation on redundancy in English, Pitts and Stroud alluded to the "immense loss of information" that occurs when information passes from our sense organs to our mental "computer" and suggested that this loss might in fact be programmed. Pitts laid emphasis on the role of "natural laws," whose very existence he took to be proof of nature's tremendous redundancy,[31] which serves as a reservoir of information. On this point as well, the line of descent that leads from cybernetics to a philosophical position like Dretske's is obvious.

The cyberneticians were neither narrow-minded technicians nor the champions of a new science bent on wiping the slate of "orthodox" science clean. Each of these views is as false as the other. They were scientists who were trying out new conceptual instruments, constantly reflecting upon the use to which these tools could be put. Though this is a rather rare situation in the scientific world, of course, it hardly justifies talk of some "epistemological rupture." The way in which the relations among information, form, chance, and meaning were discussed well bears out this contention.

Between Form, Chance, and Meaning

It is March 1950: we are at the seventh Macy Conference. Claude Shannon has just presented the results of his recent experiments on the redundancy of written English. They involved asking a subject to make letter-by-letter guesses about a text he has never seen before. Shannon took care to point out at the outset that the notion of quantity of information was defined independently of the meaning of the message. It is fascinating to watch how this exclusion of meaning, on which information theory fundamentally rests, gradually came to be ignored during the discussion that followed. It was inevitable that meaning would force its way back in, triggering an important debate over whether it is possible to unarbitrarily separate signal from noise.[32] The tension was plain between those such as Pitts who adopted a "subjective" (or engineering) point of view, according to which the designer of a communications system can unilaterally decide which part is signal and which part is noise, and those such as Bateson who looked at the problem from the "objective" point of view of the organized system or organism being studied, according to which a system can acquire meaning as a result of random perturbations, independently of the freedom of the observer to attribute meanings to the system. Bateson mentioned the case of typing errors that lead to "meaningful distortions." Pitts snapped, "You can correct [them] astoundingly well." For some participants, however, it was obvious that if a new meaning had been created through error or chance, it had to be preserved, not corrected for.[33]

The idea began to dawn on some of the participants that chance and meaning might be two sides of the same coin and that organization is a mixture of redundancy and variety, of regularities and anomalies. Licklider cited the case of communication between two persons. In response to Marquis's claim that "the best communication occurs if you say what the listener expects you to say," Licklider disagreed, saying that the optimum should be located between two extremes: if the "correlation" between speaker and listener is zero, the listener has no expectation and understands nothing; if it is one, there is no need to listen. Von Foerster went on to consider the case of a language. There must be, he suggested, an optimal level of redundancy. The less redundancy there is in a language, the more information it can transmit; but the greater the redundancy, the more structured it is. Others were quickly to forget this insight, arguing that the less redundant a language (such as English), the more it had developed away from its "primitiveness."[34]

The notion that organization exists only as a mix of order and disorder was to be at the heart of the second cybernetics, first with the formulation of the principle of "order from noise" by von Foerster in 1960[35] and then with Atlan's development of the theory of self-organization.[36] Already in 1951, in the "Note by the Editors" that prefaced the transcript of the eighth Macy Conference, von Foerster wrote, "[I]nformation can be considered as order wrenched from disorder."[37] This theme permeated Wiener's entire work as well, as the following passage from his autobiography testifies:

> We are swimming upstream against a great torrent of disorganization, which tends to reduce everything to the heat-death of equilibrium and sameness described in the second law of thermodynamics. What Maxwell, Boltzmann, and Gibbs meant by this heat-death in physics has a counterpart in the ethics of Kierkegaard, who pointed out that we live in a chaotic moral universe. In this, our main obligation is to establish arbitrary enclaves of order and system. These enclaves will not remain there indefinitely by any momentum of their own after we have once established them. Like the Red Queen, we cannot stay where we are without running as fast as we can.
>
> We are not fighting for a definitive victory in the indefinite future. It is the greatest possible victory to be, to continue to be, and to have been. No defeat can deprive us of the success of having existed for some moment of time in a universe that seems indifferent to us.
>
> This is no defeatism, it is rather a sense of tragedy in a world in which necessity is represented by an inevitable disappearance of differentiation. The declaration of our own nature and the attempt to build up an enclave of organization in the face of nature's overwhelming tendency to disorder is an insolence against the gods and the iron necessity that they impose. Here lies tragedy, but here lies glory too.[38]

At the Macy Conferences, the representatives of the personality and culture movement simply lapped up lyrical evocations of this sort. At the seventh conference, Lawrence Frank tried to claim Wiener's authority for the sententious view that every culture creates a world based solely on the background noise of events, selecting from the surrounding chaos certain signals that it processes as messages and to which it chooses to assign meaning.[39]

Gilbert Simondon, in a very fine work first published in 1958, *Du mode d'existence des objets techniques*, based his argument on an extensive reading of the cybernetics literature that included the transactions of the Macy Conferences—something so rare that it can scacely be allowed to go unmentioned. Distancing himself from the movement, he wrote, "Cybernetics risks seeing its usefulness as an interdisciplinary scientific inquiry (the purpose that Norbert Wiener assigned to its research) undermined in part as a result of its initial postulate identifying living beings and self-regulated technological objects."[40] It is all the more remarkable, then, in

view of his criticisms of the philosophy of cybernetics, that Simondon
should have credited cybernetics with the idea that

> [i]nformation is . . . midway between pure chance and absolute regularity.
> One might say that form, conceived as absolute regularity, both spatially and
> temporally, is not information but a condition of information; it is what ac-
> commodates information, the *a priori* that receives information. . . . But in-
> formation is not form, nor a set of forms; it is the variability of forms, the
> contribution of variation in relation to form. It is the unpredictability of vari-
> ation in form, not the pure unpredictability of variation in general.[41]

Apart from Wiener, however, the cyberneticians were not very receptive
to the idea that under certain circumstances chance could produce meaning. The British physicist Donald MacKay, who (along with Alan Turing,
Grey Walter, and Ross Ashby) had participated in an informal discussion
group in London called the Ratio Club, was to learn this only too well
upon being invited by McCulloch to take part in the eighth conference, in
March 1951. When he proposed the idea of an automaton endowed with the
capacity to make inductive inferences by means of random strategies,
MacKay found himself severely criticized by Leonard Savage, who, as a
statistician, one might have thought would be sympathetic to it. Savage
argued at length that building chance into a mechanism could do nothing
to assist it in mimicking a particular human behavior, and in any case
could not improve its efficiency in solving problems.[42] But it was the cyberneticians' shocked reaction to Ross Ashby's performance at the ninth
conference the following year that most clearly revealed their prejudices
with regard to the question of chance.[43]

Claude Shannon, as we remarked a moment ago, had worked out a
theory of information that excluded all reference to meaning. It was inevitable, then, that others would attempt to construct a complementary theory dealing with semantic information. Two of these attempts were presented and discussed at the Macy Conferences: MacKay's own theory, at
the eighth, and that of Rudolf Carnap and his disciple Yehoshua Bar-
Hillel at the tenth.[44] But it was Shannon's theory that the experimental
psychologists who allied themselves with the cyberneticians nonetheless
preferred to use as a conceptual framework. They therefore came under
attack from their Gestaltist or "holistic" colleagues, who sought time and
time again to prove to them that the meanings that they thought they had
neutralized would reappear, no matter what steps they might take to
guard against this, to interfere with their experiments. At the sixth conference, John Stroud described the experiments that he was conducting for
the Navy aimed at estimating the maximum quantity of information (in
Shannon's sense) that a person is capable of absorbing per unit of time.

Klüver was easily able to show that these results were neither very meaningful nor very interesting, for the capacity for absorbing information varied enormously depending on whether a subject was presented with a meaningless succession of symbols or with a sequence whose elements taken together made sense. Following von Foerster's presentation of his quantum mechanical theory of memory (the theory that had brought him to McCulloch's attention in the first place), Klüver returned to the attack, charging that "really pure 'nonsense,' that is, material utterly and completely divorced from meanings and associations, seems to have remained an ideal that has never been realized."[45] The "holistic" point of view, in these discussions, was always directed *against* the cybernetic approach.

The conflict between those who, like Shannon, Stroud, and Licklider, believed in the *practical* possibility of abstracting from meaning and those who held this to be impossible was not only about the nature of information. Two distinct conceptions of rationality were opposed to each other. The cleavage between the two did not, however, run along the lines we have observed previously: it was not a question in this case of cyberneticians against the "holists" or Gestaltists, nor of "apriorists" against psychologizers, nor of McCulloch's style of thought against Wiener's. It concerned instead two quite different attitudes toward economic rationality. Decisive advances in axiomatization and mechanization were being made at the time in connection with this issue: first with the publication of von Neumann and Morgenstern's *Theory of Games and Economic Behavior* (1944), and then with the elaboration of the foundations of decision theory by Leonard Savage, whose *Foundations of Statistics* appeared only in 1954. The emergence of formalized theories of both games and decisions was therefore to play a part in bringing about the birth of both cybernetics and, later, cognitive science. The most ambitious effort at synthesizing the two remains to this day that of Herbert Simon, himself a pioneer of the study of administrative behavior as well as of artificial intelligence. But during the period of the first cybernetics, the relation between the two approaches was conflictual. In opposition to that cast of mind peculiar to economists, which combines an obsessive concern for logical rigor with a deliberately impoverished view of human relations—a style of thinking represented at the Macy Conferences by von Neumann, Savage, Lazarsfeld, to a certain degree Pitts, and the communications engineers Shannon, Stroud, and Licklider—there emerged an unlikely coalition made up of Wiener, McCulloch, and Bateson. McCulloch, in particular, took advantage of every possible opportunity to denigrate utility theory, which flattened all the components of desires and choice along a single dimension. (He saw red when, at the eighth conference, Savage provided a memorable example of the mischievous style of humor special to economists, who do not shrink from uttering what most of us prefer to conceal: "The value of information? Why, this is nothing other than its *cash* value!")[46] McCulloch, it needs to be remembered, was very attached to the theory of "axiological anomaly" that he had recently devised. He had succeeded in constructing a network of six neurons that embodied in a coherent way what, from the point of view of rational choice theory, was incoherent: circularity of preferences. Thus an agent preferring an option A to an option B, and option B to an option C, may actually prefer C to A. In this scheme, there being no common hierarchical scale of values, but rather a "heterarchy" of values, the good is not reducible to a common measure of utility.[47] Bateson and Wiener, for their part, used a rough version of Russell's theory of logical types to criticize applications of game theory, pointing out that one can win a battle and still lose the war—and also that even if one wins the war, one can lose one's soul in the process.[48]

Cooperation and Cognition

The linking up of the themes of information and rationality took place at the eighth conference, the occasion of an astonishing discussion that followed the presentation of a paper by the psychosociologist Alex Bavelas. Bavelas had been a student of the Gestaltist Kurt Lewin, one of the regular members of the group from the beginning, but who died shortly before the third conference. In his book *The Cybernetics Group*, Steve Heims amusingly describes the intellectual journey that led from Lewin, himself a student of Husserl and Stumpf, and a member of the Psychological Institute in Berlin, to his pupil Bavelas by the punning phrase "*Gestalten* Go to Bits" (taking "bits" in the double sense of fragments of a whole that has broken up, and of units of information).[49] Having come to the United States as a refugee in 1933, Lewin was to have a considerable influence on American psychology from the 1930s through the 1950s. Like Alfred Schutz, he tried at first to build a social science (or more precisely, a social psychology) on the basis of Husserlian phenomenology: corresponding to Schutz's concept of *Lebenswelt*, for example, was Lewin's concept of "life space." But Lewin's ambition was to make psychology a mathematical and experimental science equal to physics, and, like his mentor Wolfgang Köhler, it was in the physical concept of a field and in mathematical topology that he placed his greatest hopes. The concepts of "group dynamics" and "action-research," each of which in its turn was to enjoy a brilliant future, were due to Lewin's genius. In 1946 he became acquainted with the basic concepts of cybernetics and game theory at the first two Macy Conferences, and immediately looked for ways to apply them to his work on the psychosociology of groups. His premature death cut short this new line of research into the mechanisms of social interaction—mechanisms that mediate the relation between a leader and a crowd, for example. What might have come of such an approach to social science, aimed at applying cybernetic tools to the phenomenological analysis of totalities, is of course impossible to say.

Alex Bavelas did not have the same stature as his teacher, but he did carry on the tradition of action-research inaugurated by Lewin in both laboratory and industrial settings. Its purpose was to analyze cooperative situations, to understand the obstacles that stood in the way of improved productivity, and to devise ways to remove these obstacles by redesigning communication systems. This type of research came to attract its own following. At the eighth conference Bavelas was invited to present to the group certain results obtained using a conceptual scheme that owed almost nothing to Lewin's "life spaces" and almost everything to information theory and cybernetic concepts. The fundamental problem had to do with getting a small group of people to carry out a task that requires the cooperation of all the members of the group. In order to carry out the task they must exchange information, subject to the constraint, however, whether the mission is undertaken in the controlled setting of the laboratory or under actual factory conditions, that not all possible channels of communication are open to them: each member therefore finds himself or herself isolated to a greater or lesser degree from the others, depending on the limit set upon the number of direct interlocutors.

Bavelas described several of these experiments. One of the simplest—assuming a group of five persons, each totally isolated from the others—proceeded in the following way. Each person was instructed to write on a piece of paper an integer between 0 and 5, such that the total of the five numbers thus produced equals 17. The experiment was conducted in two versions. In the first, the person directing the experiment announces the total obtained after each try: the members of the group then try again until the desired total of 17 is obtained. In the second version, the director of the experiment simply says, "Sorry—try again," and they try again as many times as it takes to come up with the right total. Bavelas's experiments plainly showed that all of the groups studied converged on the correct answer more quickly in the second case rather than the first.

In the context of the Macy Conferences, such apparent paradoxes had the effect of revealing profound differences of attitude between the participants and between their views of the world. Unhappily in the case of the eighth conference, then, three important figures—Wiener, von Neumann, and Bateson—were absent. The discussion that followed Bavelas's presentation divided the others into roughly two camps. On the one side were Shannon, Savage, and Bigelow, who could find no interpretation for the results other than the *irrationality* of the people involved. For them, the only conceivable rationality was that of the algorithm. Suppose one asks a machine to solve a particular problem: it is unimaginable that the machine would do less well if supplied with supplementary information. This is tantamount to saying that the value of an additional unit of information can never be negative. (Nonetheless Savage, suspecting the difficulties posed by coordination, had the wit to ask: what if *five* machines were asked to solve the problem?) On the other side were Bavelas, MacKay, Kubie, Klüver, and several others, who searched for ways to make sense of the result. Kubie raised the possibility that unconscious processes were at work, questioning whether details that appear "meaningless" to the experimenter might not unconsciously be assigned a meaning by the subjects; he declined to rule out parapsychological influence.

Bavelas himself, interestingly enough, suggested a logic of specularity or mirrorlike effects. In the first version of the experiment, on being told the total obtained, each member of the group reacts by putting himself in the place of the others, assuming that the others do the same with regard to him. Thus, on being told, for example, that their total is too low, each one knows it has to go up. But since each person will assume that everyone else knows this, some may be tempted to write down a number that is lower than the one they wrote down last time, in which case the result may turn out not to go up; on the other hand, if one member worries that too many of the others will be tempted to do just this, and so writes down 5 in order to compensate for their undercorrection, it may turn out, depending on what the others actually do, that the total is too high; and so on. Accordingly, Bavelas conjectured, an indeterminacy develops that the group as a whole tries to reduce: each member privately elaborates a theory of how the group operates, each one assuming a role and assigning roles to the others. Here one sees the operation of a general rule of psychosociology: no human group long remains without a social structure.[50] MacKay, who saw himself as an ecumenicist, sought to mediate the dispute by linking up Bavelas's interpretation with Shannon's theory of information. But the cyberneticians, faithful to their dogma, would not hear of it: no machine had ever been known to identify with another machine, nor had inequalities or hierarchies ever been known to arise within a society of automata. A confused discussion of von Neumann's theory of games followed, the upshot of which was that it could not shed any light on situations of this type since they involved cooperation (or coordination) rather than conflict.

The attitude one notices here on the part of the cyberneticians with regard to the question of rationality is only a case in point of the peculiar form of narrowmindedness we have noted all along, which was to retard progress in the very fields that were animated by the spirit of cybernetics in the years ahead. In fact it was not until the 1960s, with the publication of *The Strategy of Conflict* by the game theorist Thomas Schelling[51] and of the philosopher David Lewis's *Convention*,[52] that "coordination games" were seen, despite their relative lack of mathematical interest, to pose fascinating problems of a cognitive nature. They involve the capacity of agents to put themselves in the place of others and to see the world (including themselves) from their point of view. The fact that this capacity can be endlessly represented in the minds of others led to the concept of "common knowledge," defined as infinite specularity.[53] This concept plays a key role today in a number of disciplines, from economics to artificial intelligence, as well as in thinking about the foundations of game theory and rational choice, and in political philosophy.[54] It is not an exaggeration to say that the renaissance enjoyed by game theory during the 1970s, which transformed it from a theory of limited application into one of the principal methods of analysis in analytic philosophy and the social sciences alike, was due to the analysis of coordination games—another missed rendezvous for cybernetics.

It is reasonable to suppose that if Donald MacKay was the only one of the cyberneticians (in the broad sense) to be at all receptive to the point of view expressed by Alex Bavelas, the reason had to do with his participation in Alan Turing's circle. Recall that the eighth conference took place in 1951. Turing had recently published (in October 1950) the article introducing the notion of an "imitation game" that we discussed in the first chapter. The message of this article, namely, that thinking is simulating—already present in the very concept of a universal Turing machine—might have been expected to be one of the credos of the cyberneticians. But it was not. Given that they entertained the possibility that a machine could think (not because they credited it with human faculties, but because they believed that thought was mechanical in nature), their taking the position they did with regard to Bavelas's work must be regarded, in retrospect, as a major disappointment.

Savage, however, upheld the honor of the group in concluding the discussion with a singularly penetrating insight. Throughout the existence of our group, he said in effect, we have been torn by two contradictory hopes: the one, sustained by Turing's "theorem" (as the cyberneticians persisted in referring to it), that for anything humans can do, we will always manage to find a machine that can do it as well; the other, that we will finally discover something human that a machine cannot reproduce.[55]

Cybernetic Totalities

Because it invented itself as the science of "teleological mechanisms," taking purposive beings as its object of study, cybernetics has often seen regarded as the offspring of the union between a "holistic" philosophy and modern science. This image is no less false than the others, as a reading of the transcripts of the Macy Conferences shows quite well.

The severest critics of cybernetics usually do not hide their fascination with the automata that it created. Thus Raymond Ruyer, speaking about the work of Ross Ashby, which we shall discuss further in connection with its role in giving birth to the second generation of cybernetics, remarked:

> It must be recognized that Ashby's homeostat adds a truly sensational element to the debate. . . . [It] is obviously nothing more than a machine, and yet it behaves as a whole that is independent of its parts, of their accidental injuries and constraints. One can readily imagine the philosophical conclusions that an organicist in the tradition of Goldstein[56] would draw from the performance of Ashby's machine if one were to play the nasty trick of asking him to interpret it without telling him that it was a machine. . . . We certainly are not claiming that Ashby's mechanist theory is at bottom correct, but we do recognize that it scored a point for cybernetics against antimechanist theories.[57]

Jean-Claude Beaune was later to refer to the "little cybernetic monsters," conceding however that they represent "a philosophical act of considerable import."[58] For Beaune, their specifically cybernetic quality consists in "transform[ing] their spectacular facticity into a logic of appearance. They are metaphors, philosophico-technical paradigms."[59]

Once having regained their composure (as if to say: "But these machines do not fool us!"), these critics go on to identify the true aim of cybernetics: to produce, like art, simulacra—imitations of an imitation, models of a model. Cybernetic totalization is not holistic: it is an artificial holism, a simulation of holism whose purpose is to demystify it. One therefore cannot reproach the cyberneticians for misleading anyone since they were the first ones, after the fact, to acknowledge the trick that they had played. Gilbert Simondon perfectly captured the emancipating nature of this exercise:

> Cybernetics . . . frees man from his immemorial fascination with the notion of finality [or teleological purpose]. Whereas appeal to a higher end, and to the order that realizes this end, used to be considered the final step in an attempt at justification—since, at a time when technological processes were merely causal, life was confused with finality—the introduction [with cybernetics and the concept of "teleological mechanisms"] of technological schemas of finality plays a cathartic role. Nothing that can be fabricated can provide a final justification.[60]

In the domain of political theory, interestingly enough, Jean-Jacques Rousseau has been defended against the accusation of totalitarianism along very similar lines. His "social contract," by purporting to reconstruct society on the basis of the consciousness and the will of its individual members, is seen as having likewise demystified the "transcendence" of the social whole by showing that it is amenable to human artfulness. On this view, there is no real difference between an apparently organic (social) whole and a fabricated whole.[61] Simondon goes on to say:

> [M]an escapes the condition of being subordinated to the finality of the whole in learning to fabricate finality, to design and fashion a purposive whole that he [is thereby in a position to] assess and evaluate, in order to avoid having to submit passively to a preexisting state of affairs. Cybernetics . . . liberates man from the prison of organization [i.e., from the constraints of an organized whole] by giving him the capacity to judge it [since he now has the power to fashion it according to his will], instead of having to submit to it, by venerating and showing respect for it, because he is incapable of conceiving or constituting it. In [being able for the first time to] consciously shape finality, man transcends his [immemorial] subordination.[62]

Cybernetic totalities are always artificial totalities, in which the parts are prior to the whole. In other words, they are nominal totalities that are made wholes only by the organizing consciousness of a third element, external to them—in this case the mind of the cybernetician, who perceives and conceives such totalities[63] (or, in Leibnizian terms, aggregates whose unity is accidental, unlike monads whose unity is substantial).[64] The stumbling block for cybernetics was an inability to imagine any other form of totality. When the cyberneticians said (as they often did, whether in connection with ecosystems, Ashby's homeostat, human societies, automata networks, Shannon's "Rat," ant colonies, or living organisms) that these things "learn," "choose," "solve," "remember," "try," "make mistakes," and so forth, this for them was neither more nor less meaningful than saying the same thing (as they also frequently did) about the brain or the human mind.[65] It certainly was not less meaningful, since the mind for them was only the set of properties of an interconnected network of neurons; nor was it more meaningful, since an ant colony was no more an overarching superorganism independent of the individual ants in it than the mind was a transcendent entity in relation to its network of neurons. That Bateson should have considered all these totalities as minds, or that McCulloch saw in them the basis for a new materialism, is a completely secondary issue: under either interpretation, spiritualist or materialist, the monism implicit in this view was intransigently held to be universal and to apply to any kind of organized totality.

We saw in the preceding chapter how the philosophy of mind, under the influence of its psycholinguistic analysis of representation, came to take the form of a nonreductionist monism (the two principal variants being functionalism and Davidson's "anomalous monism"). Few cognitive phi-

losophers today are prepared to join the first cyberneticians in defending
a full-blown reductionist monism; that is, to assert that mind and brain
are identical, both being machines—indeed, one and the same machine.
Among those who are, one sees that the slope that leads from the mind-
brain identity thesis to the "eliminativist" position is a slippery one. On
this latter view, which is advocated by "neurophilosophers" such as Patricia Churchland and Paul Churchland,[66] mental terms such as *belief, desire*, or *pain* designate nothing whatsoever, being purely mythical categories on the order of *witch* and *succubus*. Among biologists, Jean-Pierre
Changeux blythely slides down this same slope in *Neuronal Man*. Speaking of neural networks, he writes, "These linkages and relationships, these
'spider's webs,' this regulatory system would function *as a whole*. Can one
say that consciousness emerges from all this? Yes, if one takes the word
'emerge' literally, as an iceberg emerges from the water. But it is sufficient
to say that consciousness *is* the functioning of this regulatory system."
Having said this, he cannot resist temptation, and immediately adds,
"Man no longer has a need for the 'Spirit' [*Esprit*]; it is enough for him to
be Neuronal Man."[67]

Cybernetics, very early in its career, was to find itself confronted by
another conception of organized totalities, richer than the one it embraced
and, in a sense, aimed against it. This confrontation took place at the
Hixon Symposium in 1948, as we have already noted, and pitted Warren
McCulloch against a group of scientists that included the neurophysiologists Karl Lashley and Ralph Gerard, the psychologists Wolfgang Köhler
and Heinrich Klüver, and above all the embryologist Paul Weiss. John von
Neumann was also present. Although he too had to endure Weiss's assaults, what needs to be kept in mind about von Neumann's performance
on this occasion is his own attack upon McCulloch, which we mentioned
earlier as well and to which we shall later return. The argument laid out by
Weiss is of the highest interest for us because, to a certain degree, it prefigured the theories of autopoiesis and autonomy that were to be developed
by the Chilean school of self-organization led by Maturana and Varela.
From the point of view of the history of ideas, it is particularly arresting to
see cybernetics challenged by a movement to which its own descendants
would later contribute.

A few words about Paul Weiss and embryology are in order here.[68]
Earlier I described the failed encounter between cybernetics and what was
to become molecular biology, or how physics, which under the impetus of
Schrödinger's *What Is Life?* was preparing to conquer biology and to impose a mechanical interpretation of the order of living things, had snubbed
cybernetics. I have insisted that one cannot infer from this missed rendezvous that there was not a profound affinity between the two enterprises.
The course of history has amply demonstrated this affinity, since it was as

a result of a cybernetic and information-processing metaphor—the genetic "program"—that molecular biology was able to establish itself as a discipline. Now, in the immediate aftermath of the war, there already existed a science of living things that, having enjoyed moments of prewar glory (such as the Nobel Prize awarded in 1935 to the German Hans Spemann for his work in the early 1920s on the triton), was to resist— unsuccessfully in the event—the mechanization of biology that was now being carried out by the physicists. This science was embryology.

A new paradox awaits us: whereas the physicists-turned-biologists conceived of the order of living things as the result of a discontinuity, order having been snatched from the jaws of the molecular disorder that underlies physical laws, the embryologists sought to conceive of biological order as naturally emerging from this very same disorder, without any gap in continuity. The former, following Delbrück and Schrödinger, believed that life obeyed its own laws, radically different from those of physics. (Niels Bohr had already argued in 1932 that life is *irreducible*, in the same sense that the quantum of action is irreducible in quantum mechanics.)[69] According to this view, life is not subject to the jurisdiction of thermodynamics, because it is mechanical, or machinelike, entirely coded in the genetic material of heredity—yielding the additional paradox that the nascent discipline of molecular biology was much more inclined than cybernetics, as we have seen, to treat information as something falling outside the domain of physical law.

To the question "Can science account for the enigma of life, this anomalous departure from the general tendency toward disorder that characterizes physical phenomena?" the embryologists, on the other hand, delivered an answer that was much more in keeping with the traditional approach of science. Embryology is concerned with the experimental analysis of the physicochemical processes responsible for the development and differentiation of the embryo. Having detected in these processes no singularity or anomaly by comparison with the processes that produce ordinary, inorganic physical objects, it had concluded already by the 1940s that the special characteristic of its object of study—the astonishing capacity of living things to become more complex—was to be attributed to a particular type of organization that it called "self-organization," a term that was to acquire a technical meaning among embryologists in the course of the following decade.[70] If Ilya Prigogine, the Nobel Prize– winning chemist who proposed a thermodynamics of irreversible, far-from-equilibrium processes (better known as the theory of "dissipative structures"), was able to speak of the "self-organization" of matter in the late 1960s, it may have been because he frequented the company of embryologists at the University of Brussels at the time.[71] In the field of thermodynamics, no less than in the field of embryology, there was a strong conviction that the entropy of chemical processes and the complexity of living things were connected, and that success in elucidating this connection did not in the least depend on applying categories borrowed from mechanical engineering or information theory.[72]

Born in 1898, Paul Weiss was one of the most prominent exponents of an approach to embryology whose time was coming to an end in the years following the Second World War. A theoretical biologist by training, faced with the challenge represented by the rising movement of molecular biology, he opposed the reductionism and determinism of the theory of genetic information while resisting the challenge to biology posed by cybernetics as well. At the end of his career, in the early 1970s, he well expressed the point of his longstanding campaign against these rival approaches by saying that when one attempts to describe biological order in terms of mechanisms and transfers of information, one has explained nothing—the problem remains in its entirety:

> The question thus remains how to get from an incredibly diversified scramble of molecular activities to the integrated overall systemic order of the cell; from the imprecise courses and variable performances of individual cells to organs which are so infinitely more similar among members of a given species than are the detailed componental performances of their unit members in morphogenesis. . . . It is in entering the domain of these problems that a concept of "information transfer" breaks down, much as a railroad train on tracks that suddenly end in a sandy wasteland, beyond which lies the point of destination, will never get there; or rather could get there only if at the end of the pre-set linear guidance along the tracks, free navigation across the intervening trackless space, steered by systems dynamics, takes over. In other words, what appeared as an unstructured space is not truly a wasteland, but is a system in which the role of linear mechanical tracks is performed by the guiding cues of the dynamic field structure of the total complex.[73]

In this we hear an echo of the severe criticism of cybernetics that Weiss had delivered not long before at the 1968 Alpbach Symposium. The theme of the conference ("Beyond Reductionism") conveys some sense of the atmosphere, in effect a glorification of general system theory. Its founder, Ludwig von Bertalanffy, was in attendance. In order to highlight the novelty of systemic approaches, Bertalanffy, in a gesture that would have seemed utterly out of place (inconceivable in fact) at the Macy Conferences, put "mechanistic" and "reductionist" science on trial: behaviorism, psychoanalysis, molecular biology, the conception of the brain as a computer; in short, all "physicalistic" approaches guilty of neglecting, or even denying, the problems of organized complexity, interactive processes, goal-directed behavior, and negentropic trends. Reading this diatribe, one is eager to know in which camp he located cybernetics—a science that was at once "mechanistic," "reductionist," and "physicalistic" and that, on the other hand, explicitly considered purposive behavior and negentropic trends as coming within its purview. Soon enough the answer becomes clear: "The best known of the various systems approaches is the theory of 'communication and control,'" he says, while hastening to express regret that systems theory was too often reduced to cybernetics.[74] With McCulloch's death the following year, in 1969, cybernetics had therefore already fallen prey to every imaginable sort of confusion.

Bertalanffy's identification of cybernetics as a systemic science of complexity is all the more stunning since a number of years earlier, in 1955, discussing the contribution made by cybernetics to the study of organized totalities, he had distinguished (in a way very much like that of embryology) between primary and secondary regulation within systems, relegating the latter, by virtue of its mechanical character, to a subordinate place. The primary type, described as "dynamic interaction," is the more important of the two; the secondary type, which takes the form of feedback mechanisms, is simply superimposed upon the first. "This state of affairs," Bertalanffy writes,

> is a consequence of a general principle of organization which may be called progressive mechanization. At first, systems—biological, neurological, psychological or social—are governed by dynamic interaction of their components; later on, fixed arrangements and conditions of constraint are established which render the system and its parts more efficient, but also gradually diminish and eventually abolish its equipotentiality. Thus, dynamics is the broader aspect, since we can always arrive from general systems laws to machinelike function by introducing suitable conditions of constraint, but the opposite is not possible.[75]

It was therefore within this "systems" framework that Weiss laid out his conception of self-organizing systems at the Alpbach Symposium. Speaking of processes of cellular synthesis, he referred to systems that were "self-contained," "self-perpetuating," and "self-sustaining." The point of speaking in this way was to discredit the notion of a genetic *program*: such processes, Weiss emphasized, "in order to occur at all, [require] the specific cooperation of their own terminal products."[76] Unlike the cyberneticians, Weiss made a very clear distinction between "machines" and "systems." The latter are natural, rather than nominal, totalities: "Systems are products of our experience with nature, and not mental constructs."[77] Nonetheless systems are not monads, and accounting for them does not amount to holism (insofar as holism treats wholes as substances or essences). This was not a return, then, to the old organicism of Aristotle or Leibniz. Weiss explained that he preferred not to follow Gerard and Koestler in using nouns to characterize the systemic nature of systems, since these terms ("orgs" and "holons," respectively, in their terminology) might be interpreted to suggest that wholes are "disembodied super-agencies" that can be distilled off and separated from the totalizing dynamic.[78] What Weiss was proposing was a new sort of organicism, peculiar to totalities that are neither monads nor simple aggregates. This approach was neither holist nor reductionist: it aimed instead at "reconciling" reductionism and holism through the adaptation of modern science to "the type of ordered complexes which we designate as systems."[79] Not only, then, did cybernetics not invent this approach; it was deliberately formulated as a weapon to be used against cybernetics.

Weiss could not find words harsh enough to criticize what he regarded as the abusive use of cybernetic metaphors in molecular biology. Speaking of biologists who interpreted the order that characterizes living things as an expression of genetic information, he wrote:

> Instead of reversing the rigorous objective methodology, which has marked the successful descent from the organism to the gene, and exploring how far one could effectively synthesize any system of higher order from nothing but genes in free interaction in an environment devoid of order, they had recourse to pretentious anthropomorphic terms, which evaded or obscured the issue. One simply bestowed upon the gene the faculty of spontaneity, the power of "dictating," "informing," "regulating," "controlling," etc., the orderless processes in its unorganized milieu, so as to mould the latter into the co-ordinated teamwork that is to culminate in an accomplished organism. It is at once evident that all those terms are borrowed from the vocabulary of *human systems behaviour*, especially the brain; in short, terms reserved for precisely the kind of complex group dynamics that cannot be pieced together by sheer summation of componental contributions. Therefore, to contend that genes can "determine" the systemic wholeness of the organism, while at the same time being driven to invok[e] the systems analogy of brain action in order to endow gene action with the required integrating power, is logically such a circular argument that we can readily dismiss it from serious scientific consideration.[80]

System and Autonomy

Let us go back to 1948 and the Hixon Symposium. The ground for the attack on cybernetics had been well prepared by Karl Lashley's purely neurophysiological critique of McCulloch's theory. The signal that enters through the sense organs, he argued in effect, does not find its way into a nervous system whose neurons are for the most part inactive or at rest, as the dominant neurological theory of the time maintained. To the contrary, the cerebral cortex is to be seen as an immense network of reverberating circuits that are constantly active. In the absence of external stimulation, this network becomes stabilized through the formation of regular *patterns* of activity that fulfill a great many integrative functions having a motor, temporal, syntactical, or some other character. The afferent impulses act upon this substrate to reorganize preexisting neuronal patterns rather than simply traveling along localized conducting pathways to produce an output. The output is the result of the interaction between a perturbational event and a global form or pattern that integrates an entire system of spontaneously interacting neurons. As Simondon later observed, the information produced is neither form, nor a set of forms, but rather consists in a variation in form. But here, the lesson was addressed to McCulloch.[81] In support of his claims, Lashley cited his own well-known experiments on monkeys and rats, which showed that important parts of the cerebral cortex can be removed without their behavior and capacities being profoundly altered as a result. From this he concluded that one cannot uphold, as McCulloch did, the thesis of spatial specialization in the brain of functions and habits.[82]

Today, Jean-Pierre Changeux insists in his turn on this spontaneous activity. He remarks that the "activity [evoked by peripheral stimulation] in fact constitutes only a fraction of the total activity that can be observed, even in the absence of obvious sensory stimulation." He goes on to say, in a passage that is perfectly consonant with Lashley's argument, that

> variations in a physical parameter in the environment are translated into variations in nerve impulses. . . . A chain of successive reactions, explicable in strictly physico-chemical terms, *regulates the spontaneous activity of the oscillator, which preexists all interaction with the outside world.* The impulses produced are therefore independent from the physical stimulus to which the organ is sensitive. The sense organs behave like regulators of molecular clocks. The stimulation that they receive from the outside world sets them forward or backward and corrects their timing. There is no direct analogy, however, between the physical stimulus received from the environment and the nervous signal produced.[83]

It was left to Weiss, at the Hixon Symposium, to formulate a critique similar to that of Lashley but in the language of self-organizing systems theory. No theory of the nervous system can claim to account for the facts, he said, that ignores its fundamental characteristic: autonomy. McCulloch, in his talk, had given the example of pressing on the eyeball, which makes us see light where there is no light. The propositional signals conveyed by the nerve impulse are thus wrong or false signals, he asserted. Weiss replied that there was no more falsity involved in this case than in the case of an impression released by radiant energy. Both situations manifest the same characteristic capacity of the central optical apparatus to produce an activity that is sensed as light, whether or not it is "adequately" stimulated or not.[84] McCulloch's view, he added, was radically different from his own: McCulloch regarded the central nervous system as a simple machine for transforming incoming messages into outgoing messages; he saw it, by contrast, as a system with its own internal coherence—a coherence whose characteristics are not the mere reflection of sensory stimulation. The question of determining whether this autonomous activity is generated by neuronal circuits, as Lashley supposed, or whether it is the result of a metabolic process expressed in the form of a global electric field, as Gerard postulated, was secondary here. What mattered, Weiss argued, was being able finally to deliver the coup de grâce to the old idea of associationist psychology that the structure of the input shaped the structure of the output. This was not to say, of course, that the nervous system is cut off from the external world; it simply meant that the input acts only as a trigger or release mechanism, which "chooses" among various modes of autonomous functioning of the system and may possibly alter them.[85] One can only admire the clairvoyance of these comments by Weiss, which already in 1948 exhibited the spirit that would animate ANN-style connectionist research in the mid-1980s. Although this research readily lends itself to a phenomenological interpretation, as we noticed in the previous chapter, it should be kept in mind that Weiss's arguments were initially deployed against cybernetics.

At the Hixon Symposium, therefore, McCulloch appeared isolated, having been found guilty of "atomism"[86] and reductionism. Weiss was later to revive his critique of atomistic explanations, proposing in their place a principle of "stratified determinism." This principle treated self-organization in the living world as the spontaneous emergence of a stable collective order among a population of elements interacting in variable and loosely determined ways. Thus Weiss wrote twenty years later, "Considering the cell as a population of parts of various magnitudes, the rule of order is objectively described by the fact that the resultant behavior of the population as a whole is infinitely less variant from moment to moment than are the momentary activities of its parts."[87]

Every living organism is a hierarchical system, Weiss explained, whose higher levels of integration are not reducible to lower levels. There are "discontinuities" among levels. Weiss's antireductionism was not advanced, however, as a holism: this would have been every bit as simplistic as the atomism he criticized to the extent that it would have substituted one ultimate level of explanation for another, replacing elements by the whole. Even if he did not use the expression, Weiss enunciated instead a doctrine of circular causality among interlocking or nested levels of integration. Of course he could not use the term "circular causality," since for him it symbolized the cybernetic approach—the target of his attack. It is nonetheless undeniable that this notion much better represents Weiss's thinking, paradoxically, than that of the cyberneticians. In a "system" (that is to say, an organism), the laws of physics allow the individual elements a number of degrees of freedom. This indeterminacy at the lower level ends up being reduced by the constraints imposed upon it by the integrated activity of the whole—constraints that themselves result from the composition of elementary activities. The whole and its elements therefore mutually determine each other. It is this codetermination that accounts for the complexity of living beings[88]—exactly the point that Francisco Varela sought to make a decade later in formulating his "principles of biological autonomy." What matters for our purposes here is that cybernetics failed to grasp this point, despite the fact that "circular causality" was the dominant theme of its founding conferences.

It is alarming to note, moreover, reviewing the official record of the Macy Conferences, to what an extent the theme of circularity itself was absent. There was, of course, talk of feedback; and the existence and role of "reverberating" neuronal circuits was, of course, regularly mentioned as well. But beyond these—the most elementary forms of circular causality—one finds very little. At the first conference, Wiener suggested building a Russellian paradox into a computer, as a result of which it would be plunged into an endless cycle of oscillations. This idea greatly appealed to Bateson, who, at the ninth conference, discussing the mechanisms of humor, declared that it would not trouble him a bit to say that an electric buzzer laughs.[89] But this is merely foolish. The index to the transcripts of the last five conferences is eloquent in its silence. Under the heading "circular," only a single reference is given: to the statement of a well-known literary critic of the period, Ivor Richards, who spoke at the eighth conference of the type of language needed to talk about language. There followed a rather pointless discussion, which, however, contained the sole reference to Gödel's incompleteness theorem in the published transcripts—a purely pro forma gesture, with no practical consequence for the debate.[90] Under "self" only one entry is listed, referring the reader to a remark made in passing by von Foerster about the possibility of self-communication.[91] When von Foerster, in his review of Steve Heims's book on von Neumann and Wiener, reproached the author for not having given circular causality its rightful place in the history of cybernetics, it is quite clear that he was confusing the original cybernetics movement with what he called second-order cybernetics.[92]

Complexity: The Model Becomes Blurred

As Gilbert Simondon rightly observed, the limits of cybernetics derived above all from the fact that right until the end it remained the prisoner of its initial assumption, which postulated "the identity of living beings and self-regulated technical objects."[93] Contrary to what is sometimes said, this was not because the cyberneticians were primarily technicians or engineers. If they took such a great interest in machines, this was not out of a concern with useful *applications* of an already established body of scientific knowledge, but because, to their way of thinking, machines represented the physical embodiment of theories, or hypotheses, of a mixed logico-mathematical type.

At the eighth conference, Shannon presented his automaton, which he had christened "Rat." The cyberneticians fell under its spell at once. Von Foerster recorded the group's "fascination of watching Shannon's innocent rat negotiate its maze" in these terms: it "does not derive from any obvious similarity between the machine and a real rat; they are, in fact, rather dissimilar. The mechanism, however, is strikingly similar to the notions held by certain learning theorists about rats and about organisms in general."[94]

Whether or not cybernetics was in fact the "metaphysics of the atomic age," as Heidegger supposed, we are now in a position to appreciate what was argued at the beginning of this book, namely, that it gave final expression to the principle of *Verum et factum convertuntur*. Jerome Lettvin's portrait of the intellectual evolution of Warren McCulloch after 1952 provides a striking confirmation of this point. In a curious exchange of roles, while the logician Pitts abandoned formal models to pursue experimental research on the nervous system, the neurophysiologist McCulloch was to devote all his efforts to theory and logic. Disappointed by the methods of the neurosciences, Lettvin tells us, "he was dedicated to knowing how the brain works in the way that the creator of any machine knows its workings. The key to such knowledge is not to analyze observation but to create a model and then compare it with observation by mapping. But the poiesis must come first, and McCulloch would rather have failed in trying to create a brain than to have succeeded in describing an existing one more fully."[95] Lettvin adds it was not by accident that McCulloch's circle at MIT at the time should have included Seymour Papert and Marvin Minsky, who would go on to be founders of artificial intelligence.

This evolution in McCulloch's thought, which may more generally be described as the progressive emancipation of the tool that the scientist uses to recreate the world from the reality of the world itself, was in a sense announced by an article on the role of models in science that Wiener and

Rosenblueth published in 1945 in the same journal that had accepted their foundational article of two years earlier.[96] The article began by recalling the importance that the activity of modeling has perennially enjoyed in science. The scientist, lacking the power to reign over a part of the world as master and possessor, constructs an image of it that is simpler but at the same time as faithful to it as possible, acquiring in this way a mastery over the image—a kind of fetish, in effect—if not over the world. In the course of the article the authors consider not only formal models, which are pure intellectual constructions, but also material models, which, like the objects they represent, are objects of the world themselves. They conclude by considering what happens when model making is pushed to the furthest extreme possible: the case of an object whose only satisfactory material model is the object itself. This case, which Wiener may have gotten from Josiah Royce, with whom he studied at Harvard from 1911 to 1913,[97] was to haunt the Macy Conferences—sometimes in very explicit ways, as the exchange between Gerard and McCulloch at the ninth conference shows. Ironically, or perhaps out of false modesty, Gerard suggested that what the mathematicians really seemed to want the neurophysiologists to do was to furnish them with the data they needed to be able to construct their models, without distancing themselves too far from reality. Reality had become a mere means to a higher end: model making. To this McCulloch replied, "The best model for the behavior of the brain is the behavior of the brain."[98] But more often, and then usually in an unreflective way, object and model exhibited an awkward tendency during these discussions to constantly switch roles. The ambivalence of the very word "model," as we have noticed, was thus revealed: the model may be either that which imitates or that which is, or deserves to be, imitated.

Typical in this regard was the extreme confusion of the debate over the concepts of digital and analogical at the seventh conference—so confused that some of the participants were beside themselves by the end. We have already referred to it as one of the most heated moments of the conferences, opposing partisans of a "continuist" conception of the nervous system and their "neuronist" adversaries. In this context "analogical" meant continuous, and "digital" discrete. More precisely, as von Neumann and Pitts explained, if the action of a continuous variable on the dynamic of a system depends solely on the fact that its value either exceeds or does not exceed a certain threshold, one can then *describe* the role that it plays in the economy of the system as being that of a "digital" variable of the yes or no (0 or 1) type; otherwise, such a variable is called "analogical." In this sense, some parts of natural reality can be said to be analogical. Inevitably, however, since one is also—especially—talking here of machines, conceived as models or representations of some natural reality, the word "analogical" can be understood as referring not to a relation internal to the system of the machine but to a relation between the machine and its real-world counterpart, the natural object it is supposed to represent. Accordingly, there is no obstacle to regarding machines as analogical in this second sense but digital in the first sense. What, then, is to be said in the case of the central nervous system? As the organ responsible for all representation, it is a natural object of a quite particular kind. In this case the two senses we have distinguished coalesce, and rather quickly we realize that we do not know what we are saying when we talk about artificial, which is to say materialized, representations of the brain.[99] At the seventh conference, it was the very notion of a model that became progressively more blurred—unsurprisingly, to the extent that it was usually supposed to involve a hierarchical relationship between an original and a reproduction. For now the difference between facts and their descriptions began to vanish, hierarchy giving way to an equivalence relation by virtue of the fact that the same formal model accounts for both.[100] The world and its representations thus found themselves flattened by logic. In this respect cybernetic models anticipated poststructuralism: they were only models of themselves, or else of other models—mirrors of mirrors, speculums reflecting no reality beyond themselves.[101]

The only one of the cyberneticians to grasp this fact and the implications of the shift in meaning that underlay it was von Neumann. From Burks we know that he came to take an interest in computing as a result of the nonlinear problems he had run up against in his research on fluid dynamics. It was his view, for example, that chemistry would achieve the rank of a pure science only when a way had been found to solve the equations of quantum mechanics. In the meantime, he said, almost everything that we know about the solutions to these equations we owe to experiments carried out on the physical systems themselves—a singular reversal since, no matter that a model is by definition simpler and more completely analyzable than the object it represents, now it is the natural object that serves as the model of the mathematical object, rather than the other way around.

This dramatic revision of the idea of a model occurred at the same time as a movement in the direction of studying "complex" objects in the sense in which von Neumann had defined the term. In the case of a complex object, the mathematical model—an artificial object—loses its status as an instrument of mastery and control because no one knows how to *solve* the system of equations that constitutes it. This means that the complexity of the real object cannot be reduced by mathematical modeling, and that only the history of the object's actual evolution in the world will enable us to grasp the full range of its properties. This revolutionary idea, which the sciences of nature (and of the artificial) were only just now to discover, was in fact an old insight of the social sciences. This should perhaps not seem

very surprising since, after all, there is no object in the physical or mechanical world that approaches the complexity of a society. It was not an
accident that in the late 1930s Friedrich von Hayek should have consulted
the following passage from Vilfredo Pareto's *Manual of Political Economy*. Pareto noted in 1906 that the general model of economic equilibrium
developed by Léon Walras and himself, which formalized the mechanism
by which prices were set in a competitive market,

> has by no means the purpose to arrive at a numerical calculation of prices.
> Let us make the most favourable assumption for such a calculation, let us
> assume that we have triumphed over all the difficulties of finding the data of
> the problem and that we know the *ophélimités* [i.e., "utilities" or desirability]
> of all the different commodities for each individual, and all the conditions of
> production of all the commodities, etc. This is already an absurd hypothesis
> to make. Yet it is not sufficient to make the solution of the problem possible.
> We have seen that in the case of 100 persons and 700 commodities there will
> be 70,699 conditions (actually a greater number of circumstances which we
> have so far neglected will further increase that number); we shall therefore
> have to solve a system of 70,699 equations. This exceeds practically the
> power of algebraic analysis, and this is even more true if one contemplates
> the fabulous number of equations which one obtains for a population of
> forty millions and several thousand commodities. In this case the roles would
> be changed: it would not be mathematics which would assist political econ-
> omy, but political economy would assist mathematics. In other words, if one
> could really know all these equations, the only means to solve them which is
> available to human powers is to observe the practical solution given by the
> market.[102]

The ideological implication, at least as far as Hayek is concerned, is
clear: only the market can tell us what it can do. The best, and simplest,
model for the behavior of the market is the behavior of the market itself.
The information that the market marshals and places at the service of
those who allow themselves to be carried forward by its dynamic is not
reducible: no one can claim to possess this information, still less govern
the "blind"—but ultimately beneficial—"forces of the social process."[103]
Hayek's critique of "constructivist rationalism" in social science can
therefore be seen as having anticipated von Neumann's critique of McCulloch's artificialist philosophy.

A mathematical model describing a complex object is itself a complex
object. One of its possible "models," as we have just seen, is the real object itself. But, thanks to von Neumann, the appearance of large calculating machines opened a new possibility: computer *simulation*. The mathematical object is now treated in its turn as a natural object. Its definition
is not "genetic": that is, one cannot deduce from the definition of such an

object all its properties. Accordingly, to know such an object, one must turn to experimentation, using the representation generated by the computer. Very early on, then, von Neumann was sensitive to the notion that our intellectual constructions, once they reach a critical threshold of complexity, are not radically different in character from the objects of the physical world. (That he should therefore have been prepared to "deconstruct" the hierarchical relation inherent in the concept of a model seems unsurprising in retrospect.) In any case it was this—essentially philosophical—notion that furnished von Neumann with the energy and motivation needed to design the electronic computer and to oversee its development.[104]

It was in the course of his work on automata theory that von Neumann was to refine this notion of complexity. Treating complexity as a magnitude of a thermodynamical type, he conjectured that below a certain threshold it is degenerative, meaning that the degree of organization can only decrease, but that above this threshold an *increase in complexity* becomes possible. Now this threshold of complexity, he supposed, is also the point at which the structure of an object becomes simpler than the description of its properties. In the usual case, which is that of simple machines, it is less complicated to describe in words what the automaton can do than to reproduce the structure of its wiring. For complex automata, the opposite is true: it would be simpler—indeed, infinitely more simple—to describe the structure of the automaton than to completely specify its behavior. Von Neumann, as we have seen, was to base his critique of the McCulloch-Pitts model at the Hixon Symposium on just this argument. In support of his conjecture, he invoked certain results of formal logic, confessing that he had subjected Gödel's ideas to a slight alteration. "It's a theorem of Gödel that the next logical step, the description of an object, is one class type higher than the object and is therefore asymptotically [?] infinitely longer to describe."[105] This passage, taken from a 1949 paper edited by Burks, is not as clear as one might wish. By "description of an object" one should understand "description of the behavior of an object," and by "object," the "structure of the object." The carelessness shown here by the great mathematician may be a sign of how blurred the concept of a model had become even in his mind.

Gödel, whom Burks consulted on this matter after von Neumann's death, proposed various ways for justifying the assertion—while acknowledging that, though they were for many years colleagues at the Institute of Advanced Study in Princeton, they had never discussed it together![106] His first thought was to invoke Tarski's 1933 theorem on the undefinability of truth. This theorem states that for any consistent language, it is impossible to characterize the set of true sentences of the language using a purely syntactical predicate. Semantics is therefore irreducible to syntax (the real point, Gödel added, of the incompleteness theorem).[107] It is significant that, in laying the groundwork for his nonreductionist (or "anomalous") monism, Donald Davidson later used Tarski's theorem to illustrate, metaphorically, what he took to be the irreducible dualism of mental properties and physical properties: the mental is to the physical as semantics is to syntax.[108]

Von Neumann's conjecture about complexity also cleared the way for a nonreductionist materialism, albeit a quite different one from Davidson's. It renders the following two propositions, for example, noncontradictory: first, that physicochemical mechanisms are capable of producing life; second, that life is (infinitely) more complex than the physicochemical processes that generate it. It then becomes coherent to embrace an ontology that is both nonsubstantialist (in this case, nonvitalist) *and* nonreductionist. This conclusion seems remarkable if one notes that nonreductionist ontologies are almost always substantialist, and nonsubstantialist ontologies almost always reductionist.

However, it would be simpler, Gödel noted, to justify von Neumann's conjecture by reference to the properties of the universal Turing machine. Given the undecidability of the halting problem, no more economical way exists to decribe the machine's behavior than to enumerate all of its possible outputs—an infinite number. Von Neumann, alone among the cyberneticians, displayed a sensitivity to this aspect of Turing's work and of formal logic in general. Whereas the others appealed to Turing's thesis (which they illegitimately took to be a "theorem") at every available opportunity, as if to strengthen their faith in the reducibility of human behavior to the functioning of a machine, he took the opposite view, pointing out the genuinely paradoxical lesson that the behavior of a machine is not as trivial as it is usually supposed to be, since no machine can completely predict it.

It is not hard to imagine the conclusions von Neumann would be led to draw from his ideas about complexity in relation to the philosophy of modeling. At the Hixon Symposium, finding himself taxed by the neurophysiologists (including McCulloch) for not stressing enough the difference between natural and artificial automata, he replied that this distinction would grow weaker and weaker over time. Soon, he prophesied, the builders of automata would find themselves as helpless before their creations as we ourselves feel in the presence of complex natural phenomena.[109] The model, which before had been hierarchically subordinated to a reality that it managed only to mimic, stood now as the equal of its referent. Consider the problem of trying to model a natural object whose complexity exceeds the critical threshold posited by von Neumann. The model, if it is to be faithful to what it represents, must also exceed this threshold. But then it will be not only a model of its object but also a model of itself, or rather of its own behavior. At this point it no longer takes much for the model to turn its attention inward, as it were, and to concentrate upon itself rather than upon its original object.

And so it was that neurophysiology came to give way to artificial intelligence. The autonomy of the model was bound to follow from the modeling of autonomous systems. On the one hand, it was a source of great excitement, for it held out the prospect of realizing a paradoxical ambition—to build an automaton, which is to say a being that is the source of its own law. Surely this ambition, to be the cause of a being that is the absolute cause of itself, was the height of the will to power. At the same time, however, it was full of danger, carrying with it the risk that man would finally lose himself in the mirror held up by a being created in his own image.

CHAPTER 6

Aspects of a Failure

The symbolic world is the world of the machine.

—JACQUES LACAN[1]

F OR SOMEONE who, like this writer, is predisposed to regard cybernetics and all that it hoped to achieve with sympathy, even gratitude, the feeling that finally emerges from a critical survey of its history is one of keen disappointment. The new discipline saw itself as the avant-garde of scientific investigation, as much by virtue of its object—the mind, this masterpiece of creation—as by virtue of its concepts, which until then had been ignored by physics (teleology, information, circular causality, feedback, and so on), and of its style, which was reflective in the sense that it reflected upon the use of its conceptual tools. Did this self-confidence amount to arrogance, born of the conviction that a decisive step in the advance of science had been taken, or was it simply an instance of the type of closed-mindedness that every scientific "paradigm," new or old, requires of its adherents? Whatever the explanation, the truth remains that cybernetics managed to botch what might have been productive encounters with any number of potential allies. What a waste this was! We have already examined its failed rendezvous with the life sciences, whether molecular biology, embryology, or neurophysiology; with psychology, which on the most charitable interpretation it regarded as little more than a neighboring territory to be annexed; and with phenomenology, whose philosophy of mind was perhaps better suited to it than the branch of analytical philosophy that bears this name today. One might also mention the absence of any contact with the physics of disordered systems, all the more since this was to be one of the sources many years later of the approach to computational modeling of the brain now called neoconnectionism. I would like to conclude this study with a brief analysis of two additional and, historically speaking, very important missed opportunities: the failure to take advantage of the perspective opened up by the notion of complexity; and the almost total neglect of supporting arguments offered by the human and social sciences.

Nonetheless, the kinship between the cybernetic project and the various revolutionary philosophical and scientific enterprises that have succeeded it (sometimes acknowledging its influence, but more often preferring to keep quiet), from general system theory to molecular biology and cognitive science, cannot be denied. That these enterprises have sometimes affirmed their identity *in reaction against* cybernetics must not obscure the fact that, when everything is said and done, they owe their very existence to the initiative taken by the men and women of the Cybernetics Group who met regularly, at the Beekman Hotel on Park Avenue in New York City, in a joint attempt to build a new science of mind.

Before we go on, one final, sad note. Those who still today regard themselves as carrying on the cybernetic cause typically come together for meetings at the invitation of groups dedicated to family psychotherapy. Family psychotherapy is certainly a respectable discipline—but that it should be practically the only discipline to host cybernetic meetings at the end of the twentieth century seems rather awkwardly to echo the misunderstanding that presided over the Macy Conferences themselves, the dream of world peace having now been reduced to the rather smaller hope of domestic peace among married couples. The men and women who were the first to believe in the possibility of opening up the realm of the mind to scientific investigation deserved a finer memorial than this.

Learning about Complexity

Von Neumann had raised the issue of complexity, but it was not owing to his influence that the other cyberneticians were to become acquainted with it. The exception, of course, was McCulloch, who was troubled by von Neumann's critique of his constructivist approach—all the more so since in 1946, with the help of Pitts, he had taken a step himself in the direction of complexity by standing his own problem on its head. In the J. A. Thompson lecture he gave that year, entitled "Finality and Form in Nervous Activity," he drew upon the result described in the 1943 paper with Pitts, namely, that every "idea" can be embodied in a neural "net." But do such networks, he asked, which are very precisely constructed for the purpose of accomplishing this or that performance, actually exist in the brain? The answer he gave was that it was unlikely they existed, because genes are not by themselves sufficient to specify the exact wiring plan of the entire system. It is therefore necessary, he concluded, to work on the assumption that networks are partly random and to inquire into the type of properties that they are capable of developing.[2] It was not certain, however, whether this change in method, as remarkable as it was, would be accompanied by a corresponding change in the attitude toward modeling. That no such change would be forthcoming became clear at the ninth conference, when Pitts, responding to Ashby, conjectured that the Turing thesis holds in the case of random networks as well.[3] There was therefore no move to get outside of the "artificialist" or "constructivist" mode of thought, according to which one assumes a particular function and then deduces from it the structure needed to bring it about.

McCulloch was the first to claim credit for this type of approach, commonly called "top-down," since it consists in moving from the properties of the whole to those of the elements and their connections. On being asked at the Hixon Symposium which was his primary interest, the nervous system or computing machines, he replied that at the level of design there was no difference between them to the extent that the tasks they were capable of executing prescribed their structure.[4] At the same time he found himself reproached for "atomism." This characterization, the justice of which he himself acknowledged, alluded to his interest in "bottom-up" approaches, which begin by contrast with a set of elements, completely specified together with their connections, and proceed to deduce from them the properties of the whole that they make up. An example of this was his assertion that the main tenets of Gestalt psychology were "deducible" from the kind of neurophysiology that he practiced.[5]

Far from being contradictory, this reversibility in the movement of his thought between the whole and its parts was the mark of what might be called a simple (as opposed to a complex) approach to reality. If the totality can be readily deduced from its elements, it is because the elements already contain the whole intelligence of the totality: they are intelligent— too intelligent, it might be objected—because they were designed *for* the totality. This can be seen especially clearly in the use of cybernetic metaphors by molecular biology: genes and enzymes are endowed with all the qualities of human thought and will, since they are considered to be capable of informing, regulating, directing, transcribing, and translating.[6] By contrast, the view of the organization of living things as self-organization must be regarded as neither bottom-up nor top-down since it implies the codetermination of the whole and its elements. The problem as it was posed by Paul Weiss, and as revived by neoconnectionists today, is one of exploring the stable collective behaviors that can be produced by a network of interconnected elements that has only randomly been defined. It is essential that "random" no longer be understood here as implying that the system is not deterministic, only that the connections among the elements of the system have been chosen at random. The connections are therefore not destined a priori to accomplish a collective result; instead, the particular totality that they ultimately produce under thus-and-such circumstances reveals a posteriori their role and meaning in the functioning of the whole.

As it turned out, the cyberneticians had to deal with this approach, so different from the one they had set for themselves. It was not presented to them in a technical way by a theoretician. They encountered it in the practical experience of certain of the scientists whom they invited to their conferences, experimentalists directly engaged with the natural or the living world. I shall limit myself here to two cases that we briefly examined earlier from another perspective.

The cybernetic interpretation of the experiments by Alex Bavelas, it will be recalled, concentrated on the task to be carried out and judged the results achieved by the group against this objective, comparing them with those of a machine. The notion that a supplementary piece of information might have the effect of making the problem harder to solve could only be regarded as a sign of irrationality. But what did Bavelas himself do as an experimentalist? Putting aside the objective that he had assigned his subjects, he looked instead at the way in which the group structured itself and explored the various forms this structure could assume. It was no longer a matter of asking how the group was going to accomplish the task that had been set for it; now the question was what unforeseen collective behaviors the group was capable of. Given this, it ceased to seem surprising that a new piece of information could increase the complexity of the possible responses and, as a consequence, the time taken to solve the initial problem: the initial problem was no longer the one that was judged interesting.

Ecology, more than any other discipline, was both sensitive and attentive to the question of complexity. Theodore Schneirla, an authority on ant colonies, and Herbert Birch, the animal communication specialist, furnished proof of this at the second and eighth conferences, respectively. We have already noted the violent reactions that Birch's presentation provoked. The most complex collective behaviors met with in animal societies, he maintained, whether the behavior of bees and the way in which they orient themselves in relation to their fellow creatures and communicate with them, or the behavior of ants on their expeditions and in their bivouacs, or of fish in their shoals—all these socially useful behaviors result in the last analysis from blind obedience to a certain mode of sensory organization that, under different circumstances, is equally capable of producing the most aberrant and destructive behaviors. From the apparent "intelligence" of the group, he concluded, one could not infer the intelligence of individual members: they do not act with the behavior of the

group in mind.[7] Recall that if the cyberneticians protested, it was not because Birch treated his animals as stupid but rather because he insisted on
reserving the property of intelligence for human beings.

The "Ashby Case," or the Return to Metaphysics

As the cyberneticians came to be acquainted somewhat with practical
examples of complexity, they began more and more to downplay the notion of feedback in favor of circular causality.[8] Feedback, if it is designed to achieve a predetermined end, in effect embodies the intelligence
of the whole, which is not necessarily the case with a loop in a complex
system. But then came the invited guest of the next-to-last conference,
Ross Ashby. Of Ashby's work I shall say little here, since it constituted
one of the keystones of the second cybernetics and therefore falls outside
the main scope of my inquiry. I shall limit myself to describing the impact of his thinking on the first generation of cyberneticians. For them
its effect was rather like an electric shock, and their reactions at the
time add an interesting final touch to the portrait I have been painting
of them.

In a sense, Ashby took the problem of complexity so seriously that he
devoted the whole of his professional life to it. He made no attempt to
conceal his fascination with the set-theoretical reconstruction of mathematics pioneered by the Bourbaki group in France, which led him to seek
the key to the problem in axiomatization. All accounts agree that he exercised considerable influence, directly or indirectly, on those thinkers active
today—and they are many—who have encountered cybernetic ideas in the
course of their work, whether or not cybernetics was always identified as
the source of these ideas.[9] The result of Ashby's assault on the problem of
complexity was to prove, unexpectedly for him, that axiomatizing complexity had the effect of making it vanish altogether.

At the ninth Macy Conference, the only one in which he took part,
Ashby presented two papers: the first, on the automaton that was to make
him famous, the "homeostat"; the second, on whether a mechanical chess
player can outplay its human designer. To the latter question he replied
affirmatively: the mechanical player can win if it relies on chance. Take
the case of an apparently uninteresting configuration of pieces on the chess
board that conceals the possibility of a decisive move, so subtle that not
even the best players can see it. Only two classes of player will discover it:
beginners, because they play erratically; and random players, since no
possibility is ruled out in advance.

It is this principle, if one may call it that, that the homeostat purported to embody in the matter of a machine. Ashby's cybernetic machine claimed to represent the interaction of an organism—the brain—and its environment. It served no purpose and was designed to carry out no task. It was the embodiment of a thought experiment aimed at illustrating a thesis that Ashby claimed to be of universal validity, namely, that life and intelligence, far from being extremely improbable accidents of evolution, inevitably develop in any isolated system. To be alive is to have the capacity to maintain a small number of "essential" variables within certain physiological limits over a very wide range of different environments. In this respect, Ashby's homeostat operates on two levels. On the first, all the connections are fixed, the system as a whole is deterministic, and its dynamic is interpreted as representing the coevolution of the brain and its environment. If in the course of that evolution one or several of the brain's essential variables move outside of their vital zone, the second level is automatically activated, and the homeostat changes its connections *at random*. It therefore becomes a *new* deterministic automaton, which may or may not have the capacity to maintain the essential variables within the desired range. The homeostat can be said to demonstrate the thesis it embodies if it succeeds, in any environment whatever, in establishing good connections—which is to say, connections that keep the brain "alive" and therefore "adapt" it to this environment.

The Macy Conference participants could not work out the trick behind Ashby's sleight of hand. Not that it was difficult to detect, but simply that Ashby's listeners were too taken aback to see it. Ashby himself was to make the notion explicit, in axiomatizing it, only later.[10] I will confine myself here to the following clue, just to give a flavor of Ashby's method and style. By definition, "adaptation" requires that the essential variables be limited to a very small subset of the states that in principle are accessible to them. Now what exactly is a finite automaton? In formal terms, it is a mathematical mapping of a finite set of internal states onto itself that is reiterated an indefinite number of times.[11] As it turns out, there are few "bijective" (one-to-one) mappings—that is, functions that preserve the cardinality of their initial set; moreover, there are proportionally even fewer as the cardinality grows larger. That means that for the very great majority of finite automata, the number of internal states effectively accessible to them decreases very rapidly in the course of their evolution. This is a trivial consequence of the mathematical definition of a mapping (or function): although different arguments of the function can be mapped onto a single value, different values of the function must correspond to different values of the argument.[12] In short, Ashby's routine consisted in passing off a conventional mathematical definition as a universal principle of nature.

Failing to see this, his listeners attacked him over what seemed to them his most egregious error: the reliance on chance as a means of simulating thought, invention, genius, adaptation to the unexpected. Quastler, Pitts, and Bigelow asked whether he was going so far as to assert that random searching or Brownian motion was the best way for an organism to devise new solutions. Ashby replied, "I don't know of any other way that [a] mechanism can do it." But really, Bigelow insisted, in what sense did Ashby think that his homeostat *learns*, when it only gropingly *finds* an equilibrium position? Would one say that a ball bearing that finally falls through an opening in a box that one shakes to help it get out has learned to find the exit? "I don't think it matters," Ashby replied. "The word learning, as we understand it in the objective sense, without considering anything obtained introspectively, is based on observations of this sort of thing happening." At this Bigelow lashed out, saying that Shannon's rat was capable of learning, but not Ashby's machine.[13]

The reader will not fail to have noticed that now the roles were exactly reversed. Ashby replied to the cyberneticians using the very arguments that they had used against Kubie and Birch. The cyberneticians were now pitiably reduced to giving out good and bad marks for a proper understanding of—mentalism! Ashby held up to the cyberneticians a distorting mirror in which they saw a caricature of themselves, while failing to see themselves in it. They saw no discontinuity between the world of machines and the world of organisms? Ashby went so far as to claim that there was nothing essential to life that could not be embodied in a technological device made up of a few interconnected electromagnets. They were champions of objectivity and antimentalism? In Ashby's scheme, objectivity was elevated to such a height that the object was lost: now elementary set theory took the place of the object, and chance the place of the algorithm. Relying on both logic and physiology, they were able to abstract from organisms the underlying logic machine? Ashby built his entire system on the notion of a function and, by virtue of just this, threw out both biology and logic. They were beginning to learn to pose problems in terms of complexity? Ashby had set out to tackle them by resorting to elementary thought experiments such as his homeostat. These experiments were so elementary as to be self-contradictory: the behavior of a truly complex machine surprises even its designer, whereas Ashby's machine surprises only those who are unable to figure out the ruse behind it. Once its "pedagogical" simplicity has been seen through, nothing remains but the trick it plays on the unsuspecting. Its purported complexity has vanished.

It was with Ashby that the venerable principle of *verum factum* came to receive its final and fullest expression in the history of science. Concepts such as "brain," "mind," "life," "organism," "evolution," "intelligence" lost all contact and relation with any physical datum whatever, having been entirely reconstructed within the framework of an axiomatized mathematical model: thus form was totally and definitively snatched from the jaws of matter. McCulloch was looking for the formal *and material* conditions of synthetic a priori judgment: the questions he asked were the very ones that biologists and psychologists asked, even if he did make use of logico-mathematical tools. The same thing can be said of Herbert Simon and his *physical*—that is to say, material—symbolic systems. With Ashby, by contrast, one enters into the pure mathematical a priori. The interdisciplinary project of cybernetics, the hope for interaction with those researchers who conducted clinical investigations into the basis of life or the workings of the mind—who entered into conversation with the objects of the world, as it were—was now transformed, for those who were to follow Ashby's lead, from a limited and difficult enterprise into a clearly impossible one. It was no longer a question of dialogue, as Isabelle Stengers has remarked.[14] "Ashby's influence [may be likened to] a scorched earth campaign: in his wake, certain kinds of hypotheses could no longer be proposed, [and] those who came after had to adapt themselves to the constraints that Ashby had laid down forever."[15]

Even if it was not always aware of the fact, cybernetics in its first incarnation was part of a larger attempt to dismantle the metaphysical vision of the world. But Ashby unhesitatingly jumped right back into metaphysics. On his view, in effect, the only legitimate point of view is that of omniscience, and the sole pertinent properties those that can withstand the scrutiny of God. A link is sometimes asserted between cybernetics and Leibniz's system. Whereas this makes little sense if applied to someone like Wiener, it is perfectly justified in the case of Ashby. For Ashby had decreed once and for all that a "machine" (whether a brain, an organism, a computer, or what have you) is nothing other than "that which behaves in a machine-like way, namely, that its internal state, and the state of its [environment], defines uniquely the next state it will go to."[16] The essence of such a mapping is that it defines an organization. By logical deduction, Ashby inferred from this that the notion of self-organization is self-contradictory and belongs only to the illusory realm of appearances. For there to be such a thing as self-organization, it would have to be the case that the machine can in fact *by itself* determine the change in the mapping that governs it. But in that case one would have to assume another mapping, operating at a level logically higher than that of the first, that modifies the initial mapping. But in this case the system would have been erroneously defined by the initial mapping—contrary to hypothesis. Novelty, liberty, and spontaneity are thus unmasked as illusions, or mistakes: observers are surprised by events only because they confine themselves to the finite point of view of those who choose "not to remove the lid of the system."[17]

This "proof," claiming to show the impossibility of self-organization, was formulated by Ashby in 1962.[18] It was to exercise a considerable influence, especially upon second-order cybernetics, which was forced to reconceive self-organization in a way that would allow it to get around the obstacle posed by Ashby's argument. (Some of the best-known work of Heinz von Foerster[19] and Henri Atlan[20] on the "order from noise" principle belongs to this tradition, in fact.) Ashby's argument is also encountered in a variety of other fields, where not infrequently it has been used by authors whom one has a hard time imagining in the company of cyberneticians.

One's surprise is perhaps not so great in the case of the German sociologist Niklas Luhmann, founder of a theory of rights based on the concept of autopoietic systems worked out by Humberto Muturana and Francisco Varela. To illustrate his thesis that normative systems are autonomous in the sense that they are informationally and operationally closed upon themselves and therefore cannot escape being enclosed by the hermeneutic circle, Luhmann cites a passage from Douglas Hofstadter's *Gödel, Escher, Bach*, which in fact expresses exactly the argument made by Ashby: "No matter how a program twists and turns to get out of itself, it is still following the rules inherent in itself. . . . A computer program can modify itself but it cannot violate its own instructions—it can at best change some parts of itself by *obeying* its own instructions."[21]

It is more surprising, however, to see the French political philosopher Régis Debray rely on Ashby's argument to make the unlikely assertion that collective self-government is a *logical* impossibility: "The government of a collective by itself—*verbi gracia* 'of the people by the people'—is a logically contradictory operation."[22] In his *Critique of Political Reason*, he goes on to affirm that "the 'secret' of our collective miseries . . . takes the form of a logical law," according to which "there can be no organized system without closure and no system can be closed by elements internal to that system alone. Contradictory as it might seem, a field can therefore only be closed by being opened up to an element external to it."[23] Even though this pronouncement is justified as "an extension of Gödel's theorem [*sic*]," Debray's reasoning does not go beyond Ashby's argument: given that a rule can be modified only by the operation of a metarule, the attempt to bring the metarule within the scope of a system's control over itself would require positing a meta-metarule, which in turn would fall outside this scope of self-control unless supplemented by a further rule, and so on. Since one would inevitably have to stop somewhere, at the level of an "inviolable" (pace Hofstadter) meta-meta-[. . .]-rule, Debray concludes that autonomy is impossible: self-government is inconceivable unless it is itself governed by some form of exteriority (i.e., in accordance with some rule external to the collectivity), in which case it is not actually self-government.

If the "archeo"-cyberneticians were shocked by Ashby, it is above all because, as we have already pointed out, he introduced the radically new idea of a network whose connections were chosen at random, not designed or selected in order to reach a predetermined end. Note that this makes Ashby's work the precursor of neoconnectionism[24]—yet another paradox! And an unlikely one, it may seem, in view of how different in spirit the two approaches are. Neoconnectionists regard their networks as complex objects in von Neumann's sense, as almost natural systems; they study the properties of such networks experimentally, manipulating them by varying their parameters, and so on. Ashby, for his part, used his automaton to draw a metaphysical line between truth and appearance. Nonetheless, it is undeniable that the most remarkable property of connectionist networks—namely, that they stabilize into attractors that restrict their dynamics to subsets of the set of possible states available to the system—is the very one relied on by Ashby, who showed that this result was interpreted in terms of self-organization only by those who chose not to adopt the omniscient point of view of the automaton with regard to itself, and that they were the only ones to be surprised by it.[25] Neoconnectionism is sometimes said to have been born with the *experimental* discovery made at the end of the 1960s by a young medical student, Stuart Kauffman, a pupil of McCulloch's, that randomly connected Boolean automata generate remarkable patterns of collective behavior, cyclical in character and exhibiting generally weak periodicity. The great biologist C. H. Waddington echoed this discovery at the "Beyond Reductionism" symposium at Alpbach, describing it exactly as Ashby would have done, using the same language, couched in the same sententious style: every system composed of a very large number of interacting elements, he said in effect, will inevitably and spontaneously develop some sort of stable behavior.[26] The difference between Ashby, who decreed the logical impossibility of self-organization, and the proponents of a theory of self-organizing systems was not apparent to those who failed to grasp that they held opposite philosophies of modeling.

The cyberneticians were shocked, as we have noted, but did they have good reasons for being shocked? Was not the epistemological rupture (in Foucault's sense) created by Ashby's approach potentially contained in the cybernetic approach itself? Cybernetics had after all already gone quite far along the road toward an autonomization of the logico-mathematical model, even if it claimed to maintain the link with physical, biological, and psychological reality. It had already taken important steps in the direction of a conceptual and rational reconstruction of the objective data of science, with all the risks of losing touch with the world as it is given to us that such a reconstruction involves. One is reminded in particular of the modern history of economic thought, which in the form of Gérard Debreu's attempt to recast the whole of economics in a Bourbaki-type framework contains an almost exact equivalent of the Ashby case. Here again, for the economists who came after Debreu, the choice was either to accept the reigning dogma or, in the best case, to be regarded as doing something other than economics; in the worst case, to be regarded as having plunged into the irrational.

The philosophy of mind that today inspires mainstream research in cognitive science runs the same risks. The abstraction of the forced and artificial thought experiments that almost exclusively provide it with material for analysis (along with the properties of ordinary language) strongly resembles that of the esoteric games to which the second generation of cyberneticians, following in the footsteps of Ashby, devoted themselves. In both cases, philosophical reflection is fed more by science fiction than by science. This might not matter so much were it not for the fact that cognitive science, like cybernetics before it, claims to speak in the name of physics. It sets itself the task of "physicalizing" or "naturalizing" intentionality, without seeing that its very French image of physics as the *reine des sciences*—as the "queen of the sciences," whom philosophers of mind have placed on a pedestal, and whose purity seems to them all the greater the more careful they are not to touch her—makes physics out to be a science of the a priori; a philosophical, conceptual, and rational enterprise having nothing to do with real, living science as it is actually done in laboratories. The physics of the laboratories bears more similarity to a program of perpetual tinkering than to a logic of concepts: faced with new problems to be solved, it invents new operations, new methods of inquiry, new ways of manipulating objects, without always worrying about the logical coherence of the new ensemble of procedures and results.

Physics, as it is actually practiced, is above all plural, fragmented. In particular, to speak of *a* physics is to miss the "differences between physics as a science of motion, grounded in the concept of energy, and [physics] as a set of statistical and kinetic approaches that define their object of study in terms of population and coupled events."[27] As it turns out, this new "physics of populations"—whether of automata or molecules—has had to abandon one of the central categories on which classical dynamics, including classical thermodynamics, had been built: the state function. Because the collective phenomena that the new science studies are not integrable in a state function,[28] the type of causality to which they are subject is neither linear causality nor the circular causality of the cyberneticians; it is instead, in Isabelle Stengers's phrase, a "causality of *coupling*" that leaves open the nature of the interaction (whether deterministic or stochastic, as in the case of the connections between elementary automata in a Boolean automata network, or assuming the form of chemical reactions and diffusion, as in the case of molecular activity) in order to inquire into the behaviors a population of coupled entities is capable of exhibiting."[29]

When philosophy of mind, for the reasons we have examined, stubbornly persists in conceiving of intentionality as a relation between a mental *state* and its object (or content), it cuts itself off from the new physics and the attempt to unite connectionist research with the physics of disordered systems and the thermodynamics of irreversible processes. Much of what presently goes on in the name of "naturalizing intentionality" is missing this crucial opportunity.

At the ninth Macy Conference, in March 1952, Ross Ashby left the paleocyberneticians dumbfounded and defenseless. In the history of cybernetics and, by extension, of cognitive science, their encounter marked the end of one era and the beginning of another.

Subjectless Processes

With the notable exception of Freud, students of the human sciences have never been very eager to root their hypotheses in the biological or physical substrates of behavior. This combination of arrogance and indifference has sometimes aroused the envy of biologists. Jean-Pierre Changeux, for example, can barely conceal his covetous desire to replant these sciences (now so much "in vogue," as he says) in "their biological subsoil."[30]

We have described cybernetics as a physicalist attempt to conquer the sciences of mind, which is to say, to supplant existing psychologies. In hindsight it is to be regretted that cybernetics was utterly lacking in ambition with regard to the human and social sciences in general. Norbert Wiener, for his part, gave up quite early on. With the passage of time, his arguments cannot but seem disappointing. The relevant statistical series under "essentially constant" conditions, he argued in *Cybernetics*, were not long enough to permit the new mathematical techniques of signal processing to be applied to questions of social organization.[31] For a movement that has been described as the science of *forms*, this amounted to taking a remarkably blinkered view of society!

The social scientists who participated in the Macy Conferences were scarcely more daring. Paul Lazarsfeld did not make much use of the new notions. Roman Jakobson was just passing through. Robert Merton and Talcott Parsons were more receptive—especially Parsons, who did in fact enthusiastically welcome cybernetics; but this was only to press it into the service of his own theory of sociological functionalism, entirely built around the notion of equilibrium, which, despite its narrow focus, came to exercise a considerable influence on sociology during the postwar period. Cybernetics, Parsons believed, represented the final stage in the unification of the physical and social sciences, a result that L. J. Henderson's influential lectures at Harvard during the 1930s, which he attended along with Merton, had prepared him to anticipate. Henderson, who was both a sociologist and a biochemist, did not hesitate to link Pareto's concept of economic equilibrium with Le Châtelier's principle in chemical thermodynamics and Cannon's theory of homeostasis. It seems fairly clear that Parsons's interest in cybernetics rested on a misunderstanding.

Then, of course, there was the American school of cultural anthropology and the personality and culture movement. I have already showed that their links with cybernetics were based on a huge misunderstanding that was to play a leading role in all ten of the Macy Conferences. The same thing may be said of Gregory Bateson's work, which, although original and important, was decidedly out of step with the spirit of cybernetics, despite his best attempts to fall in line. As for the others, Warren McCulloch included, their training in the human and social sciences was not extensive enough to enable them to appreciate how much they might have profited from deeper exposure to these disciplines, still less to suspect the inspiration that they might have taken from them. An encounter between cybernetics and these sciences nonetheless could, and should, have taken place—and in a much more ambitious way than I have indicated up to this point.

I have insisted on the fact that cybernetics provided the formal means for conceiving the category of *subjectless processes*. Now this category, which is to be found both in the free-market social philosophy of Friedrich von Hayek and at the heart of Louis Althusser's Marxist structuralism, has been a key source of innovation in postwar philosophy and social thought. Two quite distinct forms of the concept may in fact be distinguished. The first is that of the "invisible hand," or what is sometimes called "the ruse of reason," long predominant in the classical liberal tradition of political philosophy and economics. Central to this tradition is the problem of complexity. Liberalism grants that society is made by human beings but holds that its complexity thwarts their attempts to control it, in the same way that a physical automaton develops in ways that are beyond the control of its designer. The debate at the Hixon Symposium that opposed Weiss and von Neumann against McCulloch has long had its equivalent in the domain of social science. McCulloch's atomism corresponds to the position known there as "methodological individualism," and the economic theory of general equilibrium can be shown to exhibit the same reversibility between top-down and bottom-up approaches that McCulloch's model displays. With regard to the concept of totalities proposed by Weiss, its analogue is easily found in the social science tradition as well, having assumed its earliest form in the work of the inventor of the doctrine of the invisible hand, Adam Smith.[32] If the sponsors of the Macy Conferences had really taken their interdisciplinary project seriously, they might have thought to restage this debate, internal to the social sciences, as a way of illuminating their own.

To be sure, this missed opportunity was made up for later, but the initiative came from the human sciences themselves. The leading figure in this regard was Friedrich von Hayek, whom I have already had occasion to cite several times. The future Nobel laureate in economics took part, in fact, in one of the conferences organized by Heinz von Foerster in the 1960s on self-organization as well as the 1968 Alpbach "Beyond Reductionism" Symposium. Since that time his notion of "spontaneous social order" has taken its place in contemporary interdisciplinary seminars alongside autopoietic systems and dissipative structures. But Hayek drew much more upon social philosophy than cybernetic ideas or particular models associated with its leading representatives. The influence ran, in fact, the other way: recall that Rosenblatt, in designing his Perceptron, acknowledged his debt to Hayek.

In fact, Hayek had no need to look any further than the liberal tradition of the Scottish Enlightenment for the idea that was the equivalent, in the social domain, of von Neumann's conjecture about complexity. This tradition regards the following two propositions as noncontradictory (in much the same way as the two propositions discussed in the last chapter concerning life and the physicochemical processes that produce it are noncontradictory):[33] first, that human beings bring society into existence through their actions; second, that society is beyond their control, because it is (infinitely) more complex than they are. Thus one can, without risk of inconsistency, be nonreductionist without having to accept holism. Although it is true that methodological individualism still figures in this interpretation, it differs from the kind that this term is usually understood to refer to, precisely because it stands opposed to reductionism. Let us speak instead, then, of *complex* methodological individualism.

For Hayek, spontaneous social order constitutes a third type of order, along with natural order and artificial order. It signifies an emergence, an effect of composition, a system-effect. The "system" is obviously not a subject, endowed with consciousness and will. The knowledge that the system exploits is irreducibly distributed over the set of its constituent elements: it cannot be synthesized in one place, for the system has no "absolute knowledge" about itself that is localized somewhere within it. This collective knowledge resides in the social order of the system insofar as it is the "result of human action but not of human design"[34] and cannot be appropriated by any individual consciousness. It is *knowledge without a subject*. It is embodied in norms, rules, conventions, institutions, which themselves are incorporated in individual minds in the form of abstract schemata: "The mind does not so much make rules as consist of rules of action. We can make use of so much experience, not because we possess such experience, but because, without our knowing it, it has become incorporated in the schemata of thought which guide us."[35]

The Alpbach symposium led Hayek to conceive this paradoxical relation between a collective subjectless knowledge and individual subjects in terms of "self-transcendence." One can hardly fail to make the connection between this notion and the phenomenological notion of "transcendence in immanence," which, as we have seen, likewise went ungrasped by cybernetics. In the case of the mind, as in the case of society, we are dealing with a form of the bootstrapping paradox, which cybernetics—in spite of itself, as it were—showed could be formulated in mechanistic terms.

I have already (in Chapter 4) described the other form that the notion of subjectless processes took. This was a product of the Nietzschean Heideggerianism that was to influence the postwar human sciences in their reaction against philosophies of consciousness, above all in France, with its successive waves of structuralism, poststructuralism, and deconstruction. Cybernetics, as I have tried to show, itself came very close to announcing the dehumanization of man. One wishes that it had been aware of this—the revolt against philosophies of consciousness notwithstanding!—and that it had actively sought out dialogue with like-minded approaches, distant though they may have been. Once again, however, it was the structuralists who took the first step. I have alluded to the case of Lévi-Strauss as well as to that of Lacan. One may take the view, of course, as I do, that the results the structuralists believed they had succeeded in establishing, using cybernetic tools for the most part—in particular, the existence of a "symbolic" level that is structured like a language and functions like a machine—do not stand up to critical analysis.[36] All this is now quite dated, it is true. It may also be argued that the postulated transcendence of the symbolic fails to capture the notion of self-transcendence that is central to the parallel tradition that runs from Smith to Hayek. Nonetheless it cannot be denied that there were deep affinities between what cybernetics set out to do and the deconstruction of the metaphysical conception of the subject carried out by the structuralists and their successors.

The Missed Rendezvous with the Human Sciences

In conclusion I would like to touch briefly on the relation as I see it between the social sciences and cognitive science today. Methodological individualism in the social sciences has one golden rule: *never treat aggregates as subjects*. Treating aggregates in this way is to make a category mistake. It is a mistake, however, that we are constantly tempted to make. Consider voting in elections, which has become the democratic procedure par excellence. Whether it is a matter of electing a president through universal suffrage, or of a referendum requiring the voter to answer yes or no to a certain question, it frequently happens that the distribution of votes is nearly equal: the winner prevails by a very small margin. In fact, a vote massively in favor of one of the options proposed may arouse the suspicion that there was something irregular about the vote itself—in the same way that a series of coin flips yielding tails appreciably more (or less) often than heads provokes the suspicion that the coin has been doctored or the toss rigged somehow. Democratic theory since the time of Montesquieu has been at pains to account for this observation. For an information theorist, however, an even vote is one that maximizes entropy, which is to say disorder. In formal terms it is equivalent to a lottery.

This interpretation may seem surprising, but it acquires still more force if one considers what rational choice theorists call the "voting paradox."[37] Except for the extremely improbable case in which ballots are equally divided between two options, the conclusion is unavoidable from an individualist perspective that no single ballot cast has any effect whatsoever: the effect of any individual vote upon the outcome is, strictly speaking, nil. Each voter is forced to accept that the answer to the question "Would the final result have been altered had I voted otherwise than I did?" is no. But what do we observe in practice? We observe that the outcome of a vote is often interpreted as the manifestation of the carefully considered choice of a collective subject: the "people," the "electorate," and so on. In the case of a referendum that goes in favor of the "yeas" by an extremely narrow margin, the usual interpretation is something like the following: "The electorate, in its wisdom, has answered yes to the question put before it, but it has also wished to issue a warning to all those who seek to move too fast." It is as though one had made a subject out of chance—a collective subject in what might be called a position of exteriority to itself, since obviously the electorate is supposed to transcend each citizen taken individually. In the life of the innumerable committees and commissions to which modern societies confide responsibility for administering public affairs, the resort to anonymous voting is very frequently only a disguised means of delegating to chance a decision that presumptively rational debate has shown itself incapable of reaching. But these forms of randomly generated consensus are considered legitimate and meaningful to exactly the extent that they produce an external or transcendent point of view, and so can be taken as the decisions of a collective subject.

This interpretive attitude—what Dennett calls the "intentional stance"—is an inevitable fact of the human condition.[38] We are forever attributing to others "mental states" (intentions, desires, beliefs, and so on), no matter whether the other is a human being, an animal, a machine—or a group of human beings. As a practical matter, this stance tends to weaken methodological individualism (or, as I would rather say, to make it more complex), since the individual subject no longer has a monopoly upon certain attributes of subjectivity. It becomes necessary to admit, in addition to the existence of these individual subjects, the existence of *quasisubjects*—which is to say, collective entities capable of exhibiting at least some of the attributes that one had thought were restricted to "real" subjects (i.e., individuals) and, in particular, the existence of mental states. One thus does not hesitate to say of an organization, or more generally of a collective entity, not only that it is capable of learning, but also that it is capable of knowing, remembering, analyzing a situation, making experiments, forming concepts, taking decisions, and acting.

Now cognitive science, from the time of its cybernetic origins up through the present day, has presented a picture of the individual subject itself as a sort of quasisubject; that is, as a collective entity manifesting the properties of subjectivity. When I think, remember, desire, believe, decide, and so on, the subject of these predicates is not a ghost in the cerebral machine, a concealed homunculus as it were; it is the machine itself—in the form, for example, of a network of neurons. On this view there is no ghost in the machine, no center of subjectivity. The attributes of subjectivity are emergent effects produced by the spontaneous, self-organized functioning of a complex organization in the form of a network. Cognitive scientists who defend this thesis, or a variant of it, resort to curious expressions: Varela speaks of "selfless minds,"[39] Dennett of "non-selfy selves,"[40] Minsky of a "society of mind."[41] But the idea, and its source in cybernetic thinking, is clear enough.

All of this is to say that the weakening, indeed the deconstruction of the metaphysical (i.e., Cartesian and Leibnizian) concept of subjectivity took place at the intersection of the social sciences and cognitive science on both a macro- and a microlevel. On the macrolevel, the attributes of subjectivity are not the monopoly of individual subjects: collective entities can exhibit them as well. On the microlevel, the attributes of subjectivity are not attributes of an alleged subject: they are emergent effects produced by the functioning of subjectless processes. In both cases the deconstruction of the subject proceeds from a recognition that a complex network of interactions among simple entities—formal neurons in the case of the individual quasisubject, schematic individuals in the case of the collective subject—is capable of exhibiting remarkable properties. For cognitive scientists who carry on the cybernetic tradition, it is *neither more nor less* justified to attribute a mental state, such as an intention, to a human being than to a group of human beings.

If one reads contemporary cognitive philosophy on consciousness and the self, one cannot help but be struck by its constant use of social and political metaphors, even electoral ones. The emergence of a self at a given moment, in the course of one of those processes that constitutes the life of the mind, is likened to the transition from being in a crowd—a crowd of mental events, of neuronal configurations—to being in an organized political community, created by the election not of a center of control but of a representative: the "head of mind," as the individual (deconstructed) "subject" might be called, playing the same role as the head of state. In this scenario, crises occasionally arise: several potential representatives emerge as rivals for power, and so on. Mental mechanisms and social mechanisms are placed on the same level, precisely to the extent they *are* mechanisms.

Cybernetics heralded all this, as the first harbinger of a new philosophy. But it was to a large extent unaware that it bore this message,[42] because it never acknowledged the contribution made by established—sometimes long established—disciplines to the analysis of its chosen subject: the life of the mind. No doubt cybernetics was too impatient, too full of itself and what it took to be its revolutionary mission, too sure of representing the avant-garde of science in its conquering march across new lands. It finds itself today quite forgotten, or, in the best case, poorly remembered—quite unjustly, in either case. But cognitive science now finds itself in the same position: if anything, it is still more sure of itself, proposing in its turn to reconstruct the human sciences by wiping clean the slate of everything that has previously been thought about the mind. If the heroic and unhappy history of cybernetics has anything to teach us, surely it is that, in addition to a bold willingness to go where no one has gone before, modesty, reasoned doubt, and mindfulness of tradition, nourished by critical reflection, are equally indispensable virtues in the quest for knowledge.

Notes

PREFACE

1. See the introduction to Jean-Pierre Dupuy, *Ordres et désordres: Enquête sur un nouveau paradigme* (Paris: Seuil, 1982).

2. Their research during this period was synthesized in two works: Henri Atlan, *L'Organisation biologique et la théorie de l'information* (Paris: Hermann, 1972; revised edition, 1990), and Francisco Varela, *Principles of Biological Autonomy* (New York: Elsevier-North Holland, 1979); see also H. Atlan, "On a formal definition of organization," *Journal of Theoretical Biology* 45 (1974): 295–304.

3. The proceedings of these conferences may be found in Paul Dumouchel and Jean-Pierre Dupuy, eds., *L'Auto-organisation: de la physique au politique* (Paris: Seuil, 1983), and Paisley Livingston, ed., *Disorder and Order* (Saratoga, Calif.: Anma Libri, 1984), respectively.

4. Thomas Nagel, *Other Minds* (New York: Oxford University Press, 1995), 105 (n. 6).

5. Ilya Prigogine and Isabelle Stengers, *La Nouvelle Alliance: metamorphose de la science* (Paris: Gallimard, 1979), available in English as *Order Out of Chaos: Man's New Dialogue with Nature* (New York: Bantam Books, 1984).

6. S. J. Heims, "An Encounter between Neo-Mechanists and the Human Sciences," in *Cahiers du CRÉA*, no. 7 (November 1985): 141–202.

7. Steve Joshua Heims, *The Cybernetics Group* (Cambridge, Mass.: MIT Press, 1991).

8. Jean-Pierre Dupuy, *Aux origines des sciences cognitives* (Paris: La Découverte, 1994).

9. Thus the theme of the conference organized at Stanford in February 1994 by Hans-Ulrich Gumbrecht, "Beyond the Two Cultures?"

10. See Paul Watzlawick et al., *Pragmatics of Human Communication* (New York: Norton, 1967). The work in family psychotherapy done by Watzlawick and his colleagues at the Mental Research Hospital in Palo Alto, California, is very well known in Europe, where they are referred to as the "Palo Alto school."

11. See Michael A. Arbib, *The Metaphorical Brain: An Introduction to Cybernetics as Artificial Intelligence and Brain Theory* (New York: Wiley Interscience, 1972).

INTRODUCTION

1. I borrow this expression from the title of Heims's previously mentioned book.

2. W. Ross Ashby, *Design for a Brain* (London: Chapman and Hall, 1952). Ashby was a member of the second cybernetics, which is not at the center of the intellectual history retraced in the present book.

3. John Searle, "Is the Brain's Mind a Computer Program?" *Scientific American* 262, no. 1 (January 1990): 26–31. In the first chapter I discuss the "Chinese Room" argument, the famous thought experiment devised by Searle to illustrate this point.

4. This thesis has recently been upheld, with exceptional force and clarity, by David Chalmers in *The Conscious Mind: In Search of a Fundamental Theory* (New York: Oxford University Press, 1996); see especially chapter 9 ("Strong Artificial Intelligence").

5. See the work bearing this title by Jean Petitot, *Physique du sens* (Paris: Éditions du Centre National de la Recherche Scientifique, 1992).

6. Jean Petitot, Francisco Varela, Bernard Pachoud, and Jean-Michel Roy, eds., *Naturalizing Phenomenology: Issues in Contemporary Phenomenology and Cognitive Science* (Stanford: Stanford University Press, 1999).

7. This was the great anthropologist Gregory Bateson. See his hymn to cybernetics, *Steps to an Ecology of Mind* (New York: Ballantine Books, 1972).

8. That the approach argued for by cybernetics is no longer even contemplated by authors today is plainly apparent when one considers Searle's position, of which Thomas Nagel—who largely approves it—has said, "His real point is that the entire materialist tradition is in truth eliminative: all materialist theories deny the reality of the mind, but most of them disguise the fact (from themselves as well as from others) by identifying the mind with something else"; see Nagel's article "Searle: Why We Are Not Computers," in *Other Minds*, 103. A philosopher of consciousness such as Searle cannot imagine the possibility of constructing a theory of mind without a subject.

9. See Petitot et al., eds., *Naturalizing Phenomenology*. Affinities also seem to exist between a neocybernetics and the philosophy of Spinoza; see Henri Atlan, "Immanent Causality: A Spinozist Viewpoint on Evolution and Theory of Action," in Gertrudis Van de Vijver et al., eds., *Evolutionary Systems: Biological and Epistemological Perspectives on Selection and Self-Organization* (Dordrecht: Kluwer, 1998).

10. See the Preface, xi.

11. Ibid., xii–xiii.

12. Thomas Nagel, "Fodor: The Boundaries of Inner Space," in *Other Minds*, 70.

13. This point is clearly established by Luc Ferry and Alain Renaut, *French Philosophy of the Sixties: An Essay on Antihumanism*, trans. Mary H. S. Cattani (Amherst: University of Massachusetts Press, 1990).

14. See Martin Heidegger, "Modern Science, Metaphysics, and Mathematics," in *Basic Writings*, ed. David Farrell Krell (New York: Harper and Row, 1977), 247–82. This is an excerpt from *Die Frage nach dem Ding* (Tübingen: M. Niemeyer, 1962).

15. See Norbert Wiener, *Cybernetics: or Control and Communication in the Animal and the Machine* (Cambridge, Mass.: MIT Press, 1948), 11.

16. Martin Heidegger, "Letter on Humanism," in *Basic Writings*, 225.

17. Probably one of the last places where a rapprochement between cognitive science and French philosophy can be imagined is the American university, even though the departments of cognitive science and literature may only be a few hundred yards apart.

18. The unwitting acceptance for publication of the New York University physicist Alan Sokal's deconstructionist interpretation of quantum physics, a deliberate piece of nonsense, by the journal *Social Text* in 1996, is perhaps the most famous example.

19. This phrase is found in the review Sartre wrote in 1943 of Albert Camus's *The Stranger*, "Explication de l'*Étranger*," reprinted in *Critiques littéraires (Situations I)* (Paris: Gallimard, 1947) and available in English in *Literary and Philosophical Essays*, trans. Annette Michelson (New York: Criterion Books, 1955). In the same review, Sartre quotes Camus meditating in *The Myth of Sisyphus* on "man's inhumanity": "Men also secrete the inhuman. Sometimes, in moments of lucidity, the mechanical aspect of their gestures and their senseless pantomime make everything about them seem stupid." Camus gives an example: "A man is talking on the telephone. We cannot hear him behind the glass partition, but we can see his senseless mimicry. We wonder why he is alive." Sartre comments: "Is there really anything sillier than a man behind a glass window? Glass seems to let everything through. It stops only one thing: the meaning of his gestures. [It is] transparent to things and opaque to meanings." Sartre makes use of this example to accuse analytic philosophy of slipping an analogous partition between ourselves and others, pretending that meaning is always present from the start in human intercourse. The point of Searle's "Chinese Room" thought experiment is not so very different.

20. "To render philosophy inhuman"—thus the task Jean-François Lyotard, one of the high priests of "postmodernism," set himself in 1984.

21. See Henri Atlan, "Intentional self-organization. Emergence and reduction: towards a physical theory of intentionality," *Thesis Eleven*, no. 52 (February 1998): 5–34; also Henri Atlan and Moshe Koppel, "The cellular computer. DNA: program or data?" *Bulletin of Mathematical Biology* 52, no. 3 (1990): 335–48.

22. The quotations that follow are from a paper delivered by Peter Sloterdijk at a conference on Heidegger at Elmau Castle in Upper Bavaria on 17 July 1999. Entitled "On the Rules of the Human Fleet," it was presented as a reply to Heidegger's "Letter on Humanism." Sloterdijk's paper was published later in the summer in *Die Zeit*, creating an uproar in Germany that has profound political implications.

23. Louis Dumont, "La genèse chrétienne de l'individualisme moderne, une vue modifiée de nos origines," *Le Débat* 15 (September–October 1981), reprinted as the first chapter of *Essais sur l'individualisme: Une perspective anthropologique sur l'idéologie moderne* (Paris: Seuil, 1983). An English translation of the original article appeared in *Religion* 12 (1982): 1–27. Dumont's book is available as *Essays on Individualism: Modern Ideology in Anthropological Perspective* (Chicago: University of Chicago Press, 1986).

24. Searle must be credited with having perceived, behind the materialist monism that cognitivism and artificial intelligence claim to exhibit, a dualism that goes ignored. However, his argument—namely, that if the mind is a program, it

lies outside of nature—can be effectively countered, as we have seen. Its vulnerability in this respect is connected with the fact that he underestimates the force and the coherence (which does not necessarily mean the correctness) of the deconstructionist paradigm.

25. Evidence of this may be found in Chalmers's *Conscious Mind*, certainly the most interesting work on this topic to have so far appeared.

CHAPTER ONE

1. Giambattista Vico, *De nostri temporis studiorum ratione* (Naples, 1709).

2. Herbert A. Simon, *Models of My Life* (New York: Basic Books, 1991), 305. See too his *Models of Man, Social and Rational: Mathematical Essays on Rational Human Behavior in a Social Setting* (New York: Wiley, 1957); *The Sciences of the Artificial* (Cambridge, Mass.: MIT Press, 1969); *Models of Discovery: And Other Topics in the Methods of Science* (Boston: D. Reidel, 1977); *Models of Thought*, 2 vols. (New Haven: Yale University Press, 1979–1989); *Models of Bounded Rationality*, 2 vols. (Cambridge, Mass.: MIT Press, 1982).

3. Simon, *Models of My Life*, 309.

4. Thomas Hobbes, *Leviathan, or the Matter, Forme and Power of a Commonwealth Ecclesiasticall and Civil*, ed. Michael Oakeshott (London: Collier Macmillan, 1962), 19.

5. Ibid., part 1, chapter 5.

6. Hannah Arendt, *The Human Condition* (Chicago: University of Chicago Press, 1958), 298.

7. Ibid., 295.

8. Ibid. The emphasis is mine.

9. Jean Ullmo, *La Pensée scientifique moderne* (Paris: Flammarion, 1969), 99. Ullmo's characterization here applies to what he calls "structure." Further on, however, he identifies model and structure (see p. 104). The interchangeable use of these terms can be attributed to the influence exercised by structuralism at the time.

10. Ibid., 104.

11. Ibid, 116–17.

12. Distancing himself from Arendt's interpretation of *verum factum*, Philippe Reynaud insists on this point in "L'idée de science de l'Esprit," the first chapter of the second section of his *Max Weber et les dilemmes de la raison moderne* (Paris: Presses Universitaires de France, 1987).

13. Thomas Hobbes, *De homine* (London, 1658), chapter 10, sec. 5; see the Gert edition of this work, reprinted in *Man and Citizen*, trans. Charles T. Wood, T. S. K. Scott-Craig, and Bernard Gert (Garden City: Anchor Books, 1972), 41–42.

14. A. M. Turing, "On computable numbers, with an application to the *Entscheidungsproblem*," *Proceedings of the London Mathematical Society* 42, serial 2 (1936): 230–65; and "A Correction," ibid. 43 (1937): 544–46; both are reprinted in Martin Davis, ed., *The Undecidable: Basic Papers on Undecidable Propositions, Unsolvable Problems and Computable Functions* (Hewlett, N.Y.: Raven Press, 1965), 115–54.

15. K. Gödel, "Über formal unentscheidbare Sätze der *Principia Mathematica und verwandter Systeme I*," *Monatshefte für Mathematik und Physik* 38 (1931): 173–98; an English translation is to be found in Davis, *The Undecidable*, among other places, including Jan van Heijenoort, *From Frege to Gödel: Source Book on Mathematical Logic, 1879–1931* (Cambridge, Mass.: Harvard University Press, 1966).

16. A. Church, "An unsolvable problem of elementary number theory," *American Journal of Mathematics* 58 (1936): 345–63; reprinted in Davis, *The Undecidable*.

17. Jean Mosconi, "La Constitution de la théorie des automates," doctoral thesis, 2 vols. (Université de Paris-I, 1989), 1:19.

18. A. M. Turing, "Computability and λ-definability," *Journal of Symbolic Logic* 2 (1937): 153–63.

19. Jean Mosconi, "Sur quelques capacités et incapacités des machines," *Bulletin de la Société française de philosophie* 85, no. 3 (July–September, 1991): 86.

20. The question of whether the world itself is recursive has occupied a number of philosophers and logicians, among them, in France, Jean-Paul Delahaye and Jean-Pierre Dubucs. An accessible introduction to this technical debate may be found in William Poundstone, *The Recursive Universe* (New York: Morrow, 1985).

21. Most famously, perhaps, Hilary Putnam: see the evolution of his thinking in the second volume of *Philosophical Papers* (New York: Cambridge University Press, 1975).

22. Herbert A. Simon, *The Shape of Automation for Men and Management* (New York: Harper and Row, 1965), 96.

23. A. M. Turing, "Computing machinery and intelligence," *Mind* 59, no. 236 (1950): 433–60; reprinted in Alan Ross Anderson, ed., *Minds and Machines* (Englewood Cliffs, N.J.: Prentice-Hall, 1964). On this topic see also Alan Hodges, *Alan Turing: The Enigma* (New York: Simon and Schuster/Touchstone Books, 1984), 415–17.

24. Jean Lassègue, in a CRÉA thesis written under the direction of Daniel Andler, has worked out in a very subtle way all the sexual implications of this assumption, relating them to the life of Alan Turing; see his article "Le test de Turing et l'énigme de la différence des sexes," in Didier Anzieu et al., eds., *Les contenants de pensée* (Paris: Dunod, 1993), 145–95.

25. The allusion is to the theoretical device employed by John Rawls in *Theory of Justice* (Cambridge, Mass.: Harvard University Press, 1971).

26. J. Searle, "Minds, brains, and programs," *Behavioral and Brain Sciences* 3, no. 3 (1980): 417–57.

27. J. Searle, "Is the Brain's Mind a Computer Program?": 29; cited in Mosconi, "Sur quelques capacités et incapacités des machines," 97.

28. Some work in developmental psychology seems to show that the capacity for *make-believe* or *mimicry* is related to the ability to project one's own mental states upon others and to *simulate* the mental states of others based on one's own, and that it constitutes an early and fundamental stage of cognitive development in the child: see A. Goldman, "Interpretation Psychologized," *Mind and Language* 4, no. 3 (1989): 161–85. For a critical discussion of this thesis, see Pascal Engel's "Théories de l'interprétation et théorie de l'esprit," which appears as the third

chapter of his *Introduction à la philosophie de l'esprit* (Paris: La Découverte, 1994), originally published as *États d'Esprit* (Aix-en-Provence: Alinéa, 1992).

29. The reader will recall the argument between Derrida and Searle in 1977, in the pages of the journal *Glyph*, on J. L. Austin's theory of language acts.

30. Vincent Descombes, *Le Même et l'Autre: Quarante-cinq ans de philosophie française (1933–1978)* (Paris: Éditions de Minuit, 1979), 163; see the English edition, *Modern French Philosophy*, trans. L. Scott-Fox and J. M. Harding (Cambridge: Cambridge University Press, 1980), 139 [translation slightly modified]. Descombes is referring here to a passage in the "Essai sur la pensée d'Emmanuel Levinas," the fourth chapter of Derrida's *L'Écriture et la Différence* (Paris: Seuil, 1967), 133. Note that Descombes has deliberately taken a liberty with this text, however, since in the passage cited Derrida is talking about pretending to speak *Greek*. The substitution of Chinese for Greek is utterly brilliant—Descombes's book appeared the year before Searle first published the Chinese Room argument!

CHAPTER TWO

1. This was the reason Minsky gave Françoise Fogelman-Soulié, who had come to MIT in July 1983 to interview him in connection with the project on the history of theories of self-organization directed by Isabelle Stengers, for refusing to elaborate on the history of artificial intelligence and cybernetics (see the preface).

2. A. Rosenblueth, N. Wiener, J. Bigelow, "Behavior, Purpose, Teleology," *Philosophy of Science* 10, no. 1 (1943): 18–24.

3. Claude E. Shannon and Warren Weaver, *The Mathematical Theory of Communication* (Urbana: University of Illinois Press, 1949); for details of the wartime research project directed by Weaver, see Steve J. Heims, *John von Neumann and Norbert Wiener: From Mathematics to the Technologies of Life and Death* (Cambridge, Mass.: MIT Press, 1980), 183–84.

4. See the introduction by Arthur Burks to his edition of John von Neumann's *Theory of Self-Reproducing Automata* (Urbana: University of Illinois Press, 1966), 11–12; also Herman H. Goldstine's classic study, *The Computer from Pascal to von Neumann* (Princeton: Princeton University Press, 1972), 252–70, 317–19.

5. See Steve P. Heims, "Gregory Bateson and the Mathematicians: From Interdisciplinary Interaction to Societal Functions," *Journal of the History of the Behavioral Sciences* 13 (1977): 143; also Heims, *The Cybernetics Group*, 289 (n. 6).

6. Rosenblueth et al., "Behavior, Purpose, Teleology," 18.

7. See, for example, Norbert Wiener, *God and Golem, Inc.: A Comment on Certain Points Where Cybernetics Impinges on Religion* (Cambridge, Mass.: MIT Press, 1964).

8. See von Foerster's 1970 paper "Molecular Ethology," reprinted in Heinz von Foerster, *Observing Systems*, ed. Francisco J. Varela (Seaside, Calif.: Intersystems Publications, 1981), 150–88.

9. See, for example, Varela, *Principles of Biological Autonomy*.

10. Rosenblueth et al., "Behavior, Purpose, Teleology," 83.

11. Philippe Breton, "La cybernétique et les ingénieurs dans les années cinquantes," *Culture technique* 12 (March 1984): 158.

12. Heinz von Foerster, Margaret Mead, and Hans Lukas Teuber, eds., *Cybernetics: Circular Causal and Feedback Mechanisms in Biological and Social Systems* [Transactions of the Eighth Conference, 15–16 March 1951, New York; hereafter referred to as "*Macy 8*"] (New York: Josiah Macy, Jr. Foundation, 1952), 168–71.

13. Rosenblueth et al., "Comportement, intention, téléologie," *Études philosophiques*, no. 2 (1961): 147–56.

14. Note that the title McCulloch gave to the collection of his major papers was *Embodiments of Mind* (Cambridge, Mass.: MIT Press, 1965).

15. The title of a talk given by McCulloch at the 1948 Hixon Symposium, reprinted with ensuing discussion in ibid., 72–141.

16. See Lloyd A. Jeffress, ed., *Cerebral Mechanisms in Behavior* [Proceedings of the Hixon Symposium, sponsored by the California Institute of Technology, September 1948, Pasadena, California; hereafter referred to as "*Hixon*"] (New York: John Wiley and Sons, 1951), 68–69.

17. Steve Heims calls attention to this in the title of his article "Encounter of Behavioral Sciences with New Machine-Organism Analogies in the 1940s," *Journal of the History of the Behavioral Sciences* 11 (1975): 368–73.

18. See Warren McCulloch, "*Mysterium Iniquiatis* of Sinful Man Aspiring into the Place of God" (1955), reprinted in *Embodiments of Mind*, 163 (my emphasis).

19: See Max Weber, *Science as a Vocation*, ed. Peter Lassman, Irving Velody, and Herminio Martins (London: Unwin Hyman, 1989), 9: "A really definitive and worthwhile achievement is nowadays always a specialized achievement. Therefore, anyone who lacks the capacity to put on blinkers, so to speak, . . . should have nothing to do with science." See also Heims, *The Cybernetics Group*, 54.

20. *Hixon*, 32.

21. McCulloch, *Embodiments of Mind*, 163.

22. This, the title of a lecture given by McCulloch in 1961, well summarizes the philosophical quest that, as he himself was at pains to point out, gave sense to the entire body of his work; reprinted in *Embodiments of Mind*, 2–18.

23. Simon confessed this at a conference devoted to his work that Jean-Louis Le Moigne organized at Montpellier in January 1984.

24. Jean-Pierre Changeux, *Neuronal Man: The Biology of Mind*, trans. Laurence Garey (Princeton: Princeton University Press, 1996), 97; originally published as *L'homme neuronal* (Paris: Librarie Arthème Fayard, 1983).

25. Changeux, *Neuronal Man*, 38. The emphasis is mine.

26. On the history of these devices, generally known as "logic machines"—but in a different sense from that in which I use the phrase in the body of this work, since they are physical machines—see Martin Gardner's classic work, *Logic Machines and Diagrams* (New York: McGraw-Hill, 1959).

27. Jean Mosconi explicitly draws attention to this point in "La Constitution de la théorie des automates," 1:59–62.

28. See Heinz von Foerster, Margaret Mead, and Hans Lukas Teuber, eds., *Cybernetics: Circular Causal and Feedback Mechanisms in Biological and Social*

Systems [Transactions of the Ninth Conference, 20–21 March 1952, New York; hereafter referred to as *"Macy 9"*] (New York: Josiah Macy, Jr. Foundation, 1953), 147–48.

29. Warren McCulloch and Walter Pitts, "A logical calculus of the ideas imminent in nervous activity," *Bulletin of Mathematical Biophysics* 5 (1943): 115–33. The article is more easily located in McCulloch's collection *Embodiments of Mind*, 19–39.

30. See the testimony of Norman Geschwind in the introductions he contributed to a planned edition of the complete works of Warren McCulloch. (Sadly this edition, scheduled for publication in 1989 by Intersystems Publications, never made it into stores or libraries, the California-based publisher having gone out of business in the interval; the collection of introductions I consulted [hereafter *McC. Intro.*] is in the personal archives of Heinz von Foerster.) On the war that, from 1870 to 1950 and beyond, opposed the "reticularists" (continuists) and the "neuronists," see Jean-Pierre Changeux's very detailed analysis in the first chapter of his *Neuronal Man*. At the Hixon Symposium in 1948, Lashley, in the discussion that followed McCulloch's talk ("Why the Mind Is in the Head"), resorted to arguments that were strongly reminiscent of those that Pierre Flourens had used against Franz Gall in 1842, more than a century earlier; see *Neuronal Man*, 16–17 and *Hixon*, 70–71.

31. In the initial version of the McCulloch-Pitts model, the weighting coefficients (today called "synaptic weights") are all equal to one, such that a neuron fires if and only if the number of impulses that it receives exceeds its threshold.

32. This precise phrase does not occur in the 1943 article, though it may be inferred: "At any instant a neuron has some threshold, which excitation must exceed to initiate an impulse" (McCulloch, *Embodiments of Mind*, 19). Jean-Pierre Changeux, in his description of the mechanisms that account for what he calls "going into action," adopts the same schema. The only difference is that the elementary organ of calculation is now no longer identified with the neuron itself but with its membrane. As Changeux himself remarks, at each stage in the history of the explanatory schemas adopted, "the level of organization is 'reduced' to a more elementary level" (*Neuronal Man*, 95; see too pages 101–3).

33. L. Kubie, "A theoretical application to some neurological problems of the properties of excitation waves which move in closed circuits," *Brain* 53, no. 2 (1930): 166–77.

34. See R. Lorente de Nó, "Analysis of the activity of the chains of internuncial neurons," *J. Neurophysiol.* 1 (1938), 207–44.

35. See L. Kubie, "The Repetitive Core of Neurosis," *Psychoanalytic Quarterly* 10 (1941): 23–43. Changeux seems to ignore Kubie's decisive role in the formation of this hypothesis; see *Neuronal Man*, 141–42 and 169.

36. See, for example, the exchange between McCulloch and Kubie in Heinz von Foerster, ed., *Cybernetics: Circular Causal and Feedback Mechanisms in Biological and Social Systems* [Transactions of the Sixth Conference, 24–25 March 1949, New York; hereafter referred to as *"Macy 6"*] (New York: Josiah Macy, Jr. Foundation, 1950), 61–62.

37. Mosconi, "La Constitution de la théorie des automates," 1:154.

38. See von Neumann's January 1952 lectures at Caltech, subsequently pub-

lished as "Probabilistic Logics and the Synthesis of Reliable Organisms from Unreliable Components," in C. E. Shannon and J. McCarthy, eds., *Automata Studies* (Princeton: Princeton University Press, 1956); also reprinted in *Papers of John von Neumann on Computing and Computer Theory*, eds. William Aspray and Arthur Burk (Cambridge, Mass.: MIT Press, 1987), 553–602. For McCulloch's reaction to the linking together of these ideas, see *Embodiments of Mind*, 11.

39. See his paper "Finality and Form in Nervous Activity," delivered as the J. A. Thompson Lecture on 2 May 1946 but not published until six years later, when it appeared under the title "Finality and Form" as publication no. 11 in *The American Lecture Series* (Springfield, Ill.: Charles C. Thomas, 1952); later reprinted in *Embodiments of Mind*, 256–75 (see especially 272–73).

40. See Mosconi's acute analysis in "La Constitution de la théorie des automates," 1:137–38.

41. Many at the time of the Macy Conferences compared Pitts's intellectual abilities with those of von Neumann. Pitts was said to be the only person at the conferences able to understand the whole of what was discussed there.

42. See S. C. Kleene, "Representations of Events in Nerve Nets and Finite Automata," in Shannon and McCarthy, eds., *Automata Studies*, 3–42.

43. See M. A. Arbib, "Turing machines, finite automata and neural nets," *JACM* 8 (1961): 467–75.

44. See McCulloch's 1964 paper, " 'What's in the Brain That Ink May Character?' " reprinted in *Embodiments of Mind*, 387–97 (especially page 393).

45. See McCulloch's 1948 paper, "Through the Den of the Metaphysician," reprinted in *Embodiments of Mind*, 142–56. The passage quoted here is found at pages 143–44.

46. McCulloch, " 'What's in the Brain That Ink May Character?' " 389, 393.

47. See for example McCulloch's discussion with von Neumann at the Hixon Symposium (*Hixon*, 58–61); also Jerome Lettvin's reminiscence, "Warren and Walter," in *McC. Intro.*, 1:5, 13.

48. John von Neumann, "Rigorous Theories of Control and Information" (the second of five lectures delivered at the University of Illinois in December 1949 under the general title "Theory and Organization of Complicated Automata"), in *Theory of Self-Reproducing Automata*, 43. The emphasis is mine.

49. Ibid., 44. Again, the emphasis is mine.

50. See Changeux, *Neuronal Man*, 95–96.

51. Ibid., 169.

52. *Macy 6*, 12.

53. Ibid., 12–26, 60–61.

54. John von Neumann and Oscar Morgenstern, *The Theory of Games and Economic Behavior* (Princeton: Princeton University Press, 1944).

55. Thus Jean-Pierre Changeux, for example, though his *Neuronal Man* contains a very detailed historical analysis, never once mentions McCulloch's name. Worse still is the complete confusion produced by Marc Jeannerod, who in *Le Cerveau-machine: Physiologie de la volonté* (Paris: Fayard, 1983) refers vaguely and in passing to threshold neural networks only to attribute their invention to the "work of Eccles, in the years 1940–1950 [*sic*]" (page 100; see also 215). Jeannerod's book is available in English as *The Brain Machine: The Development of Neuro-*

172 NOTES TO CHAPTER TWO

physiological Thought, trans. David Urion (Cambridge, Mass.: Harvard University Press, 1985).

56. See Lettvin's introduction to the first volume of *McC. Intro.*, 1–2, as well as his piece "Warren and Walter," 12.

57. Howard Gardner's book, *The Mind's New Science* (New York: Basic Books, 1985), is mainly anecdotal.

58. See Frank Rosenblatt, *Principles of Neurodynamics: Perceptrons and the Theory of Brain Mechanisms* (Buffalo: Cornell Aeronautical Laboratory, 1961; Washington, D.C.: Spartan Books, 1962).

59. Ibid., 16–20.

60. Marvin Minsky and Seymour Papert, *Perceptrons* (Cambridge, Mass.: MIT Press, 1969).

61. In an epilogue to the 1988 edition of *Perceptrons*, entitled "The New Connectionism," Minsky and Papert defend themselves against the accusation of having earlier expressed "pessimism" about all future research on the Perceptron.

62. Marvin Minsky, *Semantic Information Processing* (Cambridge, Mass.: MIT Press, 1969).

63. See Hubert Dreyfus, *What Computers Can't Do* (New York: Harper and Row, 2nd ed., 1979), 130.

64. See Daniel Memmi, "Connectionisme, Intelligence Artificielle et modélisation cognitive," *Intellectica*, no. 9–10 (1990) [special issue devoted to "Connectionist Models"]: 41–79. On the same question one may profitably consult as well Daniel Andler's essay "Introduction—Calcul et représentation: les sources," in D. Andler, ed., *Introduction aux sciences cognitives* (Paris: Éditions Gallimard, 1992), 9–46; and, by the same author, "Connexionisme et cognition: À la recherche des bonnes questions," *Revue de synthèse* 4, no. 1–2 (January–June 1990), 95–127.

65. To be more precise, Rosenblatt used the adjective "connectionist," which Donald Hebb had used still earlier in his 1949 book, *The Organization of Behavior*. It was in this work that Hebb proposed a celebrated learning rule that is still regarded as relevant today in neural network models: a connection is reinforced (i.e., its weight is increased) if it links two neurons fired at the same time. For an anthology of the founding texts of connectionism, see James A. Anderson and Edward Rosenfeld, *Neurocomputing: Foundations of Research*, 2 vols. (Cambridge, Mass.: MIT Press, 1988).

66. See Daniel Andler, "From Paleo- to Neo-Connectionism," in Gertrudis Van de Vijver, ed., *New Perspectives on Cybernetics: Self-Organization, Autonomy, and Connectionism* (Dordrecht: Kluwer, 1992), 125–46.

67. See Burks's introduction to his edition of von Neumann's works on the theory of automata, *Theory of Self-Reproducing Automata*, 6–12. Von Neumann drafted a preliminary version of his thinking on the subject in June 1945 in a report that was never published, "First Draft of a Report on the EDVAC"; extracts from this may be found, however, in Brian Randell, ed., *The Origins of Digital Computers: Selected Papers* (New York: Springer-Verlag, 1973; 3rd ed., 1982); see too the extended discussion in Goldstine, *The Computer from Pascal to von Neumann*, 191–224.

68. See Heims, "Encounter of Behavioral Sciences with New Machine-Organism Analogies in the 1940s," 371.

69. On the controversial impact of von Neumann's thinking on public policy while he was alive and afterward, particularly with regard to American nuclear strategy during the Cold War, see William Poundstone, *Prisoner's Dilemma: John von Neumann, Game Theory, and the Puzzle of the Bomb* (New York: Doubleday, 1992); also Heims, *John von Neumann and Norbert Wiener*.

70. Reprinted in *Hixon*, 1–41; the unfinished statement of the theory as it stood at the time of von Neumann's death was published posthumously as *The Computer and the Brain* (New Haven: Yale University Press, 1958).

71. See *Hixon*, 22–24.

72. See Burks's introduction to his edition of von Neumann, *Theory of Self-Reproducing Automata*, 19, 25–28.

73. On this point see Lettvin's introduction to the first volume of *McC. Intro.*, 16–17.

74. In the first edition of this book I wrongly reproached the American philosopher Daniel C. Dennett for having underestimated the importance of cybernetics in the history of the cognitive sciences. I stand corrected: he has in fact always paid due homage to cybernetics, and indeed made a point of including Warren McCulloch among his first mentors in his autobiographical essay "Self-Portrait," in *Brainchildren: Essays on Designing Minds* (Cambridge, Mass.: MIT Press, 1998), 355–366. My sincerest apologies to Dan Dennett for this false imputation, to which I was misled by the fact that an essay reprinted in the same book, "The Logical Geography of Computational Approaches: A View from the East Pole," makes no explicit reference to cybernetics.

CHAPTER THREE

1. Gregory Bateson, *Steps to an Ecology of Mind*, 484. This remark is quoted from a paper ("From Versailles to Cybernetics") delivered in 1966.

2. See "A Note by the Editors," *Macy 8*, xix. Bateson is mistaken in claiming in the foreword to his *Steps to an Ecology of Mind* (page ix) that Julian Bigelow was also present.

3. See Wiener, *Cybernetics*, 12.

4. See Fremont-Smith's communication to Steve Heims, reported in *John von Neumann and Norbert Wiener*, 468, n. 13.

5. These themes were the subject of conferences held by the foundation in 1949: see *Macy 6*, 9.

6. For Rosenblueth, accepting McCulloch's offer would have meant losing his Mexican citizenship; see Heims, *The Cybernetics Group*, 44, 49.

7. See Heims, *John von Neumann and Norbert Wiener*, 185–86. Wiener mistakenly puts the date of this meeting "in the late winter of 1943–1944" in the introduction to his *Cybernetics*, 15.

8. Rosenblueth, unable to leave Mexico City, was absent. See Wiener, *Cybernetics*, 15, and Heims, "Gregory Bateson and the Mathematicians," 143.

9. See Wiener's 24 January 1945 letter to Rosenblueth, cited in Heims, *John von Neumann and Norbert Wiener*, 186.

10. See ibid., 189.

11. See Heims, *John von Neumann and Norbert Wiener*, 202; "Gregory Bateson and the Mathematicians," 145; *The Cybernetics Group*, 24–26.

12. See Heims, "An Encounter between Neo-Mechanists and the Human Sciences."

13. Here and in what follows I use the term "cycle" (or "round") for the sake of convenience in order to distinguish the first five conferences, of which we have almost no record, from the last five, for which we have full proceedings. The participants in the series of ten meetings organized by McCulloch were officially referred to by the Macy Foundation as the "Cybernetics Group" (as opposed to the other groups working in parallel on the various topics mentioned previously)—hence the title of Heims's book.

14. See Heims, "Gregory Bateson and the Mathematicians," 151.

15. This information is from an unpublished paper by Steve J. Heims, "Mechanists and Social 'Scientists' (1946–1953)"; see also *The Cybernetics Group*, 183.

16. See "A Note by the Editors," *Macy 8*, xix.

17. Roy Waldo Miner, ed., "Teleological Mechanisms" [Proceedings of a Conference held by the New York Academy of Sciences on 21–22 October 1946], *Annals of the New York Academy of Sciences* 50, no. 4 (13 October 1948): 192.

18. Wiener's paper was entitled "Time, Communication, and the Nervous System"; see ibid., 197–220.

19. See "A Note by the Editors," *Macy 8*, xix.

20. See Wiener's introduction, *Cybernetics*, 11–12. He does not mention the earlier (and quite different) use of the word by Ampère, making reference instead to Maxwell's 1868 Royal Society paper on "governors."

21. See "A Note by the Editors," *Macy 8*, xix–xx. This note erroneously gives the year of the fourth conference as 1948.

22. Von Foerster recounts this story in his contribution to the introductions to McCulloch's complete works: see "Circular Causality: The Beginnings of an Epistemology of Responsibility," *McC. Intro.*

23. See the account of Jerome Lettvin (who came along with McCulloch from Chicago to Cambridge in 1952) in "Warren and Walter," *McC. Intro.*, 8. See too Heims, *John von Neumann and Norbert Wiener*, 190 (n. 34). The growing rivalry between Wiener and von Neumann should be noted as well: see ibid., 208. See also Heims, *The Cybernetics Group*, 137–40.

24. This letter, headed "An Account of the First Three Conferences on Teleological Mechanisms" and signed by McCulloch, is contained in the personal archives of Heinz von Foerster. McCulloch's continuing insistence on the theme "teleological mechanisms" is interesting: the term had in fact been dropped from the title of the fourth conference, which was announced as "Circular Causal and Feedback Mechanisms in Biological and Social Systems."

25. See "Appendix I: Summary of the Points of Agreement Reached in the Previous Nine Conferences on Cybernetics," identifying McCulloch as the author, in Heinz von Foerster, Margaret Mead, and Hans Lukas Teuber, eds. *Cybernetics: Circular Causal and Feedback Mechanisms in Biological and Social Systems* [Transactions of the Tenth Conference, 22–24 April 1953, Princeton; hereafter referred to as "*Macy 10*"] (New York: Josiah Macy, Jr. Foundation, 1955). This summary was likewise distributed in advance to participants in the tenth conference. *Macy 10* also contains a cumulative index to the five published volumes of *Transactions* (covering conferences held between 1949 and 1953).

26. In particular the McCulloch archives at the library of the American Philo-sophical Society in Philadelphia.

27. See Heims, "Encounter of Behavioral Sciences," and *The Cybernetics Group*, 235–38.

28. See "A Note by the Editors," *Macy 8*, xx.

29. See Heims, "An Encounter between Neo-Mechanists and the Human Sciences," 369.

30. See Heims, *John von Neumann and Norbert Wiener*, 206.

31. See the introductory remarks by Frank Fremont-Smith in Heinz von Foerster, Margaret Mead, and Hans Lukas Teuber, eds., *Cybernetics: Circular Causal and Feedback Mechanisms in Biological and Social Systems* [Transactions of the Seventh Conference, 23–24 March 1950, New York; hereafter referred to as "*Macy 7*"] (New York: Josiah Macy, Jr. Foundation, 1951), 7–8.

32. Published as *Beyond Reductionism: New Perspectives in the Life Sciences*, eds. Arthur Koestler and J. R. Smythies (London: Hutchinson, 1969; New York: Macmillan, 1970).

33. Jean Piaget, invited but unable to attend, was represented by Bärbel Inhelder.

34. This will inevitably be unfair to certain participants. In any case we shall systematically include the regular "members" of the group but only some of those who figure on the list of "guests." The original list of regular members, in alphabetical order together with the fields they represented, was as follows: Gregory Bateson (anthropology), Julian Bigelow (electrical engineering), Gerhardt von Bonin (neuroanatomy), Lawrence Frank (social sciences), Frank Fremont-Smith (medicine/foundation administration), Ralph Gerard (neurophysiology), Molly Harrower (psychology [resigned after fifth conference]), George Hutchinson (ecology), Heinrich Klüver (psychology), Lawrence Kubie (psychoanalysis), Paul Lazarsfeld (sociology [dropped after sixth conference]), Kurt Lewin (social psychology [died shortly before third conference]), Rafael Lorente de Nó (neurophysiology), Warren McCulloch (neuropsychiatry), Margaret Mead (anthropology), John von Neumann (mathematics), Filmer Northrop (philosophy), Walter Pitts (mathematics), Arturo Rosenblueth (physiology), Leonard Savage (mathematics), and Norbert Wiener (mathematics). To this list it is necessary to add the names of members who joined the group later (with the number of the first conference in which they participated indicated in brackets along with their field): Alex Bavelas (social psychology [5]), Henry Brosin (psychiatry [2]), Heinz von Foerster (electrical engineering [6]), Donald Marquis (psychology [2]), Theodore Schneirla (comparative psychology [2]), and Hans Lukas Teuber (psychology [4]). The list of guests (noting in brackets the number of the conference[s] attended) included, among others, Harold Abramson (medicine [6]), Ross Ashby (psychiatry, [9]), Yehoshua Bar-Hillel (mathematical logic [10]), Herbert Birch (comparative [animal] psychology, [8]), Eilhard von Domarus (neuropsychiatry [5]), Max Delbrück (biophysics [5]), Erik Erikson (psychoanalysis [3]), Leon Festinger (social psychology [3]), Roman Jakobson (linguistics [5]), Clyde Kluckhohn (anthropology [3,4]), Wolfgang Köhler (psychology [4]), Joseph Licklider (psychology [7]), William Livingston (medicine [2]), Donald MacKay (physics [8]), Henry Quastler (computer science [9, 10]), Claude Shannon (engineering [7, 8, 10]), John Stroud

(psychology [6, 7]), W. Grey Walter (neurology [10]), Heinz Werner (developmental psychology [7]), Jerome Wiesner (computer science [9]), and John Z. Young (neuroanatomy [9]). For further detail see Heims, *The Cybernetics Group*, 285–86.

35. Leonard J. Savage, *Foundations of Statistics* (New York: Wiley, 1954).

36. Erwin Schrödinger, *What Is Life? The Physical Aspect of the Living Cell* (Cambridge: Cambridge University Press, 1944).

37. The expression is due to Heinz von Foerster (see "Circular Causality" in *McC. Intro.*); it was apparently meant to signify von Neumann's desire to preserve a measure of independence from his fellow cyberneticians—an insider who yet remained in some sense outside the group.

38. See the November 1946 correspondence between von Neumann and Wiener cited in Heims, *John von Neumann and Norbert Wiener*, 204.

39. From a 1973 letter from Delbrück to Heims cited in ibid., 205, 475, and also in *The Cybernetics Group*, 95.

40. McCulloch, *Embodiments of Mind*, 163. The work of Henri Atlan has not only thoroughly illuminated this chapter of intellectual history, it has cast new light in other directions as well: in addition to *L'Organisation biologique et la théorie de l'information*, see *Entre le cristal et la fumée: Essai sur l'organisation du vivant* (Paris: Seuil, 1979).

41. See *Macy 6*, 150–57.

42. See von Foerster, "Circular Causality," in *McC. Intro.*, 8–9.

43. The sole existing collection of Von Foerster's writings, already referred to, is the (admittedly ambiguously titled) volume *Observing Systems*.

44. Quoted at chap. 2, n. 19.

45. See Heims, "Gregory Bateson and the Mathematicians," 146–47 and 149–51.

46. Heims made this point to me in conversation.

47. See *Macy 6*, 9–10; *Macy 7*, 7–8; *Macy 8*, vii–viii.

48. From Frank's forward to Miner, ed., "Teleological Mechanisms," 194. The quote is from an 1885 address by Haldane, cited earlier by Sir Frederick Gowland Hopkins, "Some chemical aspects of life," *Science* 78, no. 2020 (1933): 227.

49. Cited in Heims, *The Cybernetics Group*, 173–74.

50. See ibid., 69–71, and the whole of chap. 7, "The Macy Foundation and Worldwide Mental Health," 164–79. As I noted in the introduction, Heims's book is for the most part devoted to analyzing the relation between science and society during the period that cybernetics was born.

51. Miner, ed., "Teleological Mechanisms," 191–92, 195–96.

52. *Macy 6*, 151.

53. See Fremont-Smith's introductory remarks at the eighth Macy Conference (*Macy 8*, viii), as well as the discussion that followed Kubie's presentation at the seventh conference (*Macy 7*, 224 and 234–35).

54. See, for example, Mead's interventions in *Macy 7*, 234, and *Macy 8*, 106.

55. See Heims, "Gregory Bateson and the Mathematicians," 143. Boring did not participate in the Macy Conferences.

56. See McCulloch, "An Account of the First Three Conferences on Teleological Mechanisms."

57. See W. Pitts and W. McCulloch, "How We Know Universals: The Perception of Auditory and Visual Forms" (1947), reprinted in McCulloch, *Embodiments of Mind*, 46–66.

58. See *Macy 8*, 104, 131; the entire discussion that followed Kubie's presentation ("Communication between Sane and Insane: Hypnosis") was one of the most heated of all the Macy Conferences.

59. See *Macy 6*, 9, 101–7.

60. See *Macy 8*, 128, 132.

61. Ibid., 128–29.

62. Ibid., 132.

63. *Macy 6*, 148.

64. See *Macy 9*, 149.

65. *Hixon*, 112.

66. See *Macy 7*, 11, 47.

67. McCulloch, "Why the Mind Is in the Head," in *Hixon*, 43; reprinted in *Embodiments of Mind*, 73.

68. In "Circular Causality" (see *McC. Intro.*), von Foerster cites the same passage from the paper read by McCulloch at the Hixon Symposium and interprets it not as a plea made in the name of physics, but as already announcing the transformation of cybernetics into epistemology.

69. See "A Note by the Editors," *Macy 8*, xi–xiii.

70. See *Macy 7*, 49.

71. See, for example, Bateson's performance during the discussion that followed Gerard's presentation on inhibitory and excitatory synapses at the ninth conference (*Macy 9*, 137–38, 140, 146).

72. See the interventions recorded in *Macy 7* of Gerard (pp. 11–12), Stroud (p. 28), and Wiener (p. 18).

73. See Bigelow's remark in *Macy 9*, 67–68, 70.

CHAPTER FOUR

1. Interview with Martin Heidegger, "Nur noch ein Gott kan uns retten," *Der Spiegel*, no. 23 (31 May 1976): 193–219.

2. See, for example, the discussion of this cognitive turn by Pascal Engel, one of the best French authorities on philosophy of mind, in his *Introduction à la philosophie de l'esprit* 7–10.

3. See Joëlle Proust, "L'intelligence artificielle comme philosophie," *Le Débat*, no. 47 (November–December, 1987): 88–102.

4. See McCulloch, *Embodiments of Mind*, xvii.

5. Mosconi, "La Constitution de la théorie des automates," 1:138.

6. See Andler, "From Paleo- to Neo-Connectionism."

7. See David E. Rumelhart, James L. McClelland, and the PDP Research Group, *Parallel Distributed Processing: Explorations in the Microstructure of Cognition*, vol. 1: *Foundations* (Cambridge, Mass.: MIT Press, 1986).

8. Proust, "L'intelligence artificielle comme philosophie," 98–99.

9. Other mental states include states of "tacit knowledge," or "sub-doxastic" states.

10. Roderick M. Chisholm, *Perceiving: A Philosophical Study* (Ithaca, N.Y.: Cornell University Press, 1957).

11. Ibid., 298.

12. For an overview of this problem and of the various theoretical positions to which it has given rise, one may profitably consult Pascal Engel's *Introduction à la philosophie de l'esprit.*

13. Reprinted in Donald Davidson, *Essays on Actions and Events* (New York: Oxford University Press, 1980).

14. Engel, *Introduction à la philosophie de l'esprit,* 10.

15. Searle, "Minds, brains, and programs," 457.

16. W. V. Quine, "Mind versus Body," in *Quiddities: An Intermittently Philosophical Dictionary* (Cambridge, Mass.: Belknap Press of Harvard University Press, 1987), 134.

17. Quoted in Investigation 5, chap. 2, sec. 10 of Edmund Husserl, *Logical Investigations,* 2 vols., trans. J. N. Findlay (London: Routledge & Kegan Paul, 1970), 2:554; originally published as *Logische Untersuchungen,* 2 vols. (Halle: M. Niemeyer, 1900–1901).

18. Franz Brentano, *Psychology from an Empirical Standpoint,* ed. Linda L. McAlister and trans. Antos C. Rancurello, D. B. Terrell, Linda L. McAlister (New York: Routledge, 1995), 88; originally published as *Psychologie vom empirischen Standpunkt* (Leipzig: Duncker & Humblot, 1874). The McAlister edition is based on Oskar Kraus's third edition of 1925; the passage cited here is quoted by Husserl in both the fifth and sixth parts of the *Logical Investigations.* On Husserl's relation to Brentano, particularly insofar as Husserl represents the point of common origin from which Heidegger split off in one direction and Sartre in another, see Alain Renaut, *Sartre: le dernier philosophe* (Paris: Grasset, 1993), 88–102.

19. Brentano, *Psychology from an Empirical Standpoint,* 80.

20. Ibid., 77.

21. Ibid., 127–28.

22. Renaut, *Sartre,* 93, 97–98; emphasis in the original.

23. See Linda L. McAlister, "Chisholm and Brentano on Intentionality," *Review of Metaphysics* 28, no. 2 (1974): 328–38. The Stanford philosopher Stefano Franchi is currently doing remarkable work on this subject. The affair is actually still more complicated, for Brentano himself was later—first in 1905 and then in the second edition of the *Psychologie,* published in 1911—to reject the thesis that "physical phenomena" are contained within consciousness (that strange *Kehre* that led Brentano to adopt a doctrine that he himself called "reism"). The problem is that Chisholm never referred to any other edition than that of 1874. Certain analytical philosophers specializing in Brentano's thought maintain that no reversal ever took place and that Brentano was a "reist" from the start. On this view, then, it was the Husserlian tradition that was gravely mistaken! See Richard Aquila, *Intentionality: A Study of Mental Acts* (State College, Pa.: Pennsylvania State University Press, 1977).

24. See W. V. Quine, *Word and Object* (Cambridge, Mass.: MIT Press, 1960), sec. 45 ("The Double Standard"), 220.

25. Ibid., 221.

26. An accessible introduction to this work can be found in Françoise Fogel-man-Soulié et al., eds., *Les Théories de la complexité: Autour de l'œuvre d'Henri Atlan* (Paris: Seuil, 1991).

27. See Stuart A. Kauffman, *The Origins of Order: Self-Organization and Selection in Evolution* (New York: Oxford University Press, 1993).

28. See Francisco J. Varela, *Principles of Biological Autonomy*.

29. See J. J. Hopfield, "Neural Networks and Physical Systems with Emergent Collective Computational Abilities" (1982), reprinted in Anderson and Rosenfeld, *Neurocomputing*, 1:457–59; also the recent work of Hopfield's student Christof Koch, *Biophysics of Computation: Information Processing in Single Neurons* (New York: Oxford University Press, 1999).

30. See Daniel J. Amit, *Modeling Brain Function: The World of Attractor Neural Networks* (Cambridge: Cambridge University Press, 1989).

31. See Jean Petitot, "Morphodynamics and Attractor Syntax: Dynamical and Morphological Models for Constituency in Visual Perception and Cognitive Grammar," in Robert F. Port and Timothy Van Gelder, eds., *Mind as Motion: Explorations in the Dynamics of Cognition* (Cambridge, Mass.: MIT Press, 1995); and his contribution to François Marty, ed., *La Philosophie transcendantale et le problème de l'objectivité* (Paris: Osiris, 1991).

32. See H. Atlan, "Intentionality in nature," *Journal for the Theory of Social Behaviour* 24, no. 1 (1994): 67–87.

33. See J. Petitot, "Phénoménologie naturalisée et morphodynamique: la fonction cognitive du synthetique a priori," *Intellectica* (special issue, "Philosophie et sciences cognitives," edited by J.-M. Salanskis), no. 17 (1992/3): 79–126; also his *Physique du sens*.

34. See Francisco J. Varela, Evan Thompson, and Eleanor Rosch, *The Embodied Mind: Cognitive Science and Human Experience* (Cambridge, Mass.: MIT Press, 1991).

35. Steve Heims has succeeded in reconstructing the essential details of this encounter, of which, it will be recalled, no written record was made. See chap. 10 of his *Cybernetic Group*, in particular pages 236–39.

36. J. Y. Lettvin, H. R. Maturana, W. S. McCulloch, and W. H. Pitts, "What the Frog's Eye Tells the Frog's Brain," *Proceedings of the IRE* 47, no. 11 (November 1959): 1940–1959; reprinted in McCulloch, *Embodiments of Mind*, 230–55.

37. See Paul Ricoeur, "Structure et herméneutique," *Esprit*, no. 11 (November 1963): 596–627.

38. See Claude Lévi-Strauss, "Introduction à l'œuvre de Marcel Mauss," in Marcel Mauss, *Sociologie et Anthropologie* (Paris: Presses Universitaires de France, 1950).

39. See n. 1 above.

40. Martin Heidegger, *The Question Concerning Technology and Other Essays*, trans. William Lovitt (New York: Harper & Row, 1977), 314; originally published in *Vortrage und Aufsatze* (Pfullingen: G. Neske, 1954).

41. See chaps. 15 and 16 ("Séminaire sur *La Lettre volée*") in Jacques-Alain Miller, ed., *Le Séminaire de Jacques Lacan*, Book 2: *Le Moi dans la théorie de Freud et dans la technique de la psychanalyse* (Paris: Seuil, 1978); an English

edition was published as *Ego in Freud's Theory and in the Technique of Psycho-analysis, 1954–55*, trans. Sylvana Tomaselli with notes by John Forrester (New York: Cambridge University Press, 1988).

42. For an assessment of this work one may consult my own article, "Self-Reference in Literature," *Poetics*, no. 18 (1989): 491–515.

43. See Lacan, *Le Séminaire*, II, 111–12.

44. Ibid., 351.

45. See Heidegger, *The Question Concerning Technology*, 314–15.

46. Philippe Breton, "La cybernétique et les ingénieurs dans les années cinqu-ante," *Culture technique*, no. 12 (March 1984), 160. See too his articles "Pourquoi les machines analogiques ont-elles disparu?" *Milieux* (June 1985), and "Quelques problèmes posés par l'émergence d'un nouveau type d'ingénieur: les ingénieurs de la connaissance," *Cahiers du CEFI* (June 1985). The great difference between the American origins of cybernetics and its reception in France is that in France it was developed chiefly in and through the engineering community, whereas engi-neers played only a very partial role in the development of cybernetics on its native soil: in this connection two recent works by Breton may be profitably con-sulted, *L'Utopie de la communication: L'émergence de "l'homme sans intérieur"* (Paris: La Découverte, 1992), and (with Serge Proulx) *L'Explosion de la communi-cation: la naissance d'une nouvelle idéologie* (Paris: La Découverte, 1989; 2nd ed., 1994).

47. Jean-Claude Beaune, *L'Automate et ses mobiles* (Paris: Flammarion, 1980), 332–33.

48. Ibid., 333.

49. Gilbert Hottois, *Le Signe et la technique: La Philosophie à l'épreuve de la technique* (Paris: Aubier, 1984), 150. Emphasis in the original.

50. Lacan, *Le Séminaire*, II, 367.

51. Jeannerod, *The Brain Machine*, 110 (author's emphasis in the original French text, added here). Note that, unwittingly chosen or not, this is a very poor title for a book that advocates a "humanist" philosophy, since such a philosophy is contradicted by the notion of the brain as a machine.

52. On the origin of the name, see Wiener, *Cybernetics*, 11–12; for Descombes's argument, see *Le Même et l'autre*, 123–24.

53. See Wiener, *Cybernetics*, 13.

54. See Heims, *John von Neumann and Norbert Wiener*, 141–42.

55. On the impression that Wiener's sometimes lax habits of thinking made upon his colleagues, see ibid., 157, 343.

56. With the exception, of course, of the "cybernetician" physiologist Rosen-blueth—and also, more strikingly, Lorente de Nó, who expressed admiration for McCulloch's performance at the Hixon Symposium (*Hixon*, 57–58); in contrast to their views are the reservations about McCulloch's work expressed by the great neurophysiologist Ralph Gerard, who had collaborated with McCulloch and Pitts and was himself a pillar of the Macy Conferences (see Gerard's interview with Heims in *John von Neumann and Norbert Wiener*, 359).

57. On the jolting effects of the war on Wiener (as compared with von Neu-mann), see chap. 9 ("The Watershed") in ibid., 179–200.

58. See ibid., chap. 13 ("Wiener, the Independent Intellectual: Technology as Applied Moral and Social Philosophy"), 330–46, and chap. 15 ("Wiener's Later Years: Again the Golem"), 372–97; and Philippe Breton, "Présupposés anthropologiques et pensée du social chez les ingénieurs: un facteur sous-estimé du développement des technologies de l'information de l'après-guerre," in *Cahiers STS* (1986).

59. A history of cybernetics centered on the tension between the distinctive styles of thought embodied by Wiener and McCulloch would give a very different picture of things than one that contrasts Wiener with von Neumann, as Heims's book does.

CHAPTER FIVE

1. *Macy 6*, 150.

2. See Leo Szilard, "Über die Entropieverminderung in einem thermodynamischen System bei Eingriffen intelligenter Wesen," *Zeitschrift für Physik* 53 (1929): 840–56. A translation appeared immediately after Szilard's death under the title "On the Decrease of Entropy in a Thermodynamic System by the Intervention of Intelligent Beings," *Behavioral Science* 9, no. 4 (1964): 301–10. The editor of this journal introduced it with the comment: "This is one of the earliest, if not the earliest paper in which the relations of physical entropy to information (in the sense of modern mathematical theory of communication) were rigorously demonstrated and in which Maxwell's famous demon was successfully exorcised: *a milestone in the integration of physical and cognitive concepts*" (my emphasis).

3. Léon Brillouin, *Science and Information Theory* (New York: Academic Press, 1956).

4. *Teleological Mechanisms*, 203. Wiener was to revert to this idea during the third Macy Conference, in March 1947; see McCulloch, "An Account of the First Three Conferences on Teleological Mechanisms."

5. See, for example, *Macy 6*, 107.

6. *Teleological Mechanisms*, 207–8.

7. *Macy 7*, 26.

8. Ibid., 20–21.

9. Ibid., 43–44.

10. Ibid., 45–46.

11. Wiener used the expressions "region of attraction" (*Macy 6*, 201) and "field of attraction" (*Macy 7*, 21).

12. *Macy 6*, 202 (my emphasis). Wiener developed these ideas at the sixth conference, from which von Neumann was absent. At the seventh, von Neumann took them up in his turn (*Macy 7*, 19–20) with enormous clarity, Wiener following close on his heels, saying that he wished only to offer "a comment on what Professor von Neumann has said" (21).

13. *Macy 7*, 18–19.

14. Changeux, *Neuronal Man*, 107.

15. Ibid., 90.

16. *Macy 6*, 88–89. The role of these hormonal messages is also discussed in Wiener, *Cybernetics*, 129–30.

17. The independent von Neumann was likewise exceptional, but his style was completely different. Wiener's two co-authors of the 1943 article, on the other hand, were surely the most rigid and dogmatic of the group. See Bigelow's outburst against Gerard, at the end of the discussion we have just commented upon, regarding the respective roles of digital and analogical processing in the central nervous system (*Macy 7*, 47).

18. McCulloch, "An Account of the First Three Conferences on Teleological Mechanisms." Wiener was playing the professor in this instance.

19. *Macy 6*, 97.

20. Here the professor was Licklider, who described himself as falling somewhere in between psychology and mathematics (*Macy 7*, 228–29).

21. *Macy 7*, 58ff. Note too the discussion with Teuber, who prefered speaking of "equivalence of stimuli" rather than "redundancy of information" (95–96).

22. Ibid., 66.

23. See Shannon's paper "The Redundancy of English," in *Macy 7*, 123ff.

24. *Hixon*, 55.

25. See chap. 7 ("Epigenesis") of Changeux, *Neuronal Man*, particularly pp. 221–23 and 247–48.

26. See *Macy 9*, particularly pp. 173 and 179–80. A more complete review of Quastler's calculations can be found in chap. 5 of Atlan, *L'Organisation biologique*.

27. Raymond Ruyer, *La Cybernétique et l'origine de l'information* (Paris: Flammarion, 1954), 25–26.

28. Ibid., 13.

29. See Fred Dretske, *Knowledge and the Flow of Information* (Cambridge, Mass.: MIT Press, 1981) and *Explaining Behavior: Reasons in a World of Causes* (Cambridge, Mass.: MIT Press, 1988); also the Jean Nicod Lectures delivered by Dretske in 1994 and subsequently published as *Naturalizing the Mind* (Cambridge, Mass.: MIT Press, 1995).

30. See McCulloch's statement in *Hixon*, 46.

31. See *Macy 7*, 154, 147.

32. See the exchange among Shannon, Licklider, Stroud, Pitts, and Savage in *Macy 7*, 154–55.

33. Ibid., 140.

34. Ibid., 141–46.

35. See von Foerster, "On Self-Organizing Systems and Their Environments" (1960), reprinted in *Observing Systems*, 1–22.

36. See Atlan, *Entre le cristal et la fumée*.

37. *Macy 8*, xiii.

38. Norbert Wiener, *I Am a Mathematician* (Garden City, N.Y.: Doubleday & Co., 1956), 324–25; cited in Heims, *John von Neumann and Norbert Wiener*, 155–56 (this in a chapter entitled, significantly, "The Foundation: Chaos or Logic?").

39. *Macy 7*, 153–54.

40. Gilbert Simondon, *Du mode d'existence des objets techniques* (Paris: Montaigne, 1989), 49; the Macy Conferences are referred to on page 263.

41. Ibid., 137.

42. See the debate between MacKay and Savage in *Macy 8*, 204–6. Savage, who defended a subjectivist conception of probabilities, did not believe that uncertainty could always be reduced to the probabilizable.

43. It is true that Wiener, the member of the group who was most sensitive to the dialectic between order and disorder, had dropped out as of the eighth conference.

44. Carnap, who had taught Pitts at Chicago, was invited to participate but had to decline for reasons of health.

45. *Macy 6*, 138; see too the debate among Stroud, Klüver, Teuber, McCulloch, and Wiener (57–59).

46. *Macy 8*, 217–18. Savage seems not to have had in mind William James's famous phrase about the cash value of ideas, referring explicitly instead to von Neumann's utility theory.

47. See McCulloch, "A Heterarchy of Values Determined by the Topology of Nervous Nets" (1945), reprinted in *Embodiments of Mind*, 40–44.

48. See Heims, *John von Neumann and Norbert Wiener*, 306–7; also *The Cybernetics Group*, 110.

49. See ibid., chaps. 9 and 10.

50. Social hierarchy, where it exists, confers particular advantages. Indeed subsequent repetition of Bavelas's experiment with groups of different nationalities showed that members of hierarchical societies, such as the Japanese, do better at coordination tasks than others. Typically, in such cases, group members are capable of detecting which one occupies the highest position in the hierarchy of the group: that is, the highest-ranking member's salience is universally recognized, and each member knows that the others know this. The group then converges very quickly on the following strategy: all members choose 3 except the highest-ranking member, who picks 5.

51. Thomas C. Schelling, *The Strategy of Conflict* (Cambridge, Mass.: Harvard University Press, 1960).

52. David K. Lewis, *Convention: A Philosophical Inquiry* (Cambridge, Mass.: Harvard University Press, 1969).

53. A proposition P is common knowledge in a given population if and only if P is true, everyone knows that P, everyone knows that everyone knows that P, and so on, ad infinitum.

54. See my book *Introduction aux sciences sociales: Logique des phénomènes collectifs* (Paris: Ellipses, 1992); and "Common Knowledge, Common Sense," *Theory and Decision* 27 (1989): 37–62.

55. See *Macy 8*, 42.

56. Kurt Goldstein (1878–1965), an American neuropsychiatrist born in Germany. Influenced by the work of the Gestaltists (Koffka, Köhler, Wertheimer), his theory of the organism in turn strongly influenced Merleau-Ponty's phenomenology.

57. Ruyer, *La Cybernétique et l'origine de l'information*, 62–63.

58. Beaune, *L'Automate et ses mobiles*, 332.

59. Ibid., 328.

60. Simondon, *Du mode d'existence des objets techniques*, 104–5.

61. See, for example, the debate between Louis Dumont (in *Essays on Individualism*) and Marcel Gauchet (in "De l'avènement de l'individu à la découverte de la société," *Annales* [May–June 1979]).

62. Simondon, *Du mode d'existence des objets techniques*, 103.

63. See in this connection the analysis of Georges Canguilhem, "Le tout et la partie dans la pensée biologique" (1966), reprinted in *Études d'histoire et de philosophie des sciences* (Paris: Vrin, 1968).

64. See the discussion in chap. 3 of Alain Renaut, *The Era of the Individual: A Contribution to a History of Subjectivity*, trans. M. B. DeBevoise and Franklin Philip (Princeton: Princeton University Press, 1997), 61–87.

65. See, for example, the discussion that followed Shannon's talk about his machine on solving labyrinth problems (*Macy 8*, 173–80). Note also Bateson's question to the ecologist Hutchinson during the discussion of Ashby's homeostat (*Macy 9*, 106), whether one could say that an ecological system "learns" according to the same logic as a homeostat (which Ashby, by the way, had just claimed *was* a brain). To this question Hutchinson responded, "Yes, definitely."

66. See Patricia S. Churchland, *Neurophilosophy: Toward a Unified Science of the Mind-Brain* (Cambridge, Mass.: MIT Press, 1986) and (with Terrence J. Sejnowski) *The Computational Brain* (Cambridge, Mass.: MIT Press, 1992); and Paul M. Churchland, "Eliminative Materialism and Propositional Attitudes," *Journal of Philosophy* 78, no. 2 (1981): 67–90, and *The Engine of Reason, the Seat of the Soul: A Philosophical Journey into the Brain* (Cambridge, Mass.: MIT Press, 1995).

67. Changeux, *Neuronal Man*, 169. Note that in French the word *esprit* means not only "spirit" but also "mind": thus Changeux slips almost imperceptibly from asserting mind-brain identity to eliminativism.

68. While collaborating on the project that gave rise to this book, the circumstances of which are described in the preface, Isabelle Stengers and I both discovered the role played by Paul Weiss, a figure less well known today than he should be. The fact that we came across Weiss independently convinced us of his importance to the history recounted here. See I. Stengers, "Les généalogies de l'auto-organisation," *Cahiers du CRÉA*, no. 8 (November 1985): 7–104.

69. See Niels Bohr, "Light and Life" (1932), reprinted in *Atomic Physics and Human Knowledge: Essays 1932–1957* (New York: Wiley, 1958).

70. See Stengers, "Les généalogies de l'auto-organisation," 64.

71. This conjecture, brilliantly developed by Isabelle Stengers in the work just cited, is not disconfirmed by Prigogine. See also note 79 below.

72. In Stengers's view, the kinship between the embryologists' theory of self-organization and that of the Brussels school of thermodynamics did not extend to the Chilean school of Maturana and Varela, nor to Atlan and his circle in France, the latter two groups, she argues, remaining hostage to the mechanist schemas of second-order cybernetics. I am inclined to downplay whatever differences there may be among them, but this is not the place to argue the point. The interested reader may consult the previously cited volume of conference proceedings (Cerisy-la-Salle, June 1981) edited by Paul Dumouchel and myself, *L'Auto-organisation*.

73. Paul A. Weiss, "The Basic Concept of Hierarchic Systems," in Paul A.

Weiss, ed., *Hierarchically Organized Systems in Theory and Practice* (New York: Hafner, 1971), 37–38; cited in Stengers, "Les généalogies de l'auto-organisation," 73.

74. Ludwig Bertalanffy, "Chance or law," in Koestler and Smythies, eds., *Beyond Reductionism*, 62. Bertalanffy lists information theory, the theory of (abstract) automata, game theory, and queuing theory along with cybernetics as alternate systems approaches—as though these theories, or in any case the first three, were not integral parts of cybernetics!

75. Ludwig von Bertalanffy, "The Meaning of General System Theory" (1955), reprinted in *General System Theory: Foundations, Development, Applications*, rev. ed. (New York: Braziller, 1973), 44; cited in Stengers, "Les généalogies de l'auto-organisation," 72. The concept of "equipotentiality" (also known as "equifinality") was defined by Bertalanffy as the property of certain processes that lead to the same goal, no matter what the point of departure and no matter what paths are followed to reach this end. Thus, for example, Hans Driesch's famous experiments in 1891 with the embryo of the sea urchin had shown that a complete larva is obtained whether one begins with a complete germ, a half-germ or a quarter-germ.

76. Paul Weiss, "The Living System: Determinism Stratified," in Koestler and Smythies, eds., *Beyond Reductionism*, 19.

77. Ibid., 10.

78. Ibid., 15 (n. 3).

79. Ibid., 10–11.

80. Ibid., 36.

81. One observes with amusement that several years later, in the "Note by the Editors" that prefaces the eighth volume of Macy Conference transcripts (1951), von Foerster was to attribute Lashley's argument to the wisdom of the cyberneticians in alliance with Lashley's learning, evidence of their common struggle against the simplistic vision of the central nervous system as a mere reflex, input-output, organ (*Macy 8*, xvi). What enabled him to sustain this interpretation was obviously the fact that at the eighth conference McCulloch, Kubie, and Lorente de Nó had drawn attention to reverberating circuits. Von Foerster, for his part, was later to become the champion of this conception of the central nervous system as an "autonomous" system capable of creating a world; see his essay "On Constructing a Reality" (1973), reprinted in *Observing Systems*, 287–309.

82. See *Hixon*, 70–71 and 112–13.

83. Changeux, *Neuronal Man*, 82–83 (emphasis added). Changeux makes reference to Lashley's experiments, but only for the purpose of ranking Lashley (like Flourens before him) in the camp of the "spiritualists" (ibid., 276). This is no doubt too pat: not everything that disagrees with reductionist and materialist monism à la McCulloch—or à la Changeux—can be lumped together. Otherwise how do we explain the conviction, expressed by Lashley at the outset of his talk at the Hixon Symposium, that mental and behavioral phenomena can be described using the concepts of mathematics and physics? Another interesting mix-up: the work of the neurobiologist Roger Sperry, a student of both Paul Weiss and Karl Lashley, which was to win him (along with Hubel and Wiesel) the 1981 Nobel Prize

186 NOTES TO CHAPTER FIVE

in Medicine, refuted the theories of both of his mentors: the experiments that he conducted on the triton showed that the wiring of the brain is very specific and that each function corresponds to a particular neuronal pathway.

84. See *Hixon*, 91.

85. Ibid., 72–74 and 140–42.

86. The expression is Köhler's: see ibid., 65.

87. See Paul A. Weiss, *Dynamics of Development: Experiments and Inferences* (New York: Academic Press, 1968), 6. Isabelle Stengers has pointed out that this passage was cited several times by Prigogine, notably in a talk given the following year, in 1969, in which the citation immediately preceded what may have been the first use by a representative of the Brussels school of thermodynamics of the term "self-organization" ("Généalogies de l'auto-organisation," 63).

88. See Weiss's remarks at the Alpbach Symposium, in Koestler and Smythies, eds., *Beyond Reductionism*, 6–9 and 45–46.

89. *Macy 9*, 11.

90. *Macy 8*, 52–54 and 80–83.

91. *Macy 8*, 124–25.

92. Heinz von Foerster, "Morality Play," *The Sciences* 21, no. 8 (October 1981): 24–25.

93. Simondon, *Du mode d'existence des objets techniques*, 49.

94. "Note by the Editors," *Macy 8*, xvii. Jean-Claude Beaune, for his part, has written, "Computers are mathematical and logical systems put into action, theories incarnate, contemporaneous with the experiments to which they give rise. . . . Every model is, de jure, a reasoning machine. The computer proposes a specifically technical and, if you will, functionalist, reinterpretation of this activity" (*L'Automate et ses mobiles*, 315).

95. Lettvin, "Warren and Walter," *McC. Intro.*, 11.

96. A. Rosenblueth and N. Wiener, "The Role of Models in Science," *Philosophy of Science* 12, no. 4 (October 1945): 316–21.

97. Cf. Royce's interpretation of the definition of infinity given by Dedekind in terms of a "self-representative system," in "The Concept of the Infinite," *Hilbert Journal* 1 (1902): 21–45. See too the use of this notion made by Borges in "Partial Enchantments of the *Quixote*," in *Other Inquisitions, 1937–1952*, trans. Ruth L. C. Simms (Austin: University of Texas Press, 1964). On its relation to the literary tradition of *mise en abyme* in general, see Dupuy, "Self-Reference in Literature."

98. *Macy 9*, 147.

99. *Macy 7*, 19–51.

100. See Lévy, "Wittgenstein et la cybernétique."

101. Cf. the chapter entitled "La double séance" in Jacques Derrida, *La Dissémination* (Paris: Seuil, 1972) or, in the English edition, *Dissemination*, trans. Barbara Johnson (Chicago: University of Chicago Press, 1981), 173–285.

102. Vilfredo Pareto, *Manuale di economia politica* (Milan: Società Editrice, 1906), quoted by Friedrich A. von Hayek, *Individualism and Economic Order* (Chicago: University of Chicago Press, 1948), 181–82. The quotation occurs in a paper by Hayek that originally appeared in *Economica* 7, no. 26 [n.s.] (May 1940).

103. Hayek, *Individualism and Economic Order*, 24.

104. See Burks's introduction to *The Theory of Self-Reproducing Automata*, 2–4, and the first paper by von Neumann collected there, "Computing Machines in General," 31–41.

105. Ibid., 47. The bracketed question mark is von Neumann's, indicating that the notion that the ratio is infinite only asymptotically (as the magnitude of the object increases) is a conjecture and nothing more. Burks comments on this passage in a letter to Gödel (p. 58).

106. Ibid., 53–56.

107. "It is this [i.e., Tarski's] theorem," Gödel wrote, "which is the true reason for the existence of undecidable propositions in the formal systems containing arithmetic" (ibid., 55).

108. See Davidson's 1970 paper, "Mental Events," in *Essays on Actions and Events*, 214–15. Davidson warns against pushing this analogy too far.

109. *Hixon*, 109–10.

CHAPTER SIX

1. Jacques Lacan, *Ego in Freud's Theory and in the Technique of Psychoanalysis, 1954–55*, trans. Sylvana Tomaselli with notes by John Forrester (New York: Cambridge University Press, 1988), 47. This is the second volume of the series *The Seminar of Jacques Lacan*, edited by Jacques-Alain Miller.

2. See McCulloch's previously cited 1946 talk, later published as "Finality and Form in Nervous Activity" (1952), especially pp. 257 and 270. It should be kept in mind that McCulloch and Pitts came up with the idea of investigating random networks before von Neumann. Equally remarkable is the thought with which McCulloch ended his paper, which represented the first salvo in the debate that rages today between neoconnectionists and partisans of "orthodox" artificial intelligence. A random network can learn, he said, and in particular can make inductive inferences, but much more would be required for it to be capable of expressing the rules it *followed* in doing this. McCulloch thought at the time, as Daniel Dennett and many others do today, that only a few years would be needed to solve the problem: see ibid., 273–75, and Dennett, "The Logical Geography of Computational Approaches," in *Brainchildren*, 215–234.

3. See *Macy 9*, 107–8.

4. See *Hixon*, 102.

5. See *Teleological Mechanisms*, 269.

6. For Paul Weiss, as we have seen, the fact that molecular biology was obliged to resort to anthropomorphic terms to account for the integrating properties of the organism, within a schema borrowed from cybernetics, was the surest possible sign of cybernetics' inherent inadequacy as a source of models of life. See his paper delivered at the 1968 Alpbach Symposium and reprinted in *Beyond Reductionism*, especially pp. 29, 36.

7. *Macy 8*, 154–57.

8. See for example the "Note by the Editors" in *Macy 8*, especially pp. xiv–xvii. In this sense Raymond Ruyer grasped only half the truth when he wrote, "The notion of feedback has, of course, been both abused and overused, confused [first]

with simple physical equilibration and [used] ultimately to absorb into cybernetics all physical equilibrium phenomena" (*La Cybernétique et l'origine de l'information*, 234). The absorption operated in the other direction as well, increasingly depriving feedback of its role as a device of control and regulation. Ruyer missed this aspect of the matter because he was in thrall, more than the cyberneticians themselves, to the notion of information.

9. At the January 1984 Montpellier colloquium on the work of Herbert Simon, organized by Jean-Louis Le Moigne, I asked the founder of artificial intelligence what influence cybernetics had had on him. "The only cybernetician who has had an impact on my work," he replied, "is Ross Ashby." The reader should keep in mind that Jacques Lacan, at the other end of the spectrum from Simon, was familiar with Ashby's work and referred to it in his 1954–1955 seminar.

10. See, for example, Ross Ashby's 1962 article, "Principles of the Self-Organizing System," in Roger Conant, ed., *Mechanisms of Intelligence: Ashby's Writings on Cybernetics* (Seaside, California: Intersystems Publications, 1981), 51–74. The article originally appeared in Heinz von Foerster and George W. Zopf, eds. *Principles of Self-Organization* (New York: Pergamon Press, 1962), 255–78; references to it below cite pages in the Conant edition.

11. Given the mapping F: $x \to y$, the automaton computes for a given initial condition x_0: $x_1 = F(x_0)$; $x_2 = F(x_1) = FF(x_0)$; $x_3 = F(x_2) = FFF(x_0)$; and so on.

12. Let $y = f(x)$ be a function such that x is its "argument" and y its "value." Now it may be the case that $y = f(x_1) = f(x_2)$ with $x_1 \neq x_2$. But for a given x, by definition, there is a single y. Hence if $y_1 = f(x_1) \neq y_2 = f(x_2)$, then $x_1 \neq x_2$.

13. See *Macy 9*, 73–108 and 151–54: the entire discussion makes wonderful reading. Von Foerster, who transcribed the debates, later admitted that the words actually used were much harsher than the ones that appear in the official record.

14. Stengers, "Les généalogies de l'auto-organisation," 49.

15. Ibid., 46.

16. Ashby, "Principles of the Self-Organizing System," 57.

17. The phrase is due to von Foerster's colleague George W. Zopf, Jr., who used it at the third of the symposiums on self-organizing systems sponsored by the Biological Computer Laboratory at Urbana-Champagne, in 1961. See Zopf's paper "Attitude and Context" in von Foerster and Zopf, eds., *Principles of Self-Organization*.

18. Ashby, "Principles of the Self-Organizing System," 62–65.

19. See von Foerster, *Observing Systems*.

20. See Atlan's *Entre le cristal et la fumée* as well as his article "The Order from Noise Principle in Hierarchichal Self-Organization," in Milan Zeleny, ed., *Autopoiesis: A Theory of Living Organizations* (New York: North Holland, 1981).

21. Douglas R. Hofstadter, *Gödel, Escher, Bach: An Eternal Golden Braid* (New York: Basic Books, 1979), 477–78 (emphasis in original); cited by Niklas Luhmann, "The Autopoiesis of Social Systems," in Gunther Teubner, ed., *Autopoietic Law: A New Approach to Law and Society* (New York: Walter de Gruyter, 1988), 12–33.

22. Régis Debray, *Critique of Political Reason*, trans. David Macey (London: New Left Books, 1983), 177; originally published as *Critique de la raison politique* (Paris: Gallimard, 1981).

23. Ibid., 169–70.

24. Recall that Rosenblatt acknowledged Ashby's influence on his Perceptron (pages 62–63 above).

25. The designers of Boolean automata networks made no attempt to conceal their surprise at the discovery of the remarkable properties of their machines. See the papers by Françoise Fogelman-Soulié and Henri Atlan delivered at the 1981 Cerisy conference and reprinted in Dumouchel and Dupuy, eds., *L'Auto-organisa-tion*, 101–14 and 115–30, respectively.

26. See *Beyond Reductionism*, 367–68; also Stuart Kauffman, "Behavior of Gene Nets," in *McC. Intro.*

27. Stengers, "Les généalogies de l'auto-organisation," 94.

28. Energy, temperature, entropy, electric potential, and the like are all instances of state functions: the value that these variables take at a given point in time for a given system depends only on the physical state of the system, independently of the particular path that led the system to its present state. A related concept in philosophy of mind is *supervenience*. A state function expresses the fact that the corresponding variable "supervenes" on the state of the system in the following sense: it is impossible for two states to agree in all of their physical characteristics and yet differ in the value they give to the variable in question.

Materialist monism, in philosophy of mind, has it that the mental supervenes on the physical. Most versions of this position restrict themselves, explicitly or implicitly, to the following formulation: mental *states* supervene on physical *states* (i.e., there cannot be two states alike in all physical respects but differing in some mental respect). Now it may well be the case that mental processes supervene on physical processes without being integrable in a state function—something that is all the more likely since what goes on in the brain is more amenable to the new physics of populations than to classical dynamics. Given this, it seems probable that the attempt to naturalize intentionality will have a better chance of success if it is carried out in accordance with the phenomenological principles described earlier, in Chapter 4, than within the framework of a psycholinguistic interpretation of intentionality.

29. Ibid., 99.

30. Changeux, *Neuronal Man*, xvii.

31. Wiener, *Cybernetics*, 25.

32. See J.-P. Dupuy, "De l'émancipation de l'économie: Retour sur le 'problème d'Adam Smith'," *L'Année sociologique* 37 (1987): 311–42.

33. See page 142 above.

34. This quote, often cited by Hayek, is due to Adam Smith's contemporary Adam Ferguson, *An Essay on the History of Civil Society* (London, 1767), 187; see, for example, Friedrich A. von Hayek, *Law, Legislation, and Liberty*, vol. 1: *Rules and Order* (Chicago: University of Chicago Press, 1973), 20.

35. Ibid., 18, 30–31. For a general exposition and critique of Hayek's philosophy of mind and its relation to social philosophy, see chap. 8 of my book *Le sacrifice et l'envie: le libéralisme aux prises avec la justice sociale* (Paris: Calmann-Lévy, 1992), 241–91. See also my article "Tangled Hierarchies: Self-Reference in Philosophy, Anthropology, and Critical Theory," *Comparative Criticism* 12 (1990): 105–23.

36. See chaps. 14 and 15 of my *Introduction aux sciences sociales*.

37. See, for instance, G. A. Quattrone and Amos Tversky, "Self-Deception and Voter's Illusion," in Jon Elster, ed., *The Multiple Self* (Cambridge: Cambridge University Press, 1987).

38. See Daniel C. Dennett, *The Intentional Stance* (Cambridge: MIT Press, 1987).

39. See chap. 6 of Varela et al., *The Embodied Mind*, 105–30.

40. Daniel C. Dennett, *Consciousness Explained* (Boston: Little, Brown and Company, 1991), 173.

41. Marvin Minsky, *The Society of Mind* (New York: Simon and Schuster, 1986).

42. In Francisco Varela's view, this is true of cognitive science still today: "Cognitive science does not yet take seriously its own findings of the lack of a Self" (*The Embodied Mind*, 124).

Bibliography

Amit, Daniel J. *Modeling Brain Function: The World of Attractor Neural Networks*. Cambridge: Cambridge University Press, 1989.

Anderson, Alan Ross, ed. *Minds and Machines*. Englewood Cliffs, N.J.: Prentice-Hall, 1964.

Anderson, James A., and Edward Rosenfeld, *Neurocomputing: Foundations of Research*. 2 vols. Cambridge, Mass.: MIT Press, 1988.

Andler, Daniel, ed. "Connexionisme et cognition: À la recherche des bonnes questions," *Revue de synthèse* 4, no. 1–2 (January–June 1990): 95–127.

———. *Introduction aux sciences cognitives*. Paris: Gallimard, 1992.

Anzieu, Didier et al., eds. *Les contenants de pensée*. Paris: Dunod, 1993.

Aquila, Richard. *Intentionality: A Study of Mental Acts*. State College, Pa.: Pennsylvania State University Press, 1977.

Arbib, Michael A. *The Metaphorical Brain: An Introduction to Cybernetics as Artificial Intelligence and Brain Theory*. New York: Wiley Interscience, 1972.

———. "Turing machines, finite automata and neural nets," *JACM* 8 (1961): 467–75.

Arendt, Hannah. *The Human Condition*. Chicago: University of Chicago Press, 1958.

Ashby, W. Ross. *Design for a Brain*. London: Chapman and Hall, 1952.

———. *Mechanisms of Intelligence: Ashby's Writings on Cybernetics*. Edited by Roger Conant. Seaside, California: Intersystems Publications, 1981.

Atlan, Henri. *Entre le cristal et la fumée: Essai sur l'organisation du vivant*. Paris: Seuil, 1979.

———. "Intentional Self-Organization. Emergence and Reduction: Towards a Physical Theory of Intentionality." *Thesis Eleven*, no. 52 (February 1998): 5–34.

———. "Intentionality in Nature." *Journal for the Theory of Social Behavior* 24, no. 1 (1994): 67–87.

———. *L'Organisation biologique et la théorie de l'information*. Revised edition. Paris: Hermann, 1990.

———. "On a formal definition of organization." *Journal of Theoretical Biology* 45 (1974): 295–304.

Atlan, Henri, and Moshe Koppel. "The cellular computer. DNA: program or data?" *Bulletin of Mathematical Biology* 52, no. 3 (1990): 335–48.

Bateson, Gregory. *Steps to an Ecology of Mind*. New York: Ballantine Books, 1972.

Beaune, Jean-Claude. *L'Automate et ses mobiles*. Paris: Flammarion, 1980.

Bertalanffy, Ludwig von. *General System Theory: Foundations, Development, Applications*. Revised edition. New York: Braziller, 1973.

Bohr, Niels. *Atomic Physics and Human Knowledge: Essays 1932–1957*. New York: Wiley, 1958.

Borges, Jorge Luis. *Other Inquisitions, 1937–1952*. Translated by Ruth L. C. Simms. Austin: University of Texas Press, 1964; New York: Washington Square Press, 1965.

Brentano, Franz. *Psychology from an Empirical Standpoint*. Edited by Linda L. McAlister and translated by Antos C. Rancurello, D. B. Terrell, Linda L. McAlister. New York: Routledge, 1995.

Breton, Philippe. "La cybernétique et les ingénieurs dans les années cinquante." *Culture technique* 12 (March 1984).

————. *L'Utopie de la communication: L'émergence de "l'homme sans intérieur"*. Paris: La Découverte, 1992.

————. "Pourquoi les machines analogiques ont-elles disparu?" *Milieux* (June 1985).

————. "Présupposés anthropologiques et pensée du social chez les ingénieurs: un facteur sous-estimé du développement des technologies de l'information de l'après-guerre." *Cahiers STS* (1986).

————. "Quelques problèmes posés par l'émergence d'un nouveau type d'ingénieur: les ingénieurs de la connaissance." *Cahiers du CEFI* (June 1985).

Breton, Philippe, and Serge Proulx. *L'Explosion de la communication: la naissance d'une nouvelle idéologie*. 2nd edition. Paris: La Découverte, 1994.

Brillouin, Léon. *Science and Information Theory*. New York: Academic Press, 1956.

Canguilhem, Georges. *Études d'histoire et de philosophie des sciences*. Paris: Vrin, 1968.

Chalmers, David J. *The Conscious Mind: In Search of a Fundamental Theory*. New York: Oxford University Press, 1996.

Changeux, Jean-Pierre. *Neuronal Man: The Biology of Mind*. Translated by Laurence Garey with new introduction by Vernon B. Mountcastle. Princeton: Princeton University Press, 1996.

Chisholm, Roderick M. *Perceiving: A Philosophical Study*. Ithaca, N.Y. Cornell University Press, 1957.

Church, Alonso. "An unsolvable problem of elementary number theory." *American Journal of Mathematics* 58 (1936): 345–63.

Churchland, Patricia S. *Neurophilosophy: Toward a Unified Science of the Mind-Brain*. Cambridge, Mass.: MIT Press, 1986.

Churchland, Patricia S., and Terrence J. Sejnowski. *The Computational Brain*. Cambridge, Mass.: MIT Press, 1992.

Churchland, Paul M. "Eliminative Materialism and Propositional Attitudes," *Journal of Philosophy* 78, no. 2 (1981).

————. *The Engine of Reason, the Seat of the Soul: A Philosophical Journey into the Brain*. Cambridge, Mass.: MIT Press, 1995.

Davidson, Donald. *Essays on Actions and Events*. New York: Oxford University Press, 1980.

Davis, Martin, ed. *The Undecidable: Basic Papers on Undecidable Propositions, Unsolvable Problems and Computable Functions*. Hewlett, N.Y.: Raven Press, 1965.

Debray, Régis. *Critique of Political Reason*. Translated by David Macey. London: New Left Books, 1983.

Dennett, Daniel C. *Brainchildren: Essays on Designing Minds*. Cambridge, Mass.: MIT Press, 1998.

————. *Consciousness Explained*. Boston: Little, Brown and Company, 1991.

————. *The Intentional Stance*. Cambridge, Mass.: MIT Press, 1987.

Derrida, Jacques. *Dissemination*. Translated by Barbara Johnson. Chicago: University of Chicago Press, 1981.

————. *Writing and Difference*. Translated by Alan Bass. Chicago: University of Chicago Press, 1978.

Descombes, Vincent. *Modern French Philosophy*. Translated by L. Scott-Fox and J. M. Harding. Cambridge: Cambridge University Press, 1980.

Dretske, Fred. *Explaining Behavior: Reasons in a World of Causes*. Cambridge, Mass.: The MIT Press, 1988.

————. *Knowledge and the Flow of Information*. Cambridge, Mass.: MIT Press, 1981.

————. *Naturalizing the Mind*. Cambridge, Mass.: MIT Press, 1995.

Dreyfus, Hubert. *What Computers Can't Do*. 2nd edition. New York: Harper & Row, 1979.

Dumont, Louis. *Essays on Individualism: Modern Ideology in Anthropological Perspective*. Chicago: University of Chicago Press, 1986.

Dumouchel, Paul, and Jean-Pierre Dupuy, eds. *L'Auto-organisation: de la physique au politique*. Proceedings of a conference held at Cerisy-la-Salle, France, in June 1981. Paris: Seuil, 1983.

Dupuy, Jean-Pierre. "Common Knowledge, Common Sense." *Theory and Decision* 27 (1989): 37–62.

————. "De l'émancipation de l'économie: Retour sur le 'problème d'Adam Smith'." *L'Année sociologique* 37 (1987): 311–42.

————. *Introduction aux sciences sociales: Logique des phénomènes collectifs*. Paris: Éllipses, 1992.

————. *Ordres et désordres: Enquête sur un nouveau paradigme*. Paris: Seuil, 1982.

————. *Le sacrifice et l'envie: le libéralisme aux prises avec la justice sociale*. Paris: Calmann-Lévy, 1992.

————. "Self-Reference in Literature." *Poetics*, no. 18 (1989): 491–515.

————. "Tangled Hierarchies: Self-Reference in Philosophy, Anthropology, and Critical Theory." *Comparative Criticism* 12 (1990): 105–23.

Elster, Jon, ed. *The Multiple Self*. Cambridge: Cambridge University Press, 1987.

Engel, Pascal. *Introduction à la philosophie de l'esprit*. Paris: La Découverte, 1994.

Ferry, Luc, and Alain Renaut. *French Philosophy of the Sixties: An Essay on Anti-humanism*. Translated by Mary H. S. Cattani. Amherst: University of Massachusetts Press, 1990.

Foerster, Heinz von. *Observing Systems*. Edited by Francisco J. Varela. Seaside, California: Intersystems Publications, 1981.

————. "Morality Play." *The Sciences* 21, no. 8 (October 1981): 24–25.

Foerster, Heinz von, ed. *Cybernetics: Circular Causal and Feedback Mechanisms in Biological and Social Systems*. Transactions of the Sixth Conference, 24–25 March 1949. New York: Josiah Macy, Jr. Foundation, 1950.

Foerster, Heinz von, Margaret Mead, and Hans Lukas Teuber, eds. *Cybernetics: Circular Causal and Feedback Mechanisms in Biological and Social Systems.* Transactions of the Seventh Conference, 23–24 March 1950. New York: Josiah Macy, Jr. Foundation, 1951.

———. *Cybernetics: Circular Causal and Feedback Mechanisms in Biological and Social Systems.* Transactions of the Eighth Conference, 15–16 March 1951. New York: Josiah Macy, Jr. Foundation, 1952.

———. *Cybernetics: Circular Causal and Feedback Mechanisms in Biological and Social Systems.* Transactions of the Ninth Conference, 20–21 March 1952. New York: Josiah Macy, Jr. Foundation, 1953.

———. *Cybernetics: Circular Causal and Feedback Mechanisms in Biological and Social Systems.* Transactions of the Tenth Conference, 22–24 April 1953. New York: Josiah Macy, Jr. Foundation, 1955.

Foerster, Heinz von, and George W. Zopf, eds. *Principles of Self-Organization.* New York: Pergamon Press, 1962.

Fogelman-Soulié, Françoise, et al., eds. *Les Théories de la complexité: Autour de l'œuvre d'Henri Atlan.* Paris: Seuil, 1991.

Gardner, Howard. *The Mind's New Science.* New York: Basic Books, 1985.

Gardner, Martin. *Logic Machines and Diagrams.* New York: McGraw-Hill, 1959.

Gauchet, Marcel. "De l'avènement de l'individu à la découverte de la société." *Annales* (May–June 1979).

Gödel, Kurt. "Über formal unentscheidbare Sätze der *Principia Mathematica* und verwandter Systeme." *Monatshefte für Mathematik und Physik* 38 (1931): 173–98.

Goldman, A. "Interpretation Psychologized." *Mind and Language* 4, no. 3 (1989): 161–85.

Goldstine, Herman H. *The Computer from Pascal to von Neumann.* Princeton: Princeton University Press, 1972.

Hayek, Friedrich A. von. *Individualism and Economic Order.* Chicago: University of Chicago Press, 1948.

———. *Law, Legislation, and Liberty.* Vol. 1. *Rules and Order.* Chicago: University of Chicago Press, 1973.

Hebb, Donald O. *The Organization of Behavior: A Neuropsychological Theory.* New York: Wiley, 1949.

Heidegger, Martin. *Basic Writings.* Edited by David Farrell Krell. New York: Harper and Row, 1977.

———. *Essais et Conférences.* Translated by André Préau and Jean Beaufret. Paris: Gallimard, 1958.

———. "Nur noch ein Gott kan uns retten." *Der Spiegel*, no. 23 (31 May 1976): 193–219.

———. *The Question Concerning Technology and Other Essays.* Translated by William Lovitt. New York: Harper & Row, 1977.

Heijenoort, Jan van. *From Frege to Gödel: Source Book on Mathematical Logic, 1879–1931.* Cambridge, Mass.: Harvard University Press, 1966.

Heims, Steve Joshua. *The Cybernetics Group.* Cambridge, Mass.: MIT Press, 1991.

———. "An Encounter between Neo-Mechanists and the Human Sciences." *Cahiers du CRÉA*, no. 7 (October 1985): 141–202.

———. "Encounter of Behavioral Sciences with New Machine-Organism Analogies in the 1940s." *Journal of the History of the Behavioral Sciences* 11 (1975): 368–73.

———. "Gregory Bateson and the Mathematicians: From Interdisciplinary Interaction to Societal Functions." *Journal of the History of the Behavioral Sciences* 13 (1977): 141–59.

———. *John von Neumann and Norbert Wiener: From Mathematics to the Technologies of Life and Death*. Cambridge, Mass.: MIT Press, 1980.

———. "Mechanists and Social 'Scientists' (1946–1953)." Unpublished paper.

Hobbes, Thomas. *Leviathan, or the Matter, Forme and Power of a Commonwealth Ecclesiasticall and Civil*. Edited by Michael Oakeshott. London: Collier Macmillan, 1962.

———. *Man and Citizen*. Translated by Charles T. Wood, T. S. K. Scott-Craig, and Bernard Gert. Garden City, N.Y.: Anchor Books, 1972.

Hodges, Alan. *Alan Turing: The Enigma*. New York: Simon and Schuster/Touchstone Books, 1984.

Hofstadter, Douglas R. *Gödel, Escher, Bach: An Eternal Golden Braid*. New York: Basic Books, 1979.

Hottois, Gilbert. *Le Signe et la technique: La Philosophie à l'épreuve de la technique*. Paris: Aubier, 1984.

Husserl, Edmund. *Logical Investigations*. 2 volumes. Translated by J. N. Findlay. London: Routledge & Kegan Paul, 1970.

Jeannerod, Marc. *The Brain Machine: The Development of Neurophysiological Thought*. Translated by David Urion. Cambridge, Mass.: Harvard University Press, 1985.

Jeffress, Lloyd A., ed. *Cerebral Mechanisms in Behavior*. Proceedings of the Hixon Symposium, sponsored by the California Institute of Technology, September 1948, Pasadena, California. New York: John Wiley and Sons, 1951.

Kauffman, Stuart A. *The Origins of Order: Self-Organization and Selection in Evolution*. New York: Oxford University Press, 1993.

Koch, Christof. *Biophysics of Computation: Information Processing in Single Neurons*. New York: Oxford University Press, 1999.

Koestler, Arthur, and J. R. Smythies, eds. *Beyond Reductionism: New Perspectives in the Life Sciences*. London: Hutchinson, 1969.

Kubie, Lawrence. "A theoretical application to some neurological problems of the properties of excitation waves which move in closed circuits." *Brain* 53, no. 2 (1930): 166–77.

———. "Repetitive Core of Neurosis." *Psychoanalytic Quarterly* 10 (1941): 23–43.

Lacan, Jacques. *Écrits*. 2 volumes. Paris: Seuil, 1966–1971.

———. *The Seminar of Jacques Lacan: Ego in Freud's Theory and in the Technique of Psychoanalysis, 1954–55*. Translated by Sylvana Tomaselli with notes by John Forrester. New York: Cambridge University Press, 1988.

Lewis, David K. *Convention: A Philosophical Inquiry*. Cambridge, Mass.: Harvard University Press, 1969.

Livingston, Paisley, ed. *Disorder and Order*. Proceedings of a conference held at Stanford University in September 1981. Saratoga, Calif.: Anma Libri, 1984.

Lorente de Nó, Rafael. "Analysis of the activity of the chains of internuncial neurons." *J. Neurophysiol.* 1 (1938): 207–44.

McAlister, Linda L. "Chisholm and Brentano on Intentionality." *Review of Metaphysics* 28, no. 2 (1974): 328–38.

McCulloch, Warren S. *Embodiments of Mind*. Cambridge, Mass.: MIT Press, 1965.

————. *Introductions to the Complete Works of Warren McCulloch*. Unpublished work edited by Norman Geschwind, Jerome Lettvin et al. in the personal archives of Heinz von Foerster.

McCulloch, Warren S., and Walter Pitts. "A logical calculus of the ideas imminent in nervous activity." *Bulletin of Mathematical Biophysics* 5 (1943): 115–33.

Marty, François, ed. *La Philosophie transcendantale et le problème de l'objectivité*. Paris: Osiris, 1991.

Mauss, Marcel. *Sociologie et anthropologie*. Paris: Presses Universitaires de France, 1950.

Memmi, Daniel. "Connectionisme, Intelligence Artificielle et modélisation cognitive." *Intellectica*, no. 9–10 (1990): 41–79.

Miner, Roy Waldo, ed. "Teleological Mechanisms." [Proceedings of a conference held by the New York Academy of Sciences on 21–22 October 1946.] *Annals of the New York Academy of Sciences* 50, no. 4 (13 October 1948): 187–278.

Minsky, Marvin. *Semantic Information Processing*. Cambridge, Mass.: MIT Press, 1969.

————. *The Society of Mind*. New York: Simon and Schuster, 1986.

Minsky, Marvin, and Seymour Papert. *Perceptrons*. Cambridge, Mass.: MIT Press, 1969.

Mosconi, Jean. "La Constitution de la théorie des automates." Doctoral thesis. 2 volumes. Université de Paris-I, 1989.

————. "Sur quelques capacités et incapacités des machines." *Bulletin de la Société française de philosophie* 85, no. 3 (July–September, 1991).

Nagel, Thomas. *Other Minds*. New York: Oxford University Press, 1995).

Neumann, John von. *Collected Works of John von Neumann*. 6 volumes. Edited by A. H. Taub. Elmsford, N.Y.: Pergamon Press, 1961.

————. *The Computer and the Brain*. New Haven: Yale University Press, 1958.

————. *Papers of John von Neumann on Computing and Computer Science*. Edited by William Aspray and Arthur W. Burks. Cambridge, Mass.: MIT Press, 1987.

————. *Theory of Self-Reproducing Automata*. Edited and completed by Arthur W. Burks. Urbana: University of Illinois Press, 1966.

Neumann, John von, and Oscar Morgenstern. *The Theory of Games and Economic Behavior*. Princeton: Princeton University Press, 1944.

Pareto, Vilfredo. *Manual of Political Economy*. Translated by Ann S. Schwier. New York: A. M. Kelley, 1971.

Petitot, Jean. "Phénoménologie naturalisée et morphodynamique: la fonction cognitive du synthetique *a priori*." *Intellectica*, no. 17 (1992/3): 79–126.

————. *Physique du sens*. Paris: Éditions du Centre National de la Recherche Scientifique, 1992.

Petitot, Jean, Francisco Varela, Bernard Pachoud, and Jean-Michel Roy, eds. *Naturalizing Phenomenology: Issues in Contemporary Phenomenology and Cognitive Science*. Stanford: Stanford University Press, 1999.

Port, Robert F., and Timothy Van Gelder, eds. *Mind as Motion: Explorations in the Dynamics of Cognition*. Cambridge, Mass.: MIT Press, 1995.

Poundstone, William. *Prisoner's Dilemma: John von Neumann, Game Theory, and the Puzzle of the Bomb*. New York: Doubleday, 1992.

———. *The Recursive Universe*. New York: Morrow, 1985.

Prigogine, Ilya, and Isabelle Stengers. *Order Out of Chaos: Man's New Dialogue with Nature*. New York: Bantam Books, 1984.

Proust, Joëlle. "L'intelligence artificielle comme philosophie." *Le Débat*, no. 47 (November–December, 1987): 88–102.

Putnam, Hilary. *Philosophical Papers*. 2 vols. New York: Cambridge University Press, 1975.

Quine, W. V. *Quiddities: An Intermittently Philosophical Dictionary*. Cambridge, Mass.: Belknap Press of Harvard University Press, 1987.

———. *Word and Object*. Cambridge, Mass.: MIT Press, 1960.

Randell, Brian, ed. *The Origins of Digital Computers: Selected Papers*. New York: Springer-Verlag, 1973; 3rd. edition, 1982.

Rawls, John. *Theory of Justice*. Cambridge, Mass.: Harvard University Press, 1971.

Renaut, Alain. *The Era of the Individual: A Contribution to a History of Subjectivity*. Translated by M. B. DeBevoise and Franklin Philip. Princeton: Princeton University Press, 1997.

———. *Sartre: le dernier philosophe*. Paris: Grasset, 1993.

Reynaud, Philippe. *Max Weber et les dilemmes de la raison moderne*. Paris: Presses Universitaires de France, 1987.

Ricoeur, Paul. "Structure et herméneutique." *Esprit*, no. 11 (November 1963): 596–627.

Rosenblatt, Frank. *Principles of Neurodynamics: Perceptrons and the Theory of Brain Mechanisms*. Buffalo: Cornell Aeronautical Laboratory, 1961; Washington, D.C.: Spartan Books, 1962.

Rosenblueth, Arturo, and Norbert Wiener. "The Role of Models in Science." *Philosophy of Science* 12, no. 4 (October 1945): 316–21.

Rosenblueth, Arturo, Norbert Wiener, and Julian Bigelow. "Behavior, Purpose, Teleology." *Philosophy of Science* 10, no. 1 (1943): 18–24.

Royce, Josiah. "The Concept of the Infinite." *Hilbert Journal* 1 (1902): 21–45.

Rumelhart, David E., James L. McClelland, and the PDP Research Group. *Parallel Distributed Processing: Explorations in the Microstructure of Cognition*. Vol. 1: *Foundations*. Cambridge, Mass.: MIT Press, 1986.

Ruyer, Raymond. *La Cybernétique et l'origine de l'information*. Paris: Flammarion, 1954.

Sartre, Jean-Paul. *Existentialism and Humanism*. Translated by Philip Mairet. London: Eyre Methuen, 1973.

———. *Literary and Philosophical Essays*. Translated by Annette Michelson. New York: Criterion Books, 1955.

Savage, Leonard J. *Foundations of Statistics*. New York: Wiley, 1954.

Schelling, Thomas C. *The Strategy of Conflict*. Cambridge, Mass.: Harvard University Press, 1960.

Schrödinger, Erwin. *What Is Life? The Physical Aspect of the Living Cell*. Cambridge: Cambridge University Press, 1944.

Searle, John. "Is the Brain's Mind a Computer Program?" *Scientific American* 262, no. 1 (January 1990): 26–31.

———. "Minds, brains, and programs." *Behavioral and Brain Sciences* 3, no. 3 (1980): 417–57.

———. "L'Esprit est-til un programme d'ordinateur?" *Pour la Science*, no. 149 (March 1990): 38–45.

Shannon, Claude E., and John McCarthy, eds. *Automata Studies*. Princeton: Princeton University Press, 1956.

Shannon, Claude E., and Warren Weaver, *The Mathematical Theory of Communication*. Urbana: University of Illinois Press, 1949.

Simon, Herbert A. *Models of Bounded Rationality*. 2 vols. Cambridge, Mass.: MIT Press, 1982.

———. *Models of Discovery: And Other Topics in the Methods of Science*. Boston: D. Reidel, 1977.

———. *Models of Man, Social and Rational: Mathematical Essays on Rational Human Behavior in a Social Setting*. New York: Wiley, 1957.

———. *Models of My Life*. New York: Basic Books, 1991.

———. *Models of Thought*. 2 vols. New Haven: Yale University Press, 1979–1989.

———. *The Sciences of the Artificial*, Cambridge, Mass.: MIT Press, 1969.

———. *The Shape of Automation for Men and Management*. New York: Harper & Row, 1965.

Simondon, Gilbert. *Du mode d'existence des objets techniques*. Paris: Montaigne, 1989.

Stengers, Isabelle. "Les généalogies de l'auto-organisation." *Cahiers du CRÉA*, no. 8 (November 1985): 7–104.

Szilard, Leo. "On the decrease of entropy in a thermodynamic system by the intervention of intelligent beings." *Behavioral Science* 9, no. 4 (1964): 301–10.

Teubner, Gunther, ed. *Autopoietic Law: A New Approach to Law and Society*. New York: Walter de Gruyter, 1988.

Turing, Alan M. "A Correction." *Proceedings of the London Mathematical Society* 43 (1937): 544–46.

———. "Computability and λ-definability." *Journal of Symbolic Logic* 2 (1937): 153–63.

———. "Computing Machinery and Intelligence." *Mind* 59, no. 236 (1950): 433–60.

———. "On computable numbers, with an application to the *Entscheidungs-problem*." *Proc. Lond. Math. Soc.* 42, serial 2 (1936): 230–65.

Ullmo, Jean. *La Pensée scientifique moderne*. Paris: Flammarion, 1969.

Van de Vijver, Gertrudis, et al., eds. *Evolutionary Systems: Biological and Epistemological Perpsectives on Selection and Self-Organization*. Dordrecht: Kluwer, 1998.

———. *New Perspectives on Cybernetics: Self-Organization, Autonomy, and Connectionism*. Dordrecht: Kluwer, 1992.

Varela, Francisco J. *Principles of Biological Autonomy*. New York: Elsevier-North Holland, 1979.

Varela, Francisco J., Evan Thompson, and Eleanor Rosch. *The Embodied Mind: Cognitive Science and Human Experience*. Cambridge, Mass.: MIT Press, 1991.

Vico, Giambattista. *De nostri temporis studiorum ratione*. Naples, 1709.

Watzlawick, Paul, et al. *Pragmatics of Human Communication*. New York: Norton, 1967.

Weber, Max. *Science as a Vocation*. Edited by Peter Lassman, Irving Velody, and Herminio Martins. London: Unwin Hyman, 1989.

Weiss, Paul A. *Dynamics of Development: Experiments and Inferences*. New York: Academic Press, 1968.

———, ed. *Hierarchically Organized Systems in Theory and Practice*. New York: Hafner, 1971.

Wiener, Norbert. *Cybernetics: or Control and Communication in the Animal and the Machine*. Cambridge, Mass.: MIT Press, 1948.

———. *God and Golem, Inc.: A Comment on Certain Points Where Cybernetics Impinges on Religion*. Cambridge, Mass.: MIT Press, 1964.

———. *I Am a Mathematician*. Garden City, N.Y.: Doubleday & Co., 1956.

———. *The Human Use of Human Beings: Cybernetics and Society*. Boston: Houghton Mifflin, 1950.

Zeleny, Milan, ed.. *Autopoiesis: A Theory of Living Organizations*. New York: North Holland, 1981.

Index

Abramson, Harold, 77, 85
adaptation, 117, 139, 149, 150
algorithms, 4–5, 10, 34, 41–42, 124–25
Alpbach Symposium, 75–76, 131, 132, 157, 158
Althusser, Louis, 19, 156
Amit, Daniel, 104
analog. *See* digital/analogical information
analytical philosophy, 91–93, 144. *See also* cognitive philosophy
Andler, David, 95–96, 102
ANN-style connectionist research, 135
anthropology, 72; cultural, 22, 43, 82, 156; social, 82, 107; structuralist, 91
anthropomorphism, 109–10, 133, 187n6
Aquinas, Thomas, 100
Arbib, M. A., 57
Arendt, Hannah, 28–29, 166n12
artificial intelligence: and cognitive science, 64, 90–91; and cybernetics, 5, 6, 21, 57; and logical rules, 65; and neoconnectionism, 187n2; and neural networks, 59, 62, 63, 95; and neurophysiology, 143; Proust on philosophy of, 93; Searle on, 6, 98–99
Ashby, W. Ross, 69, 87, 121, 127; and complexity, 148–55; influence of, 62–63, 109, 188n9; at Macy Conferences, 76, 148, 155; and second-order cybernetics, 46, 148, 152
Atlan, Henri, 103, 105, 120, 152, 184n32
Attractor Neural Network (ANN) School, 103–4, 135
attractors. *See* self-behaviors
automata theory, 28, 35, 39, 66, 108; and complexity, 137, 141, 143; and cybernetics ambiguity, 109–10; and finite-state automata, 46–47, 58, 149; natural *vs.* artificial, 50–51; and systems theory, 185n74; von Neumann's theory of, 67, 142. *See also* networks
automatism, 39, 55
autonomy: and behavior, 46–47; and mod-

els, 31, 143; and nervous system, 134–35, 185n81; of networks, 63, 103, 104; and spontaneity, 110; of systems, 7, 133–36, 152
autopoiesis. *See* self-organizing systems
axiological anomaly theory, 123
axiomatization, 122, 148–49

Bar-Hillel, Yehoshua, 76, 121
Bateson, Gregory, 25, 80, 87, 128, 136, 156; and information theory, 103, 119, 122, 123; at Macy Conferences, 70, 72, 77, 88, 124
Bavelas, Alex, 77, 123–26, 147
Beaune, Jean-Claude, 109, 127, 186n94
behavior: and chance, 121; and communication, 48; and complexity, 142–43, 147, 150; and contents, 50; and feedback, 45–47; and intentionality, 97; of machines, 47, 49; and meaning, 47, 50; and networks, 58, 68, 104, 146; of self-organizing systems, 153; and simulation, 9; spontaneity as, 110
behaviorism, 45–49, 50, 91, 103
Benedict, Ruth, 82
Bertalanffy, Ludwig von, 75, 131–32, 185nn74,75
bifurcation theory, 7, 115
Bigelow, Julian, 48, 50, 80, 124, 150; and cybernetics, 44, 67; at Macy Conferences, 70, 71, 89
biological organization theories, 46
biology: and autonomy, 136; and cybernetics, 20, 21, 77–78, 81, 129; and mathematical modeling, 57; and neural networks, 61; and science of mind, 84
Birch, Herbert, 48, 77, 147–48
Boas, Frank, 82
Bohr, Niels, 77, 130
Boltzmann, Ludwig, 120
Borges, Jorge Luis, 28
Boring, Edward, 84
bounded rationality theory, 27

Macy Conferences (*cont.*)
  self-organization at, 20; Shannon's "Rat"
  automaton discussed at, 137; and social
  sciences, 155, 156; Turing thesis discussed
  at, 53–54
mapping, 137, 149, 151
Marquis, Donald, 77, 119
Marxist structuralism, 156
Massachusetts Institute of Technology
  (MIT), 70–71
materialism, 4, 11–12, 15, 38; and cognitive
  science, 22, 25; nonreductionist, 102, 128,
  142
matter, 7, 12, 14
Maturana, Humberto, 46, 103, 106, 129, 152,
  184n72
Mauss, Marcel, 107
Maxwell, Clerk, 58, 61, 78, 120, 181n2
Mead, George Herbert, 82
Mead, Margaret, 70, 72, 77, 80, 82, 84, 113
meaning: and behavior, 47, 50; and causality, 5–6, 9, 10; in cognitivism, 11, 12, 13;
  and communication, 48; in cybernetics,
  4, 5–6, 7–8, 11, 14, 21; Heidegger on, 17;
  and information theory, 118, 119–23; and
  intentionality, 11, 155; and perception,
  106; and representation, 96; and self-
  behavior, 104–5; and simulation, 9–10;
  and syntax, 142; and theory of self-organization, 120; and Turing machines, 38–39;
  and unconscious, 125
Memmi, Daniel, 64–65
memory, 37, 48, 55, 56, 58, 64, 117
mental activity. *See* thought
mental events, 51–52, 85, 97–98
mental health, 22, 24, 82
mentalism, 48–49, 50, 150
mental states: in cognitive science, 160; and
  cybernetics, 49; in developmental psychology, 167n28; and epistemology, 92;
  in folk psychology, 13; and intentionality,
  95–98, 102, 155; and language, 102; and
  methodological individualism, 159–60;
  and physical states, 189n28; types of,
  178n8
Merton, Robert, 72, 155
metaphysics: and cybernetics, 107–8, 148–
  55; deconstruction of, 42, 160; and humanism, 17, 18, 19–20, 21; and psychologism, 91; and second-order cybernetics,
  87–88; of subjectivity, 107–10
Milgram, Maurice, 103

mind, the: and behavior, 47; in cybernetics, 6, 7; in functionalism, 40–41; and
  knowledge of universals, 56; the life of,
  161; as logic machine, 52–54, 55, 65; machines and science of, 84; and meaning,
  12; mechanization of, 14, 20–22; and
  neural networks, 59, 128; and reality,
  49–50; Searle on, 165n24; and the subject, 107; and theory of automata, 58;
  and Turing machines, 41; and *verum
  factum* principle, 150; von Neumann on,
  68
mind and matter, problem of, 4, 31, 38, 90,
  98–99, 129
mind-brain identity thesis, 129
Minsky, Marvin, 43, 57, 63, 69, 137, 160
models: and artificial intelligence, 93; and
  autonomy, 31, 143; cognitive science debate on, 64–65; and complexity, 137–43;
  and cybernetics, 4, 7, 12, 113, 127; and
  economic theory, 61; McCulloch on, 51;
  Macy Conferences debate on, 76–80;
  and phenomena, 32, 47; purpose of, 27–
  31; as reasoning machines, 185n83; and
  representations, 31–33; and self-organization systems, 153; and simulation, 9,
  32, 40–41; and structuralism, 166n9;
  Turing machines as, 33–41; and *verum
  factum* principle, 28–29. *See also* neural
  networks
molecular biology, 20, 78, 129–30, 133, 145,
  146, 187n6
monism: anomalous, 97–98, 99, 128, 142;
  materialist, 165n24, 189n28; nonreductionist, 102, 128; reductionist, 129
Moore, G. E., 105
Morgenstern, Oscar, 61, 67
Morris, Charles, 77
Mosconi, Jean, 35, 37, 56, 94

Nagel, Thomas, 15–16, 164n8
natural sciences, 28, 139
neoconnectionism, 65, 69, 103, 153, 187n2;
  and cybernetics, 144, 146
neocybernetic movement. *See* second-order
  cybernetics
nervous system: and autonomy, 134–35,
  185n81; as communication network, 54;
  and cybernetics, 87; cycles in, 55; and
  digital/analogical information, 114–15,
  138–39; and information theory, 116–17;
  and McCulloch, 61–62, 146; as machine,

110; and mathematical modeling, 57; and organization, 59; spontaneous activity in, 110, 134–35
networks, 53, 104–5, 160; random, 56, 145–46, 153, 187n2. *See also* neural networks
neural networks, 6, 8; and circularity, 123; cognitive science debate on, 64–65; and connectionism, 95–96; as discontinuist approach, 114; and epistemology, 94; excitation threshold in, 55, 115, 170nn31, 32; and *Gestalten*, 85; and ideas, 145; and intentionality, 103; learning in, 56, 172n65; McCulloch's development of, 56–61, 65, 103; mind as, 128; and neurobiology, 61–62; and phenomenology, 105; and representation, 95; research on, 62–65; signal processing in, 133–34; and subjectless processes, 107, 160; and totality, 129; von Neumann on, 68
neurons, 50, 52, 54, 62, 64–68, 104; as logical calculators, 95; McCulloch on, 58–59; parallel organization of, 66–67
neurosciences, 54, 64, 90–91, 143; neurology, 49, 57, 61, 63, 86; neurophilosophy, 129
Newell, Alan, 27, 38, 63, 93
New York Academy of Sciences, 72, 75, 81, 83
noise, 56, 118, 119–20
Northrop, Filmer, 77, 105

observer, role of the, 46, 79–80, 119
omniscience, 151, 153
order from noise principle, 119–20, 120, 152, 183n43
organized systems, 59, 67–68, 81, 151, 160; and information, 114, 118; and second-order cybernetics, 119–20. *See also* self-organizing systems

Papert, Seymour, 57, 58, 63, 94, 137
parallel processing, 66, 95
Pareto, Vilfredo, 140, 156
Parsons, Talcott, 72, 155–56
Peirce, Charles Sanders, 105
perception, 48, 55, 85, 100–1, 106, 118
Perceptron, 62–63, 95, 157
personality and culture movement, 82–83, 85–86, 120, 156
Petitot, Jean, 104, 105
phenomenal reality, 29–31
phenomenology: and ANN-style connection-

ist research, 135; and cybernetics, 14, 102–7, 124, 144; and intentionality, 99, 101, 189n28; and psychologism, 91
philosophy: and artificial intelligence, 93; and cognitive science, 90–91; and cybernetics, 81, 107; of language, 92, 94, 96–97; and psychology, 91, 92
philosophy of mind. *See* cognitive philosophy
physical causality, 11, 14
physical events, 97–98
physicalism, 113–18
physical phenomena, 12, 100–101, 113, 178n23
physical states, 189n28
physics, 57, 83–84, 97, 129, 154, 155; and cybernetics, 11, 22, 47, 51, 78, 81, 84–89, 113, 144
Pitts, Walter, 33, 84–86, 95–96, 105, 106, 145, 150; and computer development, 66; and cybernetics, 49, 51–52, 67; on digital/analogical information, 114, 138; evolution of thought of, 137; and information theory, 117, 118, 119, 122; and logic machines, 54, 55, 56; at Macy Conferences, 70–71, 73–74, 78; and neural networks, 56–58, 60–61, 65, 103; and random networks, 145, 187n2; and Turing thesis, 53–54; and von Neumann, 66, 68, 171n41
Planck, Max, 106
Poe, Edgar Allan, 108
political theory, 28, 43, 127–28, 152, 156
Popper, Karl, 29–30, 40, 93
positivism, 17, 80, 91
poststructuralism, 16, 18, 108, 139
prediction theory, 45
Prigogine, Ilya, 130
probability theory, 68
Proust, Joëlle, 93, 94, 96
psychiatry, 82, 86
psychoanalysis, 22, 79–80, 85–86, 91
psychologism, 91–92, 101
psychology: and artificial intelligence, 93; associationist, 135; and causal processes, 14; and cybernetics, 12–13, 49, 78, 83, 84, 144, 145; developmental, 167n28; folk, 12–13, 14, 49; and intentionality, 96, 97; and Macy Conferences, 77; and philosophy, 91–92; and physics, 85–86. *See also* behaviorism; Gestalt psychology
Pylyshyn, Zenon, 38, 96

Quastler, Henry, 76, 117, 150
Quine, Willard Van Orman, 92, 97, 99, 102, 118

Ramón y Cajal, Santiago, 54, 117
randomness, 56, 148, 149, 150
Rashevsky, Nicholas, 57
"Rat" automaton, 79, 137
rational choice theory, 43, 123, 159
rationality, 13, 27, 84, 122, 124–26
reality, 17, 49–50, 138, 146
reason, 13, 14, 16, 28, 34, 64
recursivity, 34, 35, 39, 58
reductionism, 80–81, 133, 135
redundancy, 117, 118, 119, 182n21
Renaut, Alain, 101
representation: in cognitivism, 13; in computation, 6; and computer simulation, 140–41; in cybernetics, 102–3; and models, 32, 33, 139; and neural networks, 63, 65; and philosophy of mind, 128; and Turing machines, 39. *See also* intentionality
reverberating circuits, 56, 108–9, 185n81
Reynaud, Philippe, 166n12
Richards, Ivor, 136
Ricoeur, Paul, 107
Rosenblatt, Frank, 62–63, 65, 69, 85, 86, 157
Rosenblueth, Arturo, 48, 80, 138; and cybernetics, 44, 45, 49, 67; and McCulloch, 50, 70, 180n56
Rousseau, Jean-Jacques, 127
Royce, Josiah, 138
Russell, Bertrand, 51, 91, 96, 105, 111
Ruyer, Raymond, 117, 127, 187n8

Sapir, Edward, 82
Sartre, Jean-Paul, 18, 99
Savage, Leonard J., 72, 76, 121, 122, 124, 125, 126
Schelling, Thomas, 125
Schneirla, Theodore, 77, 147
Schrödinger, Erwin, 77, 78, 129, 130
Schutz, Alfred, 123
Searle, John, 6, 9–10, 42, 98–99, 164n8, 165nn19, 24
second-order cybernetics: and Ashby, 148, 152; and behaviorism, 46; and chaos theory, 78; and Lacan, 109; and mental function, 103; and metaphysics, 87–88, 154; and neural networks models, 63; and organization, 119–20; and role of the ob-

server, 79–80; roots of, 10–11, 76; and self-organization, 11, 20, 63, 152, 184n72. *See also* von Foerster, Heinz
self, the, 160–61, 190n42
self-behaviors, 7, 8, 104–5, 153
self-consciousness, 88
self-organizing systems: at Alpbach Symposium, 76; Ashby on, 151–52; Chilean school of, 103, 106, 129, 184n72; and cybernetics, 80, 137; and embryology, 130–31, 184n72; and order from noise principle, 119–20; and second-order cybernetics, 11, 20, 63, 152, 184n72; theory of, 7, 20, 146, 153, 160; and Weiss, 129–36, 146
self-reproduction, 67–68
self-transcendence, 158
semantics. *See* meaning
Shannon, Claude, 33, 45, 57, 76, 107, 124; and information theory, 114, 119, 121, 122; on machines and logic, 52–53; "Rat" automaton of, 79, 137
Sherrington, Charles Scott, 55
signal processing, 6, 45, 46, 133–35, 155
Simon, Herbert, 63, 93, 122, 151; and cybernetics, 52, 188n9; "Travel Theorem" of, 27–28; on Turing machines, 38, 39
Simondon, Gilbert, 120–21, 127, 128, 134, 137
simulation: and cognitive philosophy, 96; in cognitive science, 9, 10, 63; computer, 140–41; in cybernetics, 18; and developmental psychology, 167n28; and knowing, 40–42; and models, 9, 32, 40–41; thinking as, 126
Smith, Adam, 156
social hierarchy, 183n50
social sciences: and cognitive science, 158–61; and complexity, 139–40; and cybernetics, 82–83, 145, 155–58; and Macy Conferences, 72; and neurology, 86; and philosophy, 91
social structure, 123–24, 125
spatial specialization thesis, 134
specularity, 125, 126
speech. *See* language
Spemann, Hans, 130
Sperry, Roger, 185n83
spontaneous social order, 157
state functions, 154, 189n28
Stengers, Isabelle, 151, 154
Stroud, John, 77, 79–80, 89, 118, 121, 122

Printed in the United States
by Baker & Taylor Publisher Services